STOP THE REVOLUTION

Also by Thomas J. McGuire

BATTLE OF PAOLI

THE PHILADELPHIA CAMPAIGN, VOLUME I
Brandywine and the Fall of Philadelphia

THE PHILADELPHIA CAMPAIGN, VOLUME II
Germantown and the Roads to Valley Forge

STOP THE REVOLUTION

*America in the
Summer of Independence*
and the Conference for Peace

Thomas J. McGuire

STACKPOLE
BOOKS

Published by
STACKPOLE BOOKS
5067 Ritter Road
Mechanicsburg, PA 17055
www.stackpolebooks.com

Printed in the United States of America

2 4 6 8 10 9 7 5 3 1

FIRST EDITION

Library of Congress Cataloging-in-Publication Data

McGuire, Thomas J.
    Stop the revolution : America in the summer of independence and the conference
for peace, September 11, 1776 / Thomas J. McGuire. — 1st ed.
        p.   cm.
    Includes bibliographical references and index.
    ISBN-13: 978-0-8117-0587-5 (hardcover : alk. paper)
    ISBN-10: 0-8117-0587-0 (hardcover : alk. paper)
    1. New York (N.Y.)—History—Revolution, 1775–1783   2. Staten Island
Peace Conference (1776)   3. United States—History—Revolution, 1775–1783.
I. Title.
E232.M44   2011
974.7'03—dc22
                                                                        2011011716

To Kyle R. Weaver
"Laudant illa, sed ista legunt"

CONTENTS

List of Maps		viii
Foreword		ix
Acknowledgments		xi
Introduction	"Come! Open the Window and come to bed."	I
CHAPTER 1	The Stranded Englishman	5
CHAPTER 2	The Patriarch	17
CHAPTER 3	The Peace Commissioner	26
CHAPTER 4	"George Washington Esqr., &c., &c., &c."	36
CHAPTER 5	*"Auf Christen-Mensch, auf, auf, zum Streit."*	49
CHAPTER 6	The Flying Camp	55
CHAPTER 7	The Lord and the Sage	70
CHAPTER 8	The Girl, the Generals, and the Toasts	79
CHAPTER 9	All the King's Horses and All the King's Men	89
CHAPTER 10	The Debacle	96
CHAPTER 11	*"Sgnik Sdneirf"*	112
CHAPTER 12	The Decoy Duck	123
CHAPTER 13	To Go or Not to Go	133
CHAPTER 14	"Between hawk and buzzard."	143
CHAPTER 15	September 11, 1776	157
CHAPTER 16	"They met, they talked, they parted."	168
Epilogue	225 Years Later	177
Notes		181
Index		203

MAPS

New York Harbor, July–August 1776   37

Staten Island   61

Battle of Long Island   99

Cresswell's Travels in America   115

Route of Cresswell to New York, September
5–10, and Route of Committee to Staten
Island, September 9–13, 1776   147

FOREWORD

In my career as a military artist, I have learned about the American Revolution largely through the study of objects: paintings, uniforms, and the equipment carried by soldiers. Tom McGuire and I share a passion for discovering the real people of the Revolution and bringing them to life. We do this through two very different mediums, painting and writing, but with the same idea in mind: to bring the people of the past to the people of the present and the future.

While many historic sites are well preserved and important to visit, Tom's work brings into the limelight other places, which have been built over today but are still of great historical importance. A visitor to Battery Park on lower Manhattan might be awed by the glass-faced skyscrapers, but never realize the name came from the artillery emplacements constructed there during the Revolution. The activities in New York during the summer of 1776 and the disastrous series of battles came perilously close to ending the dream of American Independence.

Why is this important? Far too often, the story of the American Revolution has been stereotyped or trivialized into a romantic fairy tale, with the result being a disconnect: How can real people relate their experiences to a romanticized fantasy? Tom's work takes the words of those who made history happen or witnessed it and weaves them together into a story that is both readable and identifiable. The summer of 1776 changed America in so many ways, and this is the story of some of that change.

The personal attempt by Admiral Lord Howe to stop the Revolution is a story little known and often relegated to a footnote, for his effort failed. But it is important to connect into the larger picture of the war, for had the admiral succeeded, the impact on world history would have been immeasurable. Here is the story of that effort, reminding us of the difficulties in achieving peace once conflict has begun. In the modern world, the date September 11 has taken on great significance in the balance between war and peace, between the possibilities of moving on and the improbability of turning back. How ironic that two hundred and twenty-five years before, within eyesight of the World Trade Center site, a conference took place that attempted to keep America as colonies.

As in his previous books, Tom combines his superb scholarship with adroit writing into yet another fascinating read.

Don Troiani
Southbury, CT

ACKNOWLEDGMENTS

I would like to thank the following individuals and institutions who were helpful in the inspiration, research, and writing of this book: Kathie Ludwig of the David Library of the American Revolution; Peter Maugle, Donna McDermott, and Barbara Pollarine of Valley Forge National Historical Park; Diane Rofini of the Chester County Historical Society; Dr. Connie Cooper of the Historical Society of Delaware; Ed Redmond of the Map Division of the Library of Congress; the Lancaster County Historical Society; the Historical Society of Pennsylvania; the manuscript department of the Library of Congress; and the National Archives (formerly the Public Record Office), London.

My friend and mentor, David McCullough, first assigned me to visit the Conference House on Staten Island while working on his book *John Adams*; that visit and David's continuing encouragement planted the first seeds of inspiration for this book more than ten years ago. My friend and editor, Kyle R. Weaver, opened the way for the creation of this work. Kyle's enthusiasm for my writing and endless good humor has made this challenge a joy, and I have dedicated this book to him as a small token of my thanks. *Laudant illa, sed ista legunt*: "Some writing is praised, but other is read." And finally, to my wife Susan, the light of my life, for the years of boundless support and thousands of miles for researching and visiting sites connected with the characters in this book.

"I imagine that all the Commissioners which are coming
are Soldiers & Sailors,
determined, if they can, to exterminate us.
There is too much Hatred and Bitterness towards us
in the Court of Britain to leave us
any Hopes of Reconciliation—
The Devil is in them and with them."

—James Read to Edward Shippen, Committee of Safety
Berks County, Pennsylvania
May 1776

"Come! Open the Window and come to bed."

"The Window was open," John Adams wrote, "and I, who was an invalid and afraid of the Air in the night blowing upon me, shut it close."

"'Oh!' says Franklin, 'don't shut the Window. We shall be suffocated,'" Adams recalled Ben Franklin saying. "Come! open the Window and come to bed, and I will convince you," the seventy-year-old doctor told him.

The moment was as poignant as the scene was inglorious, to the point of comical. In a crowded New Jersey tavern, two of the most famous leaders of the American Revolution were forced to share a bed in a small, stuffy room—"a Chamber little larger than the bed, without a Chimney and with only one small window."[1] No special privileges for these congressmen clad in nightshirts, their balding heads capped or uncapped as each saw fit, arguing over whether to open or shut the window. No entourage of bodyguards or escorts accompanied them, and they had no authority, inclination, or opportunity to commandeer more elegant quarters. Like everyone else, they had to take what was available. First come, first served. Perhaps they were lucky to get a room and a bed at all.

In a typical American tavern of that era, patrons not only had to pay extra to sleep in a bed, but shared it with whoever else paid. Many travelers slept on the floor by the big fireplace in the main room to save money, and shared common food at common tables. "Accommodations" in taverns were meant in the most literal sense of the word: to make fit; adjust; adapt. And

The Indian Queen Tavern is traditionally thought to be where John Adams and Benjamin Franklin spent the night of September 10, 1776. The tavern was moved from its original location in downtown New Brunswick to East Jersey Olde Towne, a museum of historic buildings in nearby Piscataway. Built of clapboard, it is typical of the better class of taverns in colonial New Jersey. PHOTO BY KYLE R. WEAVER

in New Brunswick, New Jersey, on the night of September 10, 1776, everyone had to adapt, for the town was jammed with soldiers—hundreds of them, young, undisciplined militiamen for the most part, coming and going at all hours.

But the circumstances of their being together in that room at that moment in history were even more striking. John Adams and Benjamin Franklin, along with Edward "Ned" Rutledge of South Carolina, were on their way to a meeting with one of the most powerful individuals in America, a man with more destructive firepower at his command than any other person in the Western Hemisphere: fifty-year-old Vice Admiral Richard Viscount Howe, commander in chief of the largest fleet ever sent abroad by the British government. Lord Howe was the older brother of Lt. Gen. William Howe, commander in chief of His Majesty's Forces in America, some thirty-two thousand British and Hessian troops, the largest European army ever to cross the Atlantic.

Together, the Howe brothers led the most powerful military force in the world at that moment, and yet they were hoping for peace and reconciliation—on England's terms. They had been granted special powers to act as peace commissioners and to grant amnesty and pardons to nearly all of the American rebels. Given the absence of an American naval force around New York City and the deplorable performance of the fledgling Continental army in its first major battle on Long Island, the brothers were being extremely reasonable in attempting to bring the War for Independence to an end without further useless bloodshed. They were willing to open a door, or even a tiny window, to achieve this end, and they hoped to seduce the American Congress and the people it represented away from their recently declared independence and back into the benevolent arms of the mother country. "It is an unusual, yea, altogether unheard of, thing," Rev. Henry Muhlenberg of Pennsylvania had written in August, "that a mother and her children should fight against one another not with rods and broomsticks but with fire and sword."[2] The Howes would have agreed, and Lord Howe truly believed that his personal effort might find some way to break the intractable deadlock between the two sides.

This is the story of that effort and the meeting that resulted, known in history as the Staten Island Conference. It takes place in the summer of 1776, a time of great change and distress. It is a picture of America at war told through the writings of numerous eyewitnesses, many of whom unknowingly crossed paths with each other and with the more famous history makers. These eyewitnesses—Nicholas Cresswell, Margaret Moncrieffe, and Henry Muhlenberg, among others—help to paint a picture of the country as it was, as they saw it. Finding the characters who wrote about what they saw and connecting them together was challenging; the picture that emerges is remarkable for its depth and its coincidences, reminding us what a small world it really was.

On September 11, 1776, in the Billopp House on the far western tip of Staten Island, Lord Howe personally met with Adams, Franklin, and Rutledge, not as representatives of Congress but as private gentlemen, for a discussion "among friends," as Ben Franklin put it. It was the last time that Britain attempted to speak to America as colonies.

CHAPTER I
The Stranded Englishman

S tranded, stuck in a cold, hostile environment thousands of miles from home on New Year's Eve, a discouraged young man picked up a quill and scratched in his journal, "This is the last day of the year 1775, which I have spent but very indifferently." He was quite mistaken in that estimate of how he spent the year, as his journal clearly shows, but at that wretched moment, all he saw was failure. "In short I have done nothing but wore out my clothes and constitution," he brooded, "and according to the present prospect of affairs, the New Year bids a forbidding aspect."[1]

It was an understandably gloomy assessment from Nicholas Cresswell, a young English adventurer stuck in Virginia during the first years of the American Revolution. "The child Independence is now struggling for birth," Sam Adams wrote of this period, and Cresswell was an accidental eyewitness to the genesis of a new nation moving to cut its ties with England.[2] This placed him in an extremely awkward position, for the political situation required the young man to hold his tongue or risk imprisonment, even physical harm.

Suspected of being a spy, Cresswell spent much of the year living under close surveillance. "I am here a prisoner at large," he scrawled in frustration on that glum New Year's Eve while at Leesburg, a small town near the Potomac River on the northwestern edge of Virginia's frontier. Nicholas desperately wanted to make his way back to England, but knew full well, "If I attempt to depart and don't succeed, a prison must be my lot."

His movements were scrutinized and he had to watch what he said, though not always successfully, especially when in his cups and politics came

5

up. Perpetually short of funds, the poor fellow had to find work; at one point, he made saltpeter (potassium nitrate), a key ingredient in the manufacture of gunpowder. While this provided him an opportunity to earn money and lessen suspicions that he was a British agent, it also disgusted him. "If I do anything to get a living," he ruminated, "perhaps I must be obliged to fight against my King and Country, which my conscience abhors." Determined not to quit, he vowed, "I will wait with patience till summer, and then risk a passage."[3]

Despite these difficulties, this hardy adventurer had managed to travel hundreds of miles through the American wilderness in 1775. Back in April, while on his way from Virginia to Fort Pitt, Cresswell dined at the Great Meadows, where George Washington first made world history by surrendering Fort Necessity in 1754, thus starting the Great War for Empire. (Of this conflict, which was the French and Indian War and the Seven Years' War combined, the French philosopher Voltaire said, "The torch that ignited the world was lit in the forests of America.") Further up the road, Cresswell picked through the bleached bones and broken skulls of Braddock's men slaughtered on the banks of the Monongahela twenty years earlier—grim evidence of the price paid to build the British Empire. He spent the next few months in the Ohio Valley, traveling down the mighty Ohio River towards Illinois, living alternately with rowdy frontiersmen and wild Indians while looking for the land of his dreams.

It was hardly an indifferent way to spend the year.

The larger picture of history often obscures the day-to-day experiences of those who live it, when great events mingle with the monotonous routines of daily life. For Nicholas Cresswell, living through the throes and convulsions of revolutionary America, his experiences were anything but routine. They were nothing short of extraordinary, especially as he crossed paths with some of the leading nationmakers in the days that changed history.

Cresswell's story of coming to America is an old, old tale, lived and retold in countless ways over the centuries. At age twenty-four, he left his parents' home in the Midlands of England, "sensible [that] a person with a small fortune may live much better and make greater improvements in America than he can possibly do in England. Especially in the Farming way, as that is the business I have been brought up to." But unlike many others who arrived with no intention of ever returning to their native lands, Nicholas had a plan. "If I like the Country," he told himself before he set out in 1774, he intended "to return immediately and endeavour to prevail

6

Nicholas Cresswell later returned to Great Britain and had this portrait painted around 1780. The artist is unknown. THE COLONIAL WILLIAMSBURG FOUNDATION

upon my Friends to give me something to begin the world with." Confident in his plans and blessed with the wisdom permitted by the luxury of choice, he reasoned, "I shall by this Voyage be better able to judge what will suit the Country or whether the Country will please me enough to fix my future residence in it or not."[4]

The timing could not have been worse for a patriotic Englishman, nor could it have been better for those who appreciate viewing history through the writings of a thoughtful and credible eyewitness. Cresswell was "determined to keep a daily and impartial Journal from this day," Tuesday, March 1, 1774, while still home in the remote hamlet of Edale, Derbyshire, "by which I hope to square my future conduct."

Neither his parents nor his friends would approve his plans, he knew full well. But, recognizing that his life was in something of a rut in rural England, Nicholas hinted that this trip might demonstrate that he was both capable and ambitious. "I understand that people in general think that I am *Non Compos Mentis*," he learned from a family friend. Even the local parson "made a Sermon on purpose for me" one Sunday. "His text was taken from the parable of the Prodigal Son," Cresswell noted, adding with some annoyance, "it is very strange that these Sons of the Clergy cannot forbear meddling in other people's affairs." Though determined "to brave them all and follow my own inclination for once," this resolute young man was dismayed by the overall lack of enthusiasm for his plan. "In short all my Friends think me mad for attempting to go abroad," he fumed.[5]

No wonder they thought that he was out of his mind. With tensions already high over colonial boycotts and defiance of British authority, news of the Boston Tea Party arrived in England shortly before Nicholas planned to set out. The king and ministry were outraged. As further proof of the viciousness of the Sons of Liberty and their treasonous hostility to lawful government, a copy of a broadside slapped up on the walls of Boston back in January was laid before the House of Commons. It read:

Brethren and Fellow Citizens!

You may depend that those odious miscreants and detestable tools to ministry and governor, the TEA CONSIGNEES (those traitors to their country, butchers, who have done, and are doing every thing to murder and destroy all that shall stand in the way of their private interest) are determined to come and reside again in the town of Boston.

I therefore give you this early notice, that you may hold yourselves in readiness, on the shortest notice, to give them such a reception as such vile ingrates deserve.

JOYCE, jun.
Chairman of the Committee
for Tarring and Feathering.

If any person should be so hardy as to tear this down, they may expect my severest resentment.

J. jun.[6]

Parliament's response to the tea party was to close the port of Boston, revoke the Massachusetts charter, recall the royal governor, and impose martial law on the entire province. More troops were ordered to occupy Boston, and Gen. Thomas Gage, commander in chief of the British army in North America, was appointed military governor of the colony. The point was to coerce the Yankees into obedience and make an example of Massachusetts as a warning to the other colonies.

As Cresswell was packing in March, both houses of Parliament debated and passed the Coercive Acts, four bills that effectively annihilated Boston and Massachusetts politically and economically. The king was only too happy to sign them into law. Though the verbal opposition from the Whigs in Parliament was eloquent—"I wish gentlemen would consider whether it is more proper to govern by military force or by management," argued Whig leader Charles James Fox—it was unavailing, for the destruction of tons of valuable tea in defiance of the government's authority to tax could not be tolerated.[7]

Nicholas was aware of the trouble in a general sense, but he was heading for Virginia, hundreds of miles from Boston. There, far from the simmering cauldron of discontent, he hoped to explore a bit, view the landscape, and get a feel for the opportunities. If things worked out, he planned to strike out on his own.

Little did he know what lay ahead of him, especially as news of the Coercive Acts spread like wildfire through the colonies. The bills raised fear and alarm; many Americans denounced them as the "Intolerable Acts." Calls for resistance went out up and down the Atlantic coast, where local associations and committees encouraged a full boycott of British goods.

With the port of Boston shut, the city faced starvation. The first large-scale disaster relief collection in American history began as tens of thousands of people from all walks of life donated food and clothing to relieve the distressed people of Boston—an important, tangible act of unity involving practically every community. Caravans of relief supplies and livestock headed overland for the beleaguered city, and militia companies everywhere began to drill more regularly. In Pennsylvania, where the provincial government did not have an established militia, thousands of men voluntarily "associated" to defend their rights and formed battalions of Associators by signing their names to Articles of Association, thus creating independent military units with a political agenda. Debates in the colonial legislatures resulted in the summoning of the First Continental Congress in Philadelphia, a general meeting of representatives "from the continent" to discuss the situation.

In the midst of it all came Nicholas Cresswell, hoping to find his fortune and himself in the process—a sanguine young Englishman landing in a continent on the verge of war with England.

He arrived in southern Maryland near the mouth of the Potomac River in May of 1774 after a mercifully swift voyage of thirty-eight days from Liverpool. "Nothing talked about but the Blockade of Boston Harbour," was his first journal entry about politics, written at the end of May. Cresswell was shocked to find that "the people seem much exasperated at the proceedings of the Ministry and talk as if they were determined to dispute the matter with the sword."[8] Surely they couldn't be serious, he thought.

After being delayed a few weeks by a fever, during which a doctor almost killed him with mercury pills, Nicholas was able to go up the Potomac to Alexandria, Virginia, in time to see a local plantation owner and former militia officer, Col. George Washington, reelected to the House of Burgesses on July 14. "The Candidates gave the populace a Hogshead of Toddy (what we call Punch in England)," he noted, a common practice on election days to treat the voters. "In the evening the returned Member gave a Ball to the Freeholders and Gentlemen of the town."

Cresswell attended the festivities hosted by Washington and met this extraordinary man, who at nearly six feet, three inches stood out in any gathering. Nicholas also recorded his first experience with the boycott against the mother country. "Coffee and Chocolate, but no Tea," he observed at the ball, noting that "this Herb is in disgrace among them at present."[9] A few weeks later, Washington was on his way to Philadelphia as a delegate to the First Continental Congress for discussion of a united response to the Coercive Acts.

Greatly impressed, Cresswell wrote much about George Washington in his journal. "His entertainments were always conducted with the most regularity and in the genteelest manner of any I ever was at on the Continent (and I have been at several of them, that is, before he was made a General)," he stated, describing the Virginian at length. "Temperance he always observed, was always cool-headed and exceedingly cautious himself, but took great pleasure at seeing his friends entertained in the way most agreeable to themselves." Of Martha Washington, Nicholas commented that "His lady is of a hospitable disposition, always good-humoured and cheerful, and seems to be actuated by the same motives with himself, but she is rather of a more lively disposition." As husband and wife, "they are to all appearances a happy pair."[10]

While on his return voyage to England a few years later, Cresswell reflected, "Washington is certainly a most surprising man, one of Nature's geniuses, a Heaven-born General, if there is any of that sort." Though Nicholas referred to him as "a great and wonderful man," by no means was he enamored with Washington's politics. In fact, he considered the Virginian to be the tool of New England radicals such as Sam and John Adams to accomplish their "diabolical purposes." Nevertheless, he was able to say, "Washington, my Enemy as he is, I should be sorry if he should be brought to an ignominious death."[11]

Early in the spring of 1775, shortly before hostilities erupted, Cresswell proceeded with his plan of seeing the country. He set out toward Fort Pitt with high hopes of making money through trade goods and land speculation, the usual way of doing business on the frontier at that time. He was in western Pennsylvania when the war broke out at Lexington and Concord on April 19, but didn't hear the news for several weeks. From Fort Pitt, he proceeded down the Ohio River to Kentucky, where he met up with a party of traders heading for Illinois.

It was a rough and colorful crowd, to say the least, an ethnic microcosm of the American nation; Cresswell's description sounds much like the opening of a long-winded joke. "Our company is increased to 14 persons and almost as many different nations," he stated, enumerating "two Englishmen, two Irishmen, one Welshman, two Dutchmen, two Virginians, two Marylanders, one Swede, one African Negro, and a Mulatto." Setting off with a mixture of anticipation and dread, "with the motley, rascally, and ragged crew I have to travel six hundred miles," he wrote from the Ohio River on June 15.[12]

They quarreled and quibbled, saw plenty of buffalo, and paddled through hundreds of miles of wilderness. One fine day, the adventurers groped around in a muddy pond for mastodon fossils at a place with the charming name of Elephant Bone Lick.[13] Over the next few weeks, Cresswell shot a panther, learned all about snakes—especially rattlesnakes—and became quite a hand at making buffalo jerky. He met many different Native Americans and, at one point, took a comely young Indian maiden as a temporary wife. The group also lost their provisions, suffered from thieves and deserters, and had a grand time. Nicholas was able to see America and Americans as he had planned—in the wild, up close, and personal.

More than once he nearly came to blows with some of his companions, especially when they talked politics. Other, more serious dangers lurked in the shadows: Because they were traveling in the wake of Dunmore's War against the Shawnee, contradictory reports of Indian atrocities tinged the expedition with apprehension. Several wanted to turn back, but not Nicholas; he was determined to forge ahead and not give in to a set of "damn'd Cowards."

One soggy, oppressive morning, after a miserable day and night of rain, the group paddled far out into the middle of the Ohio River. Up ahead in the mist, they made out the forms of four fully loaded Indian canoes steadily coming toward them. Unsure if the natives were friendly or hostile, they turned away and headed for land, only to discover six more crowded canoes between them and the shore. The adventurers were outnumbered and effectively surrounded, and the red men appeared to be heavily armed.

They panicked; the "motley, rascally, and ragged crew" hastily prepared for battle by dumping their trading supplies and most of their provisions in the river. The overnight rain had wet half of their firearms, rendering them useless. As they madly scrambled to find dry muskets, each man's character was revealed, and they ran the full spectrum.

Cresswell took command of three canoes and braced himself for a fight to the finish. "Jacob Nalen (a Swede) commanded a canoe . . . Williams, the Welshman, commanded the other," Nicholas recounted, while "Clifton, tho' a young boy, behaved with the greatest resolution." Others were not so brave. Joseph Boassiers, an American, got his musket wet and was "weeping, praying, saying Ave Mary's [Hail Marys] in abundance, at the same time hugging a little wooden crucifix he pulled from his bosom most heartily." An Irishman named Tom O'Brien dropped to the bottom of the canoe with Boassiers, pulled out a string of rosary beads, "and prayed and howled in Irish."

Outraged by these displays of cowardice, in the heat of the moment, "[I] set the muzzle of my Gun to O'Brien's head, threatening to blow his brains out if he did not immediately take his paddle," Cresswell wrote. Fortunately, "it had the desired effect, he begged for his life, invoked St. Patrick, took his paddle and howled most horribly." O'Brien's blubbering helped to break the tension, for "dangerous and desperate as we imagined our situation to be," Nicholas snickered, "I could not forbear laughing to see the condition of this poor fellow."

Usually impassive, especially with strangers, even the Indians burst out laughing as they viewed the panic, a measure of just how ludicrous the spectacle appeared to them. They proved to be a hunting party of friendly Delawares (Lenni Lenape) led by a brave named Catfish and accompanied by several squaws, "some of them very handsome," Cresswell couldn't help but notice. The natives were armed mostly with poles and canoe paddles, "but our fears had converted them into Guns," he sheepishly admitted. The episode had a happy ending as the group "proceeded up the River very merry at the expense of our cowardly companions," whose sniveling soon turned to bragging about what they *would* have done had a fight actually started.[14]

All of that was in the distant past for Nicholas as he faced 1776. He managed to enjoy the New Year's festivities in Leesburg over the next few days, though politics were never far from his mind. A few days later, he went down to Alexandria and was there trying to figure out a way to get home when copies of one of the most important publications in American history arrived from Philadelphia.

"Friday, January 19, 1776. A pamphlet called 'Commonsense' makes a great noise," he noted in his journal. *Common Sense* quickly became the most widely read and influential political pamphlet of its time, with more than one hundred thousand copies printed in three months, and twenty-five editions—half a million copies—by year's end. In a nation of less than three million people, it was the all-time bestseller in colonial America, containing some of the most radical and dangerous political ideas in human history. It also created a groundswell among the American people in favor of permanent separation from Britain.

Nicholas was horrified by *Common Sense*, calling it "One of the vilest things that ever was published to the world. Full of false representations, lies, calumny, and treason, whose principles are to subvert all Kingly Governments and erect an Independent Republic." His reaction was like many others who read it. "I believe the writer to be some Yankey Presbyterian, Member of the Congress," he concluded, with John Adams foremost in his mind as the author. Little did he know that it was written by a radical English Deist, Thomas Paine, a former revenue collector who left England a few months after Cresswell in 1774. What Nicholas did know was that, in Virginia, "The sentiments are adopted by a great number of people who are indebted to Great Britain," which to him rendered the whole movement a treasonous, disgraceful sham, fueled by nothing more than greed and self-interest.

"Nothing but Independence talked of," Cresswell wrote a few days later, especially after news of the burning of Norfolk, Virginia, by British naval forces on New Year's Day inflamed the local population. His chance of escaping to England evaporated when all ships in Alexandria bound for Britain or Ireland were stopped. By the end of the week, "Nothing but

Independence will go down," he reiterated, adding, "the Devil is in the people."[15]

Lord Dunmore, the royal governor of Virginia, called for a slave insurrection and made overtures to Native Americans to rise against frontier settlements. News that Parliament was raising large battalions of Scottish Highlanders for service in America drove home the message that London had no qualms about using "savages," whether black, red, or white, against American Whigs. Further reports that the ministry was hiring thousands of Hessian and other German soldiers (after failing to secure twenty thousand Russian troops) convinced many Americans that the royal government was prepared to crush them, no matter the cost in money or honor, and that there was no chance for reconciliation except by absolute submission to "the royal brute."

By June, the stage was set in Congress for open debate on independence. In Philadelphia on June 7, Richard Henry Lee of Virginia moved a resolution, "that these United Colonies are, and of right ought to be, free and independent States." The final breach came on July 2 when Congress adopted the resolution after impassioned debates, especially between John Adams and John Dickinson, a Pennsylvania delegate. Dickinson felt that independence was going too far and could not bring himself to agree with it, but he still believed that resistance in defense of American rights as Englishmen was his duty. After absenting himself from the final vote, Dickinson left Congress once the Declaration of Independence was adopted and marched off to war as colonel of the First Battalion of Philadelphia Associators.

In his journal, Cresswell sarcastically referred to Congress as "the Great Sanhedrim" or Sanhedrin, a mocking reference to the Jewish assembly from Biblical times. He was back in Leesburg when, on Tuesday, July 9, 1776, he received "News that the Sanhedrim had declared the thirteen united Colonies Free and Independent States." Nicholas saw this as the fulfillment of a long-laid scheme plotted by the radical New Englanders. "That this was intended by the Northern Colonies from the first, I am well convinced," he wrote, "and the following two Letters confirm me in that opinion."[16]

The letters had been intercepted by royal agents nearly a year earlier. John Adams was their author, and both were published in Tory newspapers to embarrass Congress and discredit Adams. They went far in accomplishing both. "I saw this profound and enlightened patriot walk our streets alone after the publication of his intercepted letters in our newspapers in 1775," Dr. Benjamin Rush recalled, Adams having become "an object of nearly universal detestation."[17]

Cresswell thought the letters important enough to copy into his journal. First was a confidential "Anonymous letter to the Honble. James Warren," in which Adams had written, "We ought to have had in our hands a month ago the whole legislative, executive and judicial of the whole Continent and have completely modelled a Constitution." Adams recommended that America raise a naval power, open all of its ports wide to the world, and also "to have arrested every Friend to Government on the Continent and held them as hostages" for the people of Boston, who were then under martial law. "And then," Adams wrote, "open the door as wide as possible for Peace and Reconciliation."

So, Adams wanted to know, what did Warren think? "Is all this extravagant? Is it wild?" he asked rhetorically, answering, "Is it not the soundest Policy?" The letter also contained acerbic personal remarks about individuals, including Adams's assessment that "a certain great fortune and piddling genius, whose fame has been loudly trumpetted, has given a silly cast to our proceedings." The "piddling genius" was John Dickinson.

Adams's second letter was to his wife Abigail, in which he says, among other things, "I wish I had given you a complete history from the beginning to the end of the Journey of the behaviour of my Compatriots," meaning his fellow congressmen. "No mortal could equal it. I will tell you in future, but you shall keep it secret. The fidgets, the whims, the caprice, the Vanity, the Superstition, the Irritability of some is enough to——." After copying all of this into his journal, Cresswell noted with some satisfaction that "Both these Letters were intercepted by the King's Officers and published in Draper's *Massachusetts Gazette* in August last."[18]

But now—Adams having weathered the embarrassment—the deed was done. "This cursed Independence has given me great uneasiness," Cresswell admitted in mid-July. Between bouts of illness, the debilitating summer "agues" and fevers, he kept hoping to find a way out. Privately venting his feelings, he seethed, "Saturday, July 20 . . . I am now got almost strong enough to shoot a Yankee Man." The next day, Nicholas was thrilled to hear "News that Lord Howe was arriving at New York with a large fleet and numerous Army." With new optimism he prayed, "God send him good health."

There were also British warships in the Chesapeake Bay, down near Gwynn's Island below the mouth of the Rappahannock River. In late July, Cresswell met with Mr. Thomson Mason, the younger brother of prominent Virginia leader George Mason, "who proffers to give me a letter of recommendation to the Governor [Patrick] Henry for liberty to go on board the Fleet in the Bay." This raised the young man's hopes yet again that he would finally be able to get home to England.

But a week later, on August 1, it all fell apart. "News that Lord Dunmore was driven from Gwinn's Island and the Fleet had left the Bay," he scrawled in frustration. "I am now at a loss again." With his plans for escape dashed once more, Nicholas confided his one last hope to his journal that day: "Determined to go to New York and endeavour to get to the Army."[19]

But how?

CHAPTER 2

The Patriarch

he old man's responsibilities were enormous, and all things considered, he handled them with remarkable ability and grace. If he was cranky at times, he could be forgiven, for his life's work involved mediating endless rounds of wrangles, "confusions," and community turmoil. At age sixty-five, he was a husband of thirty-one years, the father of eleven children (seven of whom lived to adulthood), grandfather of thirteen, and one of the most respected leaders not only in Philadelphia but along the Atlantic seaboard. Fluent in German, Dutch, and English, he served as a bridge between people, as well as heaven and earth. When folks got sick, he visited them, compounded herbal medicines for them, and prayed with them, providing comfort for body and soul. When they wanted to get married, or have their children baptized, or be buried, he was there for them. And when the war came, despite his ambivalence, he stood with them, all the while deploring it and the evil forces that brought it about.

He was a patriarch in the best sense of the word.

In 1776, Rev. Henry Melchior Muhlenberg was the senior Lutheran churchman in America. Three decades before, at age thirty-one, he had been sent from Halle, Germany, to revive the fledgling Lutheran congregations in Pennsylvania. Within a year of landing in 1742, he built the Augustus Lutheran Church at Trappe in what was then near-wilderness thirty miles northwest of Philadelphia. More than two and a half centuries later, the congregation endures in the midst of suburban sprawl, and the little stone church dedicated in 1743 remains the oldest unchanged Lutheran church building in America. Muhlenberg is now regarded as the American church's virtual founder.

After his arrival in America, the pastor traveled far and wide. Over the next thirty years, he established congregations from New York to Georgia, working to sustain them through dire hardships as well as in good times. Muhlenberg's journal, thousands of pages faithfully kept for four decades, is extraordinary for its details of events, erudite theological arguments, weather data, and astute observations of social conditions. In its revelation of one man's real-life struggle for righteousness in a world wracked by violence and sin, the journal is priceless.

Lately, though, he often felt like a "fifth wheel," a "worn-out horse," an "old fogey"—terms he himself used in the journal, albeit in German—or, at best, "old man Muhlenberg." By early 1775, returning to Philadelphia utterly worn out from weeks of mediating a tedious clerical dispute in Georgia, Muhlenberg saw himself winding down a long and useful life. He came back to several congregations fractured by internal dissention in a city about to become the epicenter of revolution.

The war disturbed Muhlenberg greatly and seemed to divide his family. Lutheran doctrine asserted the supremacy of governmental authority, especially the divine right of kings and the duty of submission by subjects, and yet he understood the grievances of the American Whigs. Two of his three sons, ministers all, strongly bickered over the issues: Frederick, from his urbane Lutheran church in New York City, and Peter, schooled Lutheran but ordained Anglican, from his rustic parish in Woodstock, Virginia. Admonishing his flock that "there is a time to pray and a time to fight," Peter allegedly removed his clerical gown in church to reveal a military uniform. Frederick admonished his older brother about his rebellious and militaristic inclinations, suggesting that one cannot serve two masters: He must choose to be either a preacher or a soldier. Furthermore, perhaps Peter's ambition to always be "the big man" was the true secret reason for his actions. The aspiring soldier fired back at the preacher, suggesting that he had been corrupted by cosmopolitan living in New York, that "sinkhole of Toryism," which needed to be "purged with fire." [1]

Peter had been elected to the House of Burgesses in 1774 at the same time George Washington was reelected, as witnessed by Cresswell. Before that, back in his rebellious adolescence, Peter had served a very brief stint in the British army with the Sixtieth Royal Americans. Now, in 1776, the Lutheran-turned-Anglican minister became colonel of the Eighth Virginia

Henry Melchior Muhlenberg, "Doctor of Holy Scripture and Senior Evangelical Lutheran Minister," was pictured on the frontispiece of Denkmal der liebe und achtung *by Justus Henry Christian Helmuth, published in Philadelphia in 1788.*

Regiment and marched off to South Carolina to defend Charleston against a British attack.

Within his family and without, "old man Muhlenberg" was clearly distressed by the times. Among other things, Henry worried that so many of the leaders coming to the fore in Pennsylvania were not believers in traditional Christian protestant doctrines—Ben Franklin, for example, was a self-proclaimed Deist—but were part of the Enlightenment, which fueled the push for radical change in politics and religious beliefs. "No wonder that present-day Christendom is overrun with so-called practical atheists, pretended Deists, Naturalists, and scoffing Philistines," the pastor complained in his journal on St. Patrick's Day in 1776, "who, orally and in writing, exhale their foul breath and express their loathing of the glorious plan of salvation."[2] He himself was an evangelical preacher, strongly influenced by Pietism and the Great Awakening and deploring the growing secularization of late-eighteenth-century thought.

As tensions in Philadelphia increased, the pastor looked to his old haunts in rural Trappe as a refuge from the turmoil. There was a good-sized property for sale on the Reading Road in Providence Township, halfway between Philadelphia and Reading and only a mile down the road from Augustus Church. It consisted of "seven to eight acres adjacent to the street, most of it laid out in orchards and vegetable gardens." Fronting on the road, Henry wrote, "is a large two-story dwelling, built of massive stones, with four rooms on the lower and four on the upper floor. Nearby is a one-story stone house and workshop, together with two draw-wells and a large stone barn and stables." For a man with such a large family and constantly busy with pastoral business, this situation was a godsend, so Muhlenberg purchased it on January 1, 1776. "The buildings were erected twenty and more years ago, when I was still living in Providence, by one of our parishioners, and must have cost him from £500 to £600," he cannily noted. "I was able, though not without difficulties, to purchase the place in my name, and as my estate and landed property, for £340."[3]

The pre-war boycotts and political situation had already severely strained the economy. Long before the war, the provincial government of Pennsylvania issued paper currency (Pennsylvania pounds and shillings, valued at about 70 percent of British sterling), but now inflation soared because of military demands and speculators hoarding goods. "The seller of the property would have preferred silver or gold coins, but this is not available any longer, for, since the war, paper money is quite the usual thing," Muhlenberg explained. "Anyone who looks down upon it, or refuses to

The Muhlenberg House on the Ridge Pike in Trappe, Pennsylvania, was built around 1755 and purchased by Henry Melchior Muhlenberg on January 1, 1776. PHOTO BY KYLE R. WEAVER

accept it as valid, is publically regarded and treated as an enemy and traitor to his country. This makes land expensive."

Continental paper money, issued by Congress and valued in Spanish silver dollars (the most common silver coins in circulation), added to the uncertainty. "One does not know how things will turn out or which party will gain the upper hand," the preacher commented. "If the Americans lose, the value of their paper money will be lost, too." He further justified the bargain by saying, "I could only give what I had received, and I was glad that the man accepted it and that, in return therefore, he transferred to me the little farm, which is more stable in value."[4]

Muhlenberg had certainly made a bargain, but moving in was a different story. The buildings had been occupied for two decades by artisans and tradesmen, and through neglect were falling into ruin. The main house was run down and utterly filthy; broken windows, clogged chimneys, and accumulated crud awaited the new owner. The tenants had until spring to move out.

In early March, two British forty-four-gun frigates, the *Roebuck* and the *Liverpool*, came up the Delaware River to within thirty miles of Philadelphia. The Pennsylvania Navy—a flotilla of small craft, each armed with one or two heavy guns—went down to exchange cannon fire with the warships near Wilmington. Apprehension gripped the city as the sounds of war thundered up the river, so Muhlenberg decided to get the country house in order as quickly as possible. Hiring several scrubwomen and workmen, the pastor went out to Trappe in late March and began renovations to make the place livable, but building materials and laborers were becoming harder to find.

The tension in the streets of Philadelphia was worsening. Back in town on May 17, "The day of prayer and fasting decreed by the Continental Congress was observed today," Muhlenberg wrote, but there was trouble. "The Quakers protested beforehand openly and in writing that they were unable for reasons of conscience to obey such human ordinances, and some of them opened their stalls and shops on this day in order to express their defiance of so-called human ordinances." Quaker beliefs at that time disdained holidays, whether religious or political, seeing them as lingering paganism or frivolous vanity and an imposition on liberty of conscience. But others in town did not see it that way, as Muhlenberg observed firsthand. "Before one knew it, however, a crowd of half-grown boys and students began to riot, walked up and down with clubs, etc., and ordered the conscientious Friends to take down their signs and close their shops for the day," he witnessed with dismay. "The obedient ones listened to the voices of the boys; stubborn ones were compelled by stones to listen."[5]

By contrast, out in Reading, the seat of Berks County sixty miles northwest of Philadelphia, "Our inhabitants observed the Fast Day very well—The Churches here were full Yesterday," Chairman James Read of the Berks Committee of Safety reported. "Our Parson has not attended Church since sometime in September last, now more than 7 Months, but the German Lutheran Minister gave us a very good Sermon in English Yesterday Evening, after he had preached twice in German to his own Congregation." The preacher "was very pathetic," Read noticed, meaning that his sermon was effectively delivered in an emotional style, "and did not fail to put us in mind of the Sins of the Land as the Occasion of the present Cloud impending over us, and to urge Repentance and then a Confidence in the Divine providence, and hopes that a Day of Deliverance and Salvation from our Enemy would shortly come." The preaching strongly echoed the sentiments of Henry Muhlenberg himself.

As for the war, "We may daily expect to hear of Hostilities on our Coasts from the Great Fleet lately seen in its Course from England to

America," Read continued. Regarding a British peace commission, rumors of which had been circulating for weeks, "I imagine that all the Commissioners which are coming are Soldiers & Sailors, <u>determined</u>, if they can, to exterminate us," he mused. It was as if Read had a pipeline into the office of Lord Germain and the ministry. "There is too much Hatred and Bitterness towards us in the Court of Britain to leave us any Hopes of Reconciliation," the chairman commented. "The Devil is in them and with them wherever they or their murderous Agents go—But they will not succeed in their iniquitous Designs," Read went on, prophetically stating, "Murders, indeed, we shall hear of in great number. But they will rouse us out of our Supineness and we shall unite and disperse our Enemies. For, I really believe, God is with us—and that he will scatter those that delight in War."[6]

The first of those soldiers and sailors, led by Lt. Gen. William Howe, arrived off Staten Island on June 29, throwing New York City into a panic. Frederick Muhlenberg decided to leave with his family and head for his father's place in Philadelphia. "Following the advice of prudent friends, Friedrich Mühlenberg arrived today from New York, bringing such household goods with him as he was able to take from the city," Henry jotted in his journal on July 2, the day that British forces began landing on Staten Island. The old man also heard an important rumor in town that day: "It is said that the Continental Congress resolved to declare the thirteen united colonies free and *independent*."[7]

Two days later, "Today the Continental Congress openly declared the united provinces of North America to be free and *independent* states," he recorded. Of the news, "This has caused some thoughtful and far-seeing *melancholici* [pessimistic people] to be down in the mouth," the astute old pastor observed; on the other hand, "it has caused some sanguine *miopes* [short-sighted people] to exult and shout for joy." In his own erudite, noncommittal way he wrote in Latin, "*In fine videbitur cuius toni*" ("It will appear in the end who has played the right tune").[8]

The first public reading of the Declaration of Independence took place in the State House Yard on July 8. "Today the united North American provinces were proclaimed *independent* from the *state* house," Muhlenberg entered in the journal, simply adding the notation "Psalm 127:1" as commentary. The passage, "Except the Lord buildeth the house, they who labour build it in vain," is important for understanding the minister's concerns, for unlike many others who were convinced that God was on the side of the revolutionaries, Muhlenberg remained skeptical that the leaders were religiously committed in acceptable ways to warrant divine support.

Further, "an election is being held in Philadelphia, and in the whole province" to create a new state government. "The inhabitants are to elect their delegates *per plurima vota* to a *convention*, which *convention* is to have its first session in Philadelphia on July 15 (unless the city is taken by surprise before that)," he cautioned, because "the large battle fleet has arrived in New York with its armed forces, which has landed on Staaten Island near New York."[9]

After the Declaration was read, a group of Philadelphia Associators went into the State House and removed the royal coat of arms from the wall behind the chief justice's chair. The symbol of kingly, divinely ordained government—figures of crowned lions and the royal motto *Dieu et Mon Droit* ("God and My Right") was carried a mile outside of town to the camp on the common at Center Square and heaved into a bonfire, to the cheers of the assembled Associators. Downtown later that evening, another crowd cheered when the royal arms over the entrance of Christ Church was pulled down and cast into a fire in front of the old courthouse at Second and Market Streets, the church bells pealing merrily away.

John Dickinson, who had argued relentlessly with John Adams in the debate and refused to sign the Declaration, now put on his uniform as colonel of the 1st Battalion of Philadelphia Associators. "In the month of July the associated citizens in the city were ordered to march into the neighboring province of new Jersey to form an army of observation, as the British military force has landed on Staaten Eiland," Henry Muhlenberg wrote. "This change has considerably emptied the city of civilian soldiers as well as the churches of men, so that my assistance was unnecessary and the completion of the house in Providence was the more necessary since it is now expected that the weaker vessels and children of my family will have to flee from Philadelphia to Providence."

The pastor had made up his mind. Just after dawn on Thursday, July 11, "I set out in an *extra* wagon on a journey to Providence, accompanied by my wife, who is still sick, and my little daughter. Paid 2s. for breakfast in an inn twelve miles from Philadelphia," probably in Plymouth Township. It was a very warm, sticky day, with temperatures already in the 70s at daybreak and wind from the southwest. There was a passing shower in mid-morning, about the time the Muhlenbergs stopped for breakfast. By early afternoon, the temperature outside Philadelphia was in the mid 80s.[10] "Arrived safely in Providence under God's protection about three o'clock in the afternoon," the minister rejoiced after the ten-hour ride in the steamy heat. He had come home again, though the place was not quite ready for them; the kitchen needed to be completed. "Sent letters to Philadelphia to secure three hundred bricks and also wrote an acquaintance in Barren Hill to send up a load of lime" to make mortar, he wrote a few days later. To the old man's chagrin, though, "It was impossible, however, to secure either lime or horse and wagon as the men and wagons and horses have departed with the army of observation." The realities of war were more evident in daily life. "They are doing as did the ancient Romans and Swedes, going from the plow to the camp," the pastor rued, "or, as God's Word says, beating their plowshares into swords."[11]

The trip out from Philadelphia had exhausted him. "Friday, July 12: Owing to fatigue, was unable to write; attributable to the trip yesterday."[12] Unknown to the pastor, a hundred miles to the northeast, the currents of history were about to shift again that same day.

CHAPTER 3

The Peace Commissioner

E yed through a spyglass from the lower end of Manhattan Island, the scene was magnificent, if not daunting. Around six o'clock on the glorious summer evening of July 12, 1776, as the sun began slowly descending over the deep green hills of Staten Island, spangling the harbor with silver and gold, a lone, majestic warship glided through the Narrows, its acres of ivory-hued canvas billowing in the wind. From the top of the foremast, a thick crimson cross of St. George rippled across the folds of a huge white banner streaming out from the webs of rigging, while below, the figurehead of a great carved and gilded bird swept back its wings, its fearsome golden beak screeching forward under glaring eyes. The man-o'-war's name arced gracefully across the ornately carved stern in bold white letters: E A G L E.

Off the port side, thousands of redcoats stood in long lines along the Staten Island shore, welcoming the ship with husky shouts of *huzza!* Great, cotton-like puffs of smoke belched forth amid the forest of masts and crowded hulls anchored by the Watering Place, followed seconds later by the deep, resounding thuds of naval cannon saluting the massive vessel. The thundering continued for some time as the guns fired in measured cadence, one after the other from each warship, rebounding and echoing across the harbor, while cheering sailors greeted the newcomer.

The *Eagle* had landed in America.

"New York July 12th 1776 ¼ past 8 PM . . . Several ships have come in to day, among them, one this Evening with a St Georges Flag at her Fore

This eyewitness image of Admiral Howe's flagship HMS Eagle *(the single large ship to the right of center) arriving in the New York harbor, titled "View of the Narrows between Long Island & Staaten Island with our Fleet at Anchor & Lord Howe coming in—taken from the height above the Watering Place Staaten Island 12th July 1776," was drawn by Capt. Archibald Robertson of the British Engineers.* SPENCER COLLECTION, THE NEW YORK PUBLIC LIBRARY, ASTOR, LENNOX AND TILDEN FOUNDATIONS

topmast head," Gen. George Washington informed President John Hancock, "which we conclude to be Admiral Howe from the circumstance of the Flag, and the several and General Salutes that were paid."[1] Congress was now alerted that Vice Admiral of the White Richard Viscount Howe, the newly commissioned commander in chief of His Majesty's Fleet in North America and older brother of Lt. Gen. William Howe, commander in chief of His Majesty's Army in North America, had arrived.

A few hours earlier, the American artillery around New York harbor had been thundering away for much of the afternoon. Two British warships, the forty-four-gun *Phoenix* and the twenty-gun *Rose*, had gone up the North River under full sail between three and five o'clock and came under heavy fire, first from the batteries at Red Hook on Long Island and the fort on Governor's Island, then from the Grand Battery and numerous other batteries in lower Manhattan and Paulus Hook in New Jersey. The ships held their fire until they came near Paulus Hook, when "they began to fire on both sides, on which the Rebels fled from their Works at Paulus's Hook, but returned at intervals to their Guns and fired them," a British officer noted.[2]

In the city, "when they came to this side of Trinity Church, they began to fire smartly," Rev. Mr. Shewkirk of the Moravian Church wrote. "The balls and bullets went through several houses between here and Greenwich," he observed, as screaming citizens fled to safety in the Bowery, at that time the upper east outskirts of town. Amid the crashing glass and splintering wood, "The smoke of the firing drew over our street like a cloud, and the air was filled with the smell of the powder," the minister noted.[3] *The New-York Gazette* reported three cannonballs striking a Captain Clarke's house in Greenwich, "one of which went thro' the Front and lodged in a Brick Wall at the Head of Miss Clarke's Bed, in her Chamber, a Second went thro' the House, and the Third destroyed several Trees before the Door, and took its Course into the Woods."[4] The only recorded fatalities were five or six Continental artillerymen killed by their own gun bursting at the lower battery in Manhattan and a cow taken out by return fire from His Majesty's ships.[5] The smoke had barely cleared when the British guns down by Staten Island announced Admiral Lord Howe's arrival on the *Eagle*.

The admiral was just under fifty years old, the youngest in the Royal Navy. At five feet, nine inches, he stood about two inches above average height, though not as tall as his brother the general, who towered over six feet. Richard Howe's swarthy, weathered complexion earned him the nickname "Black Dick," and he was the archetype of an eighteenth-century British admiral. His demeanor was described as solemn, almost grave, with deep-set brown eyes under bushy eyebrows and a bald crown. It was said that his sailors knew a battle was in the offing whenever Black Dick's countenance lightened with the shadow of a smile. His looks were so rugged that the great portrait artist Sir Joshua Reynolds remarked to Howe's sister Caroline that the admiral would be an "incomparable" subject to paint because "a pretty man does not make a good portrait."[6]

The admiral's flagship was a behemoth, a sixty-four gun "double-decker" with a crew of five hundred and twenty men. While not the largest ship in the Royal Navy (she ranked as a third-class ship of the line), the *Eagle* was of the largest class of British warships in the American theater and one of the newest. She was launched in 1774 and commissioned on February 7, 1776, just two days after Lord Howe officially accepted his commission from the king. The ship's captain was the Honorable Henry Duncan, assisted by four lieutenants: Samuel Reeve, John Howarth, Harry Harwood, and Philip Brown.[7]

Vice Admiral of the White Richard Viscount Howe by John Singleton Copley. NATIONAL
MARITIME MUSEUM, GREENWICH, LONDON

Two months and one day earlier, the *Eagle* had departed England from
Portsmouth, weighing anchor at St. Helens Roadstead off the Isle of
Wight. Lord Howe's civilian secretary, Ambrose Serle, kept a journal in
which he recorded the thrills and tedium of sea travel, the monotonous
weeks of sameness standing in dramatic counterpoint to the terrors of five
gut-wrenching days and nights at the mercy of a hurricane. They came
across icebergs, one so astonishing in its grandeur that the ship's mate drew
a watercolor of it in the logbook. "Wednesday, June 12: Two very large
Islands of ice we came up to this morning," Serle noted. "One was of a very
particular Construction, and at least as large as Westminster Abbey."[8] Like
countless other sea travelers over the centuries, when the ship neared the
North American coast, Serle was struck by the sweet aroma of pine trees,
remarking that it was a welcome change from the shipboard smells of tar
and rope and the effluvia of five hundred men living in the hold.

The admiral's demeanor and personal example set the tone on the ship. "The Deportment of a Chief inspires the Conduct of all his Subordinates; and it is remarkably the Case on board the *Eagle*," Serle remarked one Sunday after divine service. "No Noise, Disorder, Swearing, or Immoralities; but an easy, manly Carriage seems to animate our whole Company." Other officers told Serle that they thought it the best ships' company in the Royal Navy. "The Admiral is no less the Glory of the Fleet, than his brother the General is the Idol of the Army."[9]

Admiral Howe's courage and steady manner were revered by the men and respected in Parliament. "Give us Black Dick and we fear nothing," echoed from the line at Spithead to the floor of the House of Commons.[10] During a particularly violent storm, the new flagship and its crew were tested to the limit in every way. "But great as she was & heavy in Bulk, she was tossed from Billow to Billow like a cork, and sported about by the Winds & the Waves like a Feather," Serle recounted. "Fear and Dread began to prevail in most Countenances. Men reeled to & fro indeed, and seemed (many of them at least) to be at their Wits End." But not the admiral: "Lord Howe possessed himself with great Composure." By contrast, "For my own part, I prepared myself for Death, and retired to my Cot," Serle frankly admitted, after saying his prayers.[11]

On that long-awaited day when they arrived off New York, the secretary was ecstatic. "Friday, July 12: This morning, the Sun shining bright, we had a beautiful Prospect of the Coast of New Jersey at about 5 or 6 Miles Distance," Serle wrote. "The Land was cleared in many Places, and the Woods were interspersed with Houses, which being covered with white Shingles appeared very plainly all along the Shore." Off the entrance of New York harbor stood Sandy Hook lighthouse, a tall, octagonal stone tower built on the hook of land jutting out from the Highlands of Neversink. "We passed Sandy Hook in the Afternoon, and about 6 o'Clock arrived safe off the East Side of Staten Island," the secretary recorded with relief. After eight weeks at sea, he was happy to see that "the Country on both Sides was highly picturesque and agreeable."

And then, there was the welcome from the British forces on Staten Island. "Nothing could exceed the Joy that appeared throughout the Fleet and Army upon our Arrival," Serle exclaimed. "We were saluted by all the Ships of War in the Harbour, by the Cheers of the Sailors all along the Ships, and by those Soldiers on the Shore. A finer Scene could not be exhibited, both of Country, Ships, and men, all heightened by one of the brightest Days that can be imagined."[12] The euphoria of everyone aboard the *Eagle* could barely be contained.

The admiral had arrived with a second commission: that of peacemaker. Lord Howe had set sail after months of wrangling in London, where he had used his extensive political influence in Parliament and at court to get command of the North American fleet, and then to secure authority to try and negotiate a peaceful settlement. He had to outmaneuver the convoluted webs of both the Ministry and the Admiralty, neither of which trusted him, for His Lordship had been an advocate of reconciliation for several years and was entirely too moderate in his view of the Americans, they felt.

The American war had polarized Parliament, and even those Tory ministers who hoped for a better solution than force were being hounded by the hard-liners, who saw anything short of demanding absolute submission by the colonists as weakness. The radical Whig opposition in the House of Commons was merciless in its denunciations of Tory policies, the expense of the war, and the extreme measures of hiring thousands of German mercenaries, which they predicted would be the ruin of the empire. The Howe brothers were both of the Whig faction, and while loyal to their duty as military leaders, they agreed that the Tories were grossly mismanaging affairs. The Howes recognized that the force required to subdue the rebellion would cause extensive destruction and embitter the population, rendering an unmanageable America nearly useless to Britain. The expense of it all would ruin both.

John Montagu, Lord Sandwich, First Lord of the Admiralty, loathed Lord Howe and his attitudes. In February 1776, Sandwich handed one of his cronies a valuable office long promised to Howe by Lord North. Seizing the opportunity, Black Dick threatened the prime minister with his own resignation and his brother's. Howe then appealed directly to the king and succeeded in being named commander in chief of the North American fleet, in place of fifty-nine-year-old Vice Admiral Molyneux Shuldham.

With command now firmly in hand, the admiral spent most of the spring of 1776 jockeying for the authority to act as a peace commissioner before the crisis with the colonies reached the point of no return. He firmly believed that his personal intervention would be the key to calming the waters and that a reasonable, moderate discussion would be the beginning of a happy reunion. Howe was correct in his assertion that the position of the radicals in America was being strengthened by the threats of force and imperious demands for submission from the conservatives in England. With the army and navy present to demonstrate the power of the mother country, the admiral was convinced that he could coax the rebels into laying down their arms while working with moderate colonial leaders to address their grievances.

Howe's carrot-and-stick approach and conciliatory attitude was seen by the Tory ministry as nothing short of meddling in policy and, at worst, a sign of weakness. Fearing that the Whig admiral and his brother might give too many concessions to the rebels and thus weaken the government's position, the ministers worked overtime drafting instructions to severely limit their commission, hoping it would result in "too little, too late." In essence, the Howes were permitted to offer pardons only—and only after the American rebels laid down their arms and unconditionally submitted to Parliament's authority. The spiteful maneuverings and bureaucratic foot-dragging in London delayed the admiral for an extra eight weeks, a loss of time that proved costly.

But now, he was here. "Where we anchored was in full View of New York, and of the Rebels' Head Quarters under Washington, who is now made their Generalissimo with full powers," Ambrose Serle noted, Washington's headquarters occasionally being at No. 1 Broadway, opposite the Bowling Green and in full view of the harbor. "As soon as we came to Anchor, Admiral Shuldham came on board, and soon after Genl. Howe, with several officers of their respective Departments."[13]

The general had been anxiously awaiting his brother's arrival. "There is great Reason to expect a numerous Body of the Inhabitants to join the Army," meaning Loyalists, "who in this time of universal Oppression, only wait for Opportunities to give Proofs of their Loyalty," he had written to Lord Germain five days earlier. But they needed tangible, active encouragement, especially now that independence was declared. "This Disposition among the People makes me impatient for the arrival of Admiral Howe, concluding the Powers with which he is furnished will have the best effect at this critical Time," William Howe commented.[14]

Lord Howe had not seen his younger brother since the general left England more than a year earlier to take command of the army in America. The newcomers were shocked to discover how badly the situation had deteriorated. "By them we learnt the deplorable Situation of His majesty's faithful Subjects," Serle commented with horror, "that they were hunted after & shot at in the Woods & Swamps, to which they had fled for these four months to avoid the savage Fury of the Rebels; that many of them were forced to take up Arms & join their Forces; and that Deserters & others flocked to the King's Army continually." Some of the royal governors, like Tryon of New York and Lord Dunmore of Virginia, had fled to the British military's protection. Others, like William Franklin, the royal governor of New Jersey and son of Benjamin Franklin, were under arrest. Still others, like John Penn, the proprietor of Pennsylvania and grandson of the founder, did little but stay out of the way.

But the real bombshell had come to Staten Island only four days earlier. "We also heard, that the Congress had now announced the Colonies to be INDEPENDENT STATES, with several other Articles of Intelligence, that proclaim the Villainy & the Madness of these deluded People," Serle was aghast to learn.[15] Lord Howe had arrived a week and a half too late.

The text of the Declaration of Independence was printed by Congress and widely distributed, and within the week made it into the newspapers. Serle read the document, his jaw dropping and rage rising with nearly every sentence. "A more impudent, false, and atrocious Proclamation was never fabricated by the Hands of Man," he seethed, going down the list of charges against George III. "Hitherto, they had thrown all the Blame and Insult upon the Parliament and ministry." Serle exploded as the king was called a tyrant, unfit to be the ruler of free people, and seeing the British people described as deaf to the voice of justice and kinship. "Now, they have the Audacity to calumniate the King and People of Britain," he spewed.[16]

Congress had adopted the resolution on independence on Tuesday, July 2, the same day that Howe's army landed on Staten Island. A one-line notice first appeared in the Philadelphia newspapers on July 3, and a New York paper, *The Constitutional Gazette*, published the same simple announcement in its Saturday, July 6 edition: "On Tuesday last the CONTINENTAL CONGRESS declared the UNITED COLONIES FREE and INDEPENDENT STATES."[17]

General Howe himself first heard the news on July 8, apparently as he was finishing a rather mundane report to Lord George Germain. "Several Men have come over to this Island & to the ships since my Letter of yesterday, and by a News Paper of the 6th I learn, that the Continental Congress, on the Tuesday preceeding, had declared the United Colonies free & independent States," he wrote almost offhandedly to the secretary of state at the end of the one-and-a-half page letter. "Having no better Authority for this Intelligence than the News Paper," Howe rather blandly told Germain, "I decline making Observations upon it."[18]

The report was immediately put on a packet ship and dispatched to England. An inscription on the back of the letter indicates that it was received in London on August 10, an incredibly swift thirty-two days later. It was the first notice received by the British government that America had declared independence.

Despite this, with Admiral Howe now in New York harbor, the peace commission could begin. While still out at sea back in June, believing the ship was just off the coast of Massachusetts (they were near Nova Scotia), Lord Howe had composed letters with information intended for circulation throughout the colonies. On Tuesday, June 18, Ambrose Serle noted in his journal, "Very busily employed yesterday and today, in preparing Letters, containing Lord Howe's Declaration, to the several Governors, to be distributed among the Colonies."[19] Taking "the earliest opportunity to inform you of my arrival" and telling the governors of his intention to meet immediately with his brother, the admiral announced his appointment as naval commander in chief, and also "having the honour to be by his Majesty constituted one of his Commissioners for restoring peace to his colonies and for granting pardons to such of his subjects therein." There were other, personal letters, some from friends in England to certain "persons of influence" including Benjamin Franklin and John Dickinson of Pennsylvania, hoping to persuade them to cooperate in bringing about a peaceful settlement.

Enclosed in each letter was a formal declaration stating that the king had appointed him and his brother, "each of us, jointly and severally, to be his Majesty's Commissioner and Commissioners for granting his free and general pardons to all those, who in the tumult and disorder of the times, may have deviated from their just allegiance, and who are willing, by a speedy return to their duty, to reap the benefits of the royal favour." It further stated "that due consideration shall be had to the meritorious services of all persons who shall aid and assist in restoring the public tranquillity" and reiterated that "pardons shall be granted, dutiful representations received, and every suitable encouragement given."[20] Helping with a successful settlement could prove to be very lucrative.

Howe had the letters made up in packets and planned to distribute them as quickly as possible. Serle noted that they were loosely closed with a "flying seal" so that anyone could open them and read them. "I had little expectation that these Letters and Declaration would reach the hands of His Majesty's Governors," the admiral later revealed to Lord Germain. "My Object was, that they should be circulated as much as possible throughout the Provinces . . . but no opportunity offered 'till I arrived off the Harbour of New York."

On July 13, Lt. Samuel Reeve was sent to Perth Amboy, New Jersey, the closest port on the mainland in the direction of Philadelphia. "I dispatched the first Lieutenant of the *Eagle*, to Amboy, with those intended for the Colonies to the Southward of New York," Howe wrote, "directing him to deliver them to any Person who might appear in Authority."[21] The letters were received in Amboy by Gen. Hugh Mercer, the American commander posted there.

That evening, Howe personally wrote another letter to someone "who might appear in Authority":

Eagle Off of Staten Island July the 13th 1776

Sir,

The Situation in which you are placed and the acknowledged liberality of your Sentiments, induce me very much to wish for an opportunity to converse with you on the Subject of the Commission with which I have the honor to be charged; As I trust that a dispassionate consideration of the Kings benevolent intentions, may be the means of preventing the further Effusion of Blood, and become productive of Peace and lasting Union between Great Britain and America.

If this proposal should be acceptable, I would advance in a Frigate to have the pleasure to receive you, as near to the Town of New York as will be most for your accommodation.

I flatter myself I shall find no difficulty in obtaining Credit to my Assurances for the perfect safety of your person, and free liberty to return on Shore at your Pleasure. Tho' I shall be equally ready to afford any more preferable Security that may be required, in case no other objection occurs to the desired Interview.

I am Sir Your sincere . . .
Howe

This letter, entrusted to Lt. Philip Brown for delivery the next day, was addressed to "George Washington, Esq., New York."[22]

CHAPTER 4
"George Washington Esqr., &c., &c., &c."

The British naval officer stood up with his hat off, bowed, and shouted across the gunwale of the barge, "I have a letter, sir, from Lord Howe to Mr. Washington."

"Sir," replied the American officer, "we have no person in our army with that address."

Lt. Philip Brown of HMS *Eagle* was dumbfounded by the answer. Bobbing up and down in the murky gray waters of New York Harbor just off Red Hook on a rainy day, impeccably dressed in a blue-and-white Royal Navy uniform with gilded buttons gleaming under an oilskin cloak, his hair carefully curled, powdered and queued, the officer was being curtly told that the urgent and important letter he carried from Admiral Lord Howe was improperly addressed.

"Sir," pleaded Brown, "will you look at the address?" He pulled the letter out of his pocket and read the address:

George Washington, Esq., New York
    "Howe"

"No, sir," reiterated Col. Joseph Reed, adjutant general of the Continental Army, "I cannot receive that letter." He, too, was impeccably dressed, in a dark blue and pale buff uniform, gilded buttons gleaming under an oilskin cloak, his hair powdered and queued in the formal military style of the era.

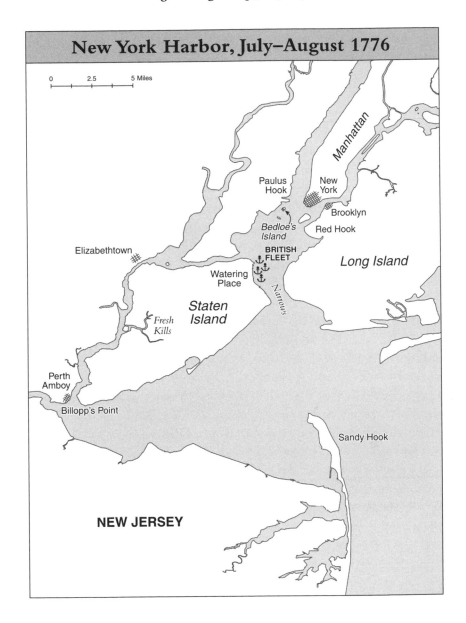

New York Harbor, July–August 1776

"I am very sorry," Brown responded with chagrin, "and so will be Lord Howe, that any error in the superscription should prevent the letter being received by *General Washington*," with "general" being the critical word. The lieutenant denied any specific knowledge of what was in the letter, but anxiously added that Lord Howe had been granted great powers. The adjutant general, unmoved, would not accept the paper.

"Why, sir," Reed told Brown, "I must obey orders."

"Oh, yes, sir, you must obey orders, to be sure."[1]

Ironically, Reed had some letters from captive British officers to their friends, including one for General Howe, which he passed over to Lieutenant Brown. Carefully observing *punctilio*, the small, essential courtesies between officers and gentlemen, the two then saluted by removing their hats with their right hands, fully extending their right arms, and bowing to each other. The gleaming red-and-gold Royal Navy barge then began rowing back towards Staten Island.

The episode had begun in the early afternoon when Lieutenant Brown left the *Eagle* under a white flag. "Mr. Brown . . . was dispatched with a Flag of Truce to Washington at New York," Lord Howe's secretary Ambrose Serle wrote in his journal. "He was stopped by three Boats at a little Distance from the Town, demanding his Business. Upon being told that he had a Letter from Lord Howe to their Commander, they ordered him to lay to, while one of the Boats went to the Shore for Directions."[2] The three whaleboats were guard boats of the harbor defense, manned by Massachusetts troops of the 21st Continental Regiment under the command of Lt. Col. Benjamin Tupper.[3]

"Col Tupper being A board of A Privateer went and meet the flag," Ensign Caleb Clapp of the 26th Continental Regiment related. "Seeing that the Letter was directed to George Washington Esqr, he answered that [he] Knew no such Person, but he woud, send an Officer a shore and se if their was any such Person, but cou'd not find any of that Name." Clapp further stated that "It was Reported that General Washington was at the Whorf, and see the letter, but wou'd not receive it, unless it was properly directed."[4]

Washington's chief of artillery, Col. Henry Knox, was an eyewitness to the scene as events unfolded. "They came within about four miles of the city and were met by some of Colonel Tupper's people," Knox told his wife Lucy, "who detained them until his Excellency's pleasure should be known."[5] That evening, Washington notified John Hancock, "About 3 OClock this afternoon I was informed that a Flag from Lord Howe was coming up and waited with two of our Whale boats untill directions should be given."

The officer from the guard boats alerted the commander in chief about the letter, evidently stating how it was addressed. "I immediately convened such of the General officers as were not upon other duty," Washington explained to Congress, "who agreed in opinion that I ought not to receive any Letter directed to me as a private Gentleman, but if otherwise and the Officer desired to come up to deliver the Letter himself as was suggested, he should come under a safe conduct." The general then sent Colonel Knox and Adjutant General Reed, accompanied by aide-de-camp Maj. Samuel Webb, with specific instructions to speak with Lieutenant Brown.[6]

After turning Brown away, the Americans noticed the British barge suddenly coming back around. Lieutenant Brown called to them again, wanting to know how the letter should be addressed. Reed responded to the effect that "all the world knew who General Washington was since last summer."[7]

"You are sensible, sir, of the rank of General Washington in our army?" Reed asked pointedly.

"Yes, sir, we are," Brown replied. "I am sure my Lord Howe will lament exceedingly this affair, as the letter is quite of a civil nature, and not a military one." The British officer anxiously added, "He laments exceedingly that he was not here a little sooner," which Knox interpreted as alluding to the Declaration of Independence.[8] Again, Brown stated how sorry he was that the letter could not be received.

"Col. Reed told him a proper direction would obviate all difficulties & that this was no new matter," Washington continued to Hancock, "this subject having been fully discussed in the course of the last year, of which Lord Howe could not be ignorant." The officers again parted with excruciating civility.

"I would not upon any occasion sacrifice Essentials to Punctilio," Washington told the president, "but in this Instance, the Opinion of Others concurring with my own, I deemed It a duty to my Country and my appointment to insist upon that respect which in any other than a public view I would willingly have waived." To have accepted the letter would set a dangerous precedent, for in essence, it would be accepting disrespect. "Nor do I doubt but from the supposed nature of the Message and the anxiety expressed they will either repeat their Flag or fall upon some mode to communicate the Import and consequence of it," Washington concluded.[9]

Was Lord Howe playing a game, "testing the waters," as it were, to see if he could snub Washington or keep him in an inferior position? The short answer is no, not snub him, but yes, keep him in his place. The distinction is important and requires an explanation.

To begin with, from the British perspective, this was a rebellion of "provincials," colonials who were English subjects but not full Englishmen. This was one of the key causes of the rebellion, for the American Whigs considered themselves as having the full rights of Englishmen and felt that Parliament was denying them those rights. Therefore, like good Englishmen they were compelled to defend them by force of arms, and when the British government demonstrated its determination to crush them by all means possible, they revoked their allegiance to Britain to create a government of their own. "That to secure these rights, Governments are instituted among Men, deriving their just powers from the consent of the governed," Thomas Jefferson had written in the Declaration of Independence, stating a fundamental, philosophical reason for why governments exist at all. He further stated "That whenever any Form of Government becomes destructive of these ends, it is the Right of the People to alter or abolish it, and to institute new Government . . . as to them shall seem most likely to affect their Safety and Happiness." Both concepts were extremely radical in 1776 and remain so in many parts of the world today.

Then, there was the class system, both in America and in England, where class status meant power. In Great Britain, it meant inherited power and privilege. Few Englishmen owned substantial property, and they were mostly of the upper class. By contrast, in America, thousands of landless Britons and other Europeans had emigrated, acquired property, and gained status.

But no American landowner had the same status as an English landowner, period. There was no House of Lords or aristocracy in America to compare with Britain; thus, provincials were provincials, no matter who they were. In Virginia, Washington had acquired certain high status as a plantation owner, militia colonel, and member of the House of Burgesses; that status counted for little if anything in England.

In that regard, Lord Howe was in a delicate position as negotiator. Any action on the part of British officials short of force could be interpreted as giving status to the rebels. At this early stage of the war, British military officers and government officials properly referred to those Americans fighting against them as rebels, distinguishing them from His Majesty's loyal subjects. To treat with the rebels on any formal level would legitimize their political status; thus came the problem of addressing them by any title other than "mister," or at best, "esquire," which meant a landed country gentleman. In this case, Howe was attempting to communicate with Washington on a "civil," or social or political level, not in his military capacity. Except for the letters to the governors, all of the other letters Howe sent ashore were addressed in the same way, but none of them were to military people.

Washington's professional military status was, at best, murky by European standards. In the 1750s, with no military background or experience at all, Washington had been granted the temporary rank of colonel in the Virginia militia by Governor Dinwiddie as an expedient in order to negotiate with the French at Fort Duquesne, who the Virginians asserted were trespassing on Virginia's (and thus England's) territory. Having some idea of where

Fort Duquesne was from his days as a surveyor, twenty-two-year-old Colonel Washington was sent with the highest military rank available from the governor to treat with a professional European officer. Unimpressed, the French commander was more amused than insulted, for he recognized right away that the young Virginian was no professional soldier. For one thing, Washington did not speak French, one of the hallmarks of a true professional.

After Washington surrendered Fort Necessity at Great Meadows on July 3, 1754, the governor demoted him to captain, upon which he resigned in disgust. The following year, Gen. Edward Braddock employed him as a volunteer aide and guide, promising him a commission in the British army at the end of the campaign. Braddock's disastrous defeat at the Monongahela on July 9, 1755, and his subsequent death removed Washington's hope of acquiring professional status as a British officer.

Those days always stayed with him, for he wrote to his fellow Virginian Col. Adam Stephen in July 1776, "I did not let the Anniversary of the 3rd or 9th of this Instt. pass off without a grateful remembrance of the escape we had at the Meadows and on the Banks of Monongahela." He told his old comrade, "The same Providence that protected us upon those occasions will, I hope, continue his Mercies, and make us happy Instruments in restoring Peace & liberty to this once favour'd, but now distressed Country."[10] Now, in 1776, for British officers to address him or anyone else in the rebel forces who had not served with European rank was deemed by them at best, inappropriate, and at worst, an insult to the profession and the social establishment that dated back hundreds of years.

From the American "rebel" perspective, having declared independence, they were no longer subservient to the British political system. This, however, was not a social revolution or class war; for the most part, the American political and military leaders, whatever their private thoughts (John Adams being a perfect example), would usually adhere to the protocols and punctilios of gentlemanly behavior and social rank when writing to or speaking with British officials (as opposed to writing or speaking *about* them). In this case, Washington was demanding no less from the Howes.

"So high is the Vanity and Insolence of these Men!" Ambrose Serle raged when Lieutenant Brown returned to the *Eagle*, the letter still in his possession. "The Truth is, the Punctilio of an Address would never have retarded the Reception of a Letter from a person, with whose high Rank & Commission they were well acquainted, and whose Bravery & Honor are so well known every where." He felt that it was a snub to Admiral Howe, who was going out on a limb to reach an accommodation. But what else could one expect from such low, scheming, provincial men, daring to place themselves on the same level and demanding entitlement? "They have uniformly blocked up every Avenue To peace," he fulminated, "and whenever they have pretended to make Advances of that kind, they have always done it in a mode, that they well knew (and, because they knew, designed) was inadmissible, upon every Principle of Honor and Decency." The gap between the two sides was ever widening. "There now seems no Alternative but War and Bloodshed, which must lay at the Door of these unhappy People," the admiral's secretary concluded. "They pretend (or rather have pretended) to seek peace, and yet renounce it . . . and declare openly for Independence & War."[11]

Congress applauded Washington's handling of the situation. The Board of War reported what transpired, and on July 17, Congress passed a resolution, "That General Washington, in refusing to receive a letter said to be sent from Lord Howe, addressed to 'George Washington, Esqr.' acted with a dignity becoming his station; and, therefore, this Congress do highly approve the same." Further, Congress ordered "that no letter or message be received, on any occasion whatsoever, from the enemy, by the commander in chief, or other, the commanders of the American army, but such as shall be directed to them in the characters they respectively sustain." Congress ordered the resolutions published, and they appeared in the July 27 edition of *The Pennsylvania Gazette*.[12]

While Congress was discussing the issue in Philadelphia, a second episode occurred in New York. This letter was from General Howe, addressed to "George Washington, Esq., &c. &c. &c.," answering a letter from Washington regarding treatment of prisoners in Canada. On July 16, "At 1 P.M. Sent a Midshipman in the Pinnace with a Flag of Truce to New York," Capt. Henry Duncan of the *Eagle* noted in his journal. This time, a very young officer-in-training, not an officer, was the courier, sent in a pinnace, or small sailboat, not the admiral's barge. "At $^1/_2$ past 7 the Flag of Truce returned," again with the letter unopened.[13]

"Another Flag of Truce was sent to-day with a letter to Washington from the General," the admiral's secretary huffed, "which was refused for the same idle and insolent Reasons as were given before." Again, the blame was attributed to rebel obstinacy, not sardonic British condescension. "It seems to be beneath a little paltry Colonel of Militia at the Head of a Banditti or Rebels to treat with the Representatives of His lawful Sovereign, because 'tis impossible for him to give all the Titles which the poor Creature requires," Serle fumed, with more than a whiff of arrogance. "If such men in such a

Cause can prosper," he seethed, "it is only the prosperity of a Night, which the morning Cloud shall chase away."[14]

Again, Washington took a firm stand in refusing the letter, which prompted the Howes to try another tack. Three days after the second letter was refused, Capt. Nisbet Balfour, one of General Howe's aides, came up toward New York under a white flag. "There appeared an insurmountable obstacle between the two Generals, by way of corresponding," the aide told Joseph Reed and Maj. Samuel Webb, formerly one of General Israel Putnam's aides, now on Washington's staff. Balfour related that "General Howe desired his Adjutant General might be admitted to an Interview with his Excellency General Washington—On which Colo. Reed, in the name of General Washington, consented," Webb wrote.[15] The British evidently had no trouble saying the word "general," only writing it.

It was Washington's opportunity to demonstrate how he intended to play the game, and he played the part to the hilt. "Saturday, July 20: Colonel Patterson, the Adjutant General, went on a Flag of truce to New York," Lt. Col. Stephen Kemble, the deputy adjutant general of the British Army and a native of New Jersey, wrote in his journal. At noon, Webb and Reed met Lt. Col. James Paterson of the 63rd Regiment in the middle of the harbor and took him into their barge. Foregoing the usual custom of blindfolding enemy officers on such visits, the British adjutant general was rowed right up to the Grand Battery at the tip of Manhattan.

The Grand Battery, so named because it was the largest collection of heavy guns defending the city, was formidable. The ramparts had been built up from within (in contrast to the usual method of digging a ditch in front and throwing the earth behind) and were mounted with thirteen 32-pounders, one 24-pounder, three 18-pounders, two 12-pounders, one 13-inch brass mortar, one 10-inch and two 8-inch iron mortars.[16] Here, Paterson "was received with great Pomp by a Guard, Conducted to Capt. Kennedy's House," which was Colonel Knox's quarters at No. 1 Broadway, not far from the battery, "where he saw a great Court, Gentlemen well dressed, &c.; had an Audience with Mr. Washington, the particulars not come to my knowledge," Kemble noted.[17]

Both Henry Knox and Joseph Reed noted the particulars in great detail. The intention was to impress the British officer that Washington and his staff were professionals, and the best way was to dazzle him with gentlemanly, formal appearances. "General Washington was very handsomely dressed and made a most elegant appearance," Colonel Knox wrote. "Colonel Paterson appeared awe-struck, as if he was before something

43

supernatural. Indeed, I don't wonder at it," the former Boston bookseller commented. "He was before a very great man indeed."[18]

Knox was not exaggerating. At nearly six feet, three inches in height and weighing just over two hundred pounds, Washington's physical appearance was striking, even in ordinary times, and he was always conscious of it, taking great pains to conduct himself appropriately. In uniform, he was awesome to behold in the truest sense of the word, with his long hair powdered white and simply styled, offsetting his gray-blue eyes and florid, noble face; a dark blue uniform coat turned up with pale buff and trimmed with plain, gold-washed buttons; looped, gold-laced epaulettes on his shoulders and a sash of sky-blue watered silk across his chest under the coat, denoting his rank as commander in chief; buff-colored smallclothes tastefully edged with simple embroidery; and polished black riding boots. Unlike European generals (and some in his own army), no elaborate embroidery or thick bullion lace adorned Washington's uniform, nor was it trimmed with velvet; it was simple and elegant. Always a stylish but restrained dresser, he carried himself with a dignity and deportment that inspired awe, even in some of the roughest characters in his army, and a force of personality that commanded respect. On horseback, he was second to none.

Throughout the war (and later, as president), Washington was addressed as "Excellency" or "Your Excellency." Reed and Knox both noted that during the interview, or "audience," Colonel Paterson repeatedly addressed Washington in this fashion. "Every other word was, 'May it please your Excellency,'" or "'if your Excellency so pleases,'" Knox told his wife. "In short, no person could pay more respect than the said adjutant-general."[19]

Paterson opened the discussion by saying that General Howe could not understand where the difficulty lay; that whenever ambassadors or representatives encountered disputes of rank, they overcame it by the use of "esquire" or "etc., etc." No disrespect was intended by the general or the admiral, the adjutant general insisted; "they held his Person & Character in the highest Esteem," Paterson said, and "the Direction with the Addition of &c. &c. &c.—implied every thing that ought to follow." He politely mentioned that in the previous year, Washington had sent a letter to "The Honorable William Howe, Esq." and it was not refused. Then, taking out General Howe's most recent letter, Paterson placed it on the table.

Washington courteously expressed his respect for General Howe and then responded. "A Letter directed to a person in a publick Character should have some Description or Indication of it," he began, "otherwise, it would appear a mere private letter." The commander in chief then told Paterson "That it was true the &c. &c. &c. implied every thing & they also implied any thing." He explained that he addressed the letter from last year in response to Howe's letter to him, addressed the same way, and that the officer who accepted the letter from Howe had done so by mistake. Because of this, Washington did not think it proper to return it, but decided to answer it with the same mode of address. The general reiterated that "he should absolutely decline any Letter directed to him as a private Person when it related to his publick Station."[20] The letter remained on the table, untouched.

"No failure of respect was intended, your Excellency," Paterson replied. He noted afterwards, "I expressed my Apprehensions that all Intercourse must consequently be cutt off between us, but that my first & principal duty was, to communicate to him the Contents of that Letter." That was acceptable; Washington was willing to listen. Paterson then recounted to the best of his recollection the contents of the letter concerning the treatment of prisoners. The discussion went back and forth in a civil fashion, each denying any knowledge of cruelty or inappropriate treatment. At the end, they were no further along on that topic, and it would be years of wrangling over accusations of poor treatment of captured personnel, especially of American prisoners.

Both agreed that communication between the generals was essential. Washington "expressed some Concern at the Idea of all Communication being at an End, as he was fully convinced how much we had already suffered for want of that free Intercourse subsisting among all civilized Nations, tho' at War." He then mentioned British mistreatment of some captured Americans at Breed's Hill. "I cou'd boldly affirm from my own Knowledge upon the Spot, that every degree of Humanity and Tenderness was exerted upon that occasion to the unfortunate people who fell into our Hands," Paterson emphatically replied.[21] He countered Washington's statement by mentioning the case of General Prescott, who had been captured by the Americans and held for exchange, that his age and infirmities might be fatal under the rigorous treatment he had received. Washington replied that he had no knowledge of Prescott's whereabouts, nor was he aware of any poor treatment. Again reaching an impasse over the discussion of prisoners, the interview began to wind down.

And then, suddenly, the whole picture changed. "As I was about to take my Leave," Paterson stated, "I told the General I could not resist the Temptation before me of exceeding the Limits of my Commission by taking the Liberty of pointing out, the Kings most gracious disposition towards the Americans so strongly manifested in the powers he had granted and the Choice he had made of Persons unconnected with Ministerial Arrangements," which could be broadly interpreted as including people who disagreed with the Tory ministry's policies.[22] He was referring to the Howe brothers.

Paterson had shifted the topic to the peace commission. "The Goodness and Benevolence of the King had induced him to appoint Lord Howe and General Howe his commissioners to accommodate this unhappy dispute," the adjutant general boldly continued, emphasizing "that they had great Powers and would derive the greatest pleasure from effecting an Accommodation." This part of the conversation was now covering the subject of Lord Howe's letter of July 12, the refusal of which had started the standoff. Paterson told Washington that he personally and sincerely "wished to have this Visit considered as making the first Advances to this desirable Object."[23] By doing this, he was now attempting to open the door.

"I am not vested with any powers on this subject," by Congress, the commander in chief answered, "but from what has appeared or transpired on this head, Lord Howe and General Howe are only to grant Pardons."

And then, Washington shocked Paterson. "Those who have committed no Fault want no Pardon," he bluntly told the British officer. "We are only defending our indisputable rights."[24]

Bold and assertive as it was, the line of reasoning was nothing new. Months earlier, there was "some talk of a Reconciliation, but am afraid it is not well grounded," Nicholas Cresswell had written in his journal on March 1 as rumors of reconciliation and independence made the rounds in Virginia.[25] In the March 8 edition of *The Virginia Gazette*, a fictitious dialogue between a delegate to Congress and the ghost of Gen. Richard Montgomery, the first Continental army general killed in the war, touched on the very issue of royal pardons, discussion of which had been circulating for months. "I still love liberty and America," the general's ghost began. "I am sent here upon an important errand, to warn you against listening to terms of accommodation from the court of Britain." The spirit of Montgomery, a former British officer who died leading the attack at the gates of Quebec on New Year's Eve, states, "No, I see no offers from Great Britain but of *pardon*. The very word is an insult to our cause. To whom is pardon offered? To virtuous freemen. For what? For flying to arms in defence of the rights of humanity. And from whom do these offers come? From a *royal criminal*." The specter then proclaimed, "You have furnished me with a new reason for triumphing in my death, for I had rather had it said that I died by his vengeance than that I lived by his mercy."[26]

While Washington's statement to Paterson was not so theatric, it came like a thunderbolt; according to Henry Knox, "This confused him."[27] Recovering quickly from the assertion, the adjutant general tactfully replied, "That would open a very wide Field for Argument," too wide a field for this occasion, he added.[28] Paterson said that Washington "heartily concurred with me, and with a great deal of marked Attention and Civility permitted me to take my Leave."[29]

Taking the letter back, Paterson courteously inquired, "Has your Excellency no particular commands with which you would please to honour me to Lord and General Howe?" Washington graciously replied, "Nothing, sir, but my particular compliments to both," which Henry Knox thought was "a good answer."[30]

The interview had lasted about an hour, during which Paterson "behaved with the greatest Politeness & Attention." The adjutant general also "express'd strong Acknowledgements that the usual Ceremony of blinding his Eyes had been dispensed with." As was customary with envoys, Washington then "strongly invited him to partake of a small Collation"— an elegant, informal meal, served with wine—"which he politely declined, alledging his late Breakfast—& an Impatience to return to Gen. Howe."[31] Henry Knox, always ready to share a good meal and a convivial glass of wine or two, lamented that "Mr. Adjutant-general disappointed us. As it grew late, he even excused himself from drinking one glass of wine."[32]

Before setting off, Paterson was introduced to the American generals present. According to one source, "When he went away he said, it is reported, to Washington and the others with him: 'Sir and gentlemen, let it be remembered that the King has made the first overture for peace; if it be rejected, you must stand by the consequences' and thus—which seems to have been the main errand—he departed."[33] Again, without a blindfold, the adjutant general of the British army was escorted by Reed and Webb to the continental barge at the Grand Battery and was rowed down the harbor, "Sociable and Chatty all the way," Webb recalled.[34]

The first attempt by the Howes to open their peace negotiations had mired first in punctilio and then bogged down in accusations about maltreatment of prisoners. Colonel Paterson's reception was a masterpiece of showmanship all sugared with punctilio and manners, demonstrating Washington's determination to set the tone of how he intended to proceed, in much the same way that Admiral Howe's demeanor set the pattern for behavior on board the *Eagle*. "This interview was more polite than interesting," General Howe commented to Lord Germain. "However," the general admitted, it did have one good effect, though seemingly small: "it induced me to change my superscription for the attainment of an end so desirable."[35] From now on, in General Howe's letters to the American commander in chief, George Washington was addressed as "General Washington, &c. &c."

A few weeks later, with communication reopened, Howe sent Washington a letter concerning the prisoner issue. At the end of it, he added a personal note, saying, "I cannot close this Letter without expressing the deepest Concern that the unhappy State of the Colonies, so different from what I had the Honor of experiencing in the Course of the last War, deprives me of the Pleasure I should otherwise have had in a more personal Communication. I am with due respect, Sir, Your most Obedient Servant, Howe."[36]

Washington responded a few days later. "Give me leave to assure you Sir, that I feel myself greatly Obliged by the polite conclusion of your Letter of the 1st Instant," assuring the British commander of the "high sense of the honor and satisfaction I should have received from your personal Acquaintence." He told Howe, a fellow survivor of Braddock's defeat, "The different State of the Colonies from what It was last War & which has deprived me of that Happiness, cannot be regretted by any One more than Sir, Your Most Obedient Servant, G. Washington."[37]

CHAPTER 5

"Auf Christen-Mensch, auf, auf, zum Streit."

◆

opular depictions of Congress's activities on July 4, 1776, often portray the delegates engaged in heated debate, then solemnly agreeing on independence and coming up to the desk, quills at the ready, to scratch their signatures on a large, ornately scribed piece of parchment as the Liberty Bell peals in the background. What actually went on in the State House that day was by no means so romantic and differed little from most other days. Congress dealt with fourteen items of business on July 4, only one of which was the adoption of the final wording of the Declaration of Independence. The debates over independence had ended two days earlier, the document was not published or publically read until a few days later, and the engrossed parchment did not yet exist; it was authorized in mid-July and signed by most delegates on August 2, without much ceremony.

There were other pressing items of business that day, the defense of Pennsylvania being one of immediate importance. The following letter was addressed to the officers of the Pennsylvania Associators meeting in Lancaster:

Philadelphia, July 4th, 1776

The Congress this morning directed us to confer with the Committees of Safety and Inspection, and the Field Officers now in town, about the proper mode of collecting the militia of this province, in order to form a flying camp, to cover Pennsylvania and New-Jersey, from the Attacks of the Enemy, who have landed on Statten-Island, and will probably direct their March this Way, if they should imagine the Attempt on New-York too hazardous. Necessity obliges us to dispense with forms, and to avail ourselves of the advantage, which we may reasonably hope from your being assembled: We, therefore, most earnestly request you immediately to collect the Forces of your several Counties, and march them down to Brunswick, where the Congress will furnish them with provisions, and allow them Continental pay. Men who have the safety of their country at heart, need no other incentive to the greatest exertions, than such as arises from its danger; for which reason, we have thought it necessary barely to inform you of the fact; with this addition, that the Militia of New Jersey are already, for the most part, in New-York; so that that province will be defenceless without your timely aid.

B. Franklin, Robt. R. Livingston, F. Hopkinson, J. Dickinson,
Committee of Congress[1]

The letter was quickly dispatched along the sixty-five-mile route. "An Express was sent from this committee near 10 oclock [P.M.] by request of Committee of Congress with a letter to the meeting of officers at Lancaster," Christopher Marshall of the Pennsylvania Board of War wrote, "in order to request them to expedite the 6,000 men appointed to compose the flying Camp and to march directly for Brunswick in the Jerseys, the place appointed for the Rendezvous of those troops."[2]

The initial outburst of excitement had drained the city of Philadelphia of its first wave of enthusiasts, and as the words of the Declaration of Independence spread into rural areas over the next few weeks, companies of volunteers began forming and heading east. In the upper reaches of Philadelphia County and Berks County, where the population was mostly German and Scots-Irish, the response was overwhelming.

To Rev. Henry Muhlenberg in Trappe, it was like a tidal wave: overwhelming and more than a little disturbing. "I have not been charged with the task of investigating and comprehending the matter in controversy," the pastor confided to his journal, "nor is it possible for me to determine which party has the highest and best right, whether the one has a better right to make serfs of the inhabitants of America by force and to reap what they have not plowed or sown, or whether the Americans have as good or even better right to defend the rights and privileges granted and stipulated to them by God the Highest and by former crowned heads."

In the summer of 1776, Muhlenberg found himself caught on the horns of the great dilemma of armed resistance, and it caused him much soul-searching. "Therefore," he consoled himself, "since the ministers neither can nor should be judges or arbitrators in such a conflict, they do best if they commit the whole thing to the only and highest Judge of heaven." He found solace in Lutheran doctrine, for "if God's governance ordains or suffers that a king or a parliament or a congress should have power over me, then I must be subject to and serve two discordant masters at the same time."[3] He wrote this as hundreds of local men and boys from the Pennsylvania countryside headed past his home and church to the scene of action.

On Sunday, July 21, after mediating a parochial wrangle at New Hannover church, ten miles northwest of Trappe, "About three o'clock in the afternoon I set out in the burning heat of the sun on my way back to Providence," the old preacher wrote. "On the way I met a company of men from Reading, a hundred strong, on the march to the *province* of Jersey. Most of them were settlers and young men born in this country and recently enlisted with others to form an army of observation in Jersey, since Rehoboam's thick finger has entrenched itself on Staaten Eiland, the island between New York, Jersey, and Pennsylvania, and requires watching as well as counterpressure." He noted that "the company camped overnight here in Providence, some in the woods but most of them in two inns."[4]

Two days later, "Again, in the evening, there arrived here a company of *riflemen*, or sharpshooters, from Reading on their march to Jersey." Muhlenberg wrote that "Most of them are native youngsters from in and around Reading who learned bushfighting like that of the Indians. They are also clad in Indian fashion and are armed with rifles and tomahawks."[5] These men were dressed in hunting shirts, long, frock-like garments made of homespun linen dyed a variety of colors or left unbleached. These were common garments in colonial America, and although much more economical than formal uniforms, time would bear out that they were not as conducive to military discipline.

But for the moment, they would serve the purpose. Washington's General Orders for July 24 stated, "as it is necessary that men should have Cloaths and appear decent and tight, he earnestly encourages the use of Hunting Shirts, with long Breeches, made of the same Cloth, Gaiter fashion about the legs, to all those yet unprovided." The general gave two good reasons for their use: First, "No Dress can be had cheaper, nor more convenient, as the Wearer may be cool in warm weather, and warm in cool weather by putting on under-Cloaths which will not change the outward dress, Winter or Summer." The second reason was psychological: "Besides which it is a dress justly supposed to carry no small terror to the enemy, who think every such person a complete marksman."[6]

The hunting shirts sported a cape over the shoulders and were decorated with strips of fringe, sometimes in multiple layers. "Their outer shirts are shaggy, almost like the pictures of satyrs, fauns, or sylvan spirits of ancient times," Muhlenberg commented.[7] Fringed trousers, leggings, moccasins, and round hats or caps decorated with animal fur and feathers completed the frontier or "Indian" garb. The riflemen's accoutrements—powder horns, shot pouches, and the like—were often trimmed with colorful beadwork, and multicolored blankets completed their marching kits.

The following Sunday, July 28, around 8 P.M., the quiet of a warm Sabbath evening was broken when "a company of militia from Cumberland Township, Berks County, marched in with drums and fifes and great shouting to continue their march to Jersey tomorrow." Muhlenberg was intrigued that they "imitate the war cries of the Indians, which sound semitonic, inhuman, barbarous, horrible, and yet beautiful, very much like the war cries of the Turks." The day being Sunday, he piously remarked, "It would, of course, sound much more powerful and heartening if they could take as their war cry the forty-sixth Psalm or the hymn, *"Ein Feste Burg ist unser Gott,"* Martin Luther's stirringly militant work, "A Mighty Fortress is Our God."[8]

Troops continued to pass through Trappe regularly, as it was located on one of the main roads from the interior of the state and about a day's march from the city. "August 2: Toward evening Colonel Grub arrived with his battalion of five hundred militia men, who camped tonight in the open field in order to march on to Jersey early in the morning."[9] These troops brought to mind an issue that was already causing a great deal of consternation among the volunteers and the generals: "As it is now time that the farmers should be preparing their fields for the sowing of winter crops and the men must go to war, there is much lamentation, and the women and gray old fathers are obliged to complete the gathering of the late harvest and put their hands to the plow."[10] The stress of war affected the entire community, and numerous unsung heroes remained at home to pick up the slack.

The village of Trappe is located in Providence Township, Montgomery County, which in 1776 was Philadelphia County. Before independence, the provincial government of Pennsylvania did not have a militia system, due largely to the influence of Quaker pacifism, so men joined companies of vol-

Augustus Lutheran Church in Trappe, Pennsylvania, was built by Henry Melchior Muhlenberg in 1742-43, and is now the oldest, unchanged Lutheran church building in America. Muhlenberg, his wife, and his three famous sons, Henry, Frederick, and Peter, are buried in the churchyard. PHOTO BY KYLE R. WEAVER

unteer Associators. Now, as the Pennsylvania Convention created a state government in place of the provincial government, and with the anticipated British attack on Philadelphia, the local Associators were starting to be called militia and were gradually being placed under state and county authority.

Depending on the population, each township typically formed a militia company led by a captain, and several companies were put together to form a battalion, commanded by a colonel. Innkeeper Jacob Peterman of Trappe was made captain of the Providence Company in the 5th Battalion Philadelphia County Militia, under the command of Col. John Bull of Norriton Township. Because all of this was new, the confusion early in the war was monumental. Within a year, all males aged sixteen years and above were required to be listed in the militia rolls regardless of political or religious viewpoints.

On Saturday, August 3, "As a company of militia, made up of residents of Providence, was to march off next Monday, the captain [Peterman] and others had requested yesterday that on Sunday afternoon I say a word of admonition in English and German in Augustus Church as a farewell to them," Muhlenberg wrote.[11] It was a very long and trying Sunday for the sixty-five-year-old pastor, filled with a spectrum of emotion and stress. After riding ten miles to New Hanover early in the morning to preach because of the continuing ugly wrangle between the pastor and the congregation, "I started to ride for Providence at half past twelve and at about half past three arrived at the Providence church where there was again a very large gathering of German and English people." The challenge of preaching in two languages was the easy part for this brilliant man: "We first sang several stanzas of the hymn, "*Auf Christen-Mensch, auf, auf, zum Streit*" ["Up, Christian Men, Up, Up to the Strife"], and then I preached in English on Ephesians 6:10 ff., about arming with divine weapons, and then in German on Deuteronomy 20: 1-4," which admonished them, "When thou goest out to battle against thine enemies, and seest horses, and chariots, and a people more than thou, be not afraid of them . . . let not your hearts be faint, fear not, and do not tremble, neither be ye terrified because of them, for the Lord your God is he that goeth with you, to fight for you against your enemies."

The scene was heart-wrenching, repeated countless times in communities all over the land. "There was much weeping, not so much for our sins, but rather more because the women were sending off their husbands, the mothers their sons, and the children their fathers to war," Muhlenberg noted. He couldn't help but point out the irony of the Americans fighting with the mother country, remarking, "It is an unusual, yea, altogether unheard of, thing that a mother and her children should fight against one another not with rods and broomsticks but with fire and sword."

The next morning, the emotional drama continued. "Today the company from Providence marched away," the minister wrote, as "many wives, children, and parents wept for their departing dear ones." Muhlenberg sympathetically noted that "one of them asked me to baptize his child before he went, namely Henrich Schrack and his wife Magdelena; child Jacob, born July 2, baptized August 5."[12] The pastor dutifully recorded the event in his journal.

The militiamen were obligated for sixty days' worth of service, and the Providence Company was heading to rendezvous in Philadelphia with the rest of the 5th Battalion. Once formed, they would go by boat up the Delaware River to Burlington or Trenton and then march overland for New Brunswick. From there, they would be assigned as needed, either to the Continental Army, which was in Manhattan and Long Island, or to the Army of Observation, a curious anomaly also known as the "Flying Camp," which was then gathering in the towns and villages of New Jersey, opposite Staten Island.

CHAPTER 6

The Flying Camp

O ne of the most challenging aspects of studying the American
Revolution is trying to understand the complex evolution of the
American military, especially in the first two years of the war.
Here was a new nation made up of thirteen separate political units, former
British colonies calling themselves states, each with a peculiar history of settlement and jealously guarding its rights. These states were of all different
shapes and demeanors, peopled by a curious variety of European, African,
and Native American ethnic groups. Conflicting religious doctrines were a
major feature in settlement patterns, with extremes ranging from the rigid,
intolerant Calvinist militancy of Puritan Massachusetts to the free-thinking
"liberty of conscience" pacifism of Quaker Pennsylvania. Between was old
New Netherland, which became New York, New Jersey, and Delaware, cen-
tering on New York City, where commerce was the founding religion of old
New Amsterdam and spiritual beliefs were an individual's personal business.

As a result, many of the colonies were hostile to one another, having
been formed by religious refugees, economic opportunists, and political or
social outcasts. Some of them quibbled endlessly about boundaries arbitrar-
ily assigned from London decades earlier with little or no knowledge of
actual conditions. To superimpose European values about land and rights
on this continent—especially English values, where status in that island
society was largely determined by property ownership and religion—was to
create a hodgepodge of conflicts and plant many of the seeds for a con-
tentious new nationality, the Americans.

Not surprisingly, the military forces being created to try and defend the newly independent states from the wrath of the British Empire reflected this loose, crazy-quilt chaos. Volunteers for the national, or Continental Army, needed to be recruited and sustained for at least a year of service and were subject to the authority of Congress. Separate from this, some states began forming regiments of state regulars for home defense, much like today's National Guard, which could be called into Continental service as requested.

Then there was the militia, which in most states was comprised of all able-bodied men over sixteen regardless of age or religious conviction, who were liable to be drafted for short terms of service, usually sixty days. Because they were requested by Congress at different times to support the Continental forces, they were often equipped at national expense. Much of that equipment quickly disappeared as their service time expired and the militiamen headed home.

The Continental Army marched to New York City after the British army of about seven thousand evacuated Boston on March 17, 1776, and sailed to Halifax, Nova Scotia, to await reinforcements. When these British forces later appeared off New York Harbor and landed on Staten Island on July 2, Washington called for the creation of an "Army of Observation," or "Flying Camp," on the New Jersey mainland. Though at first it seemed clear that New York was Howe's immediate target, Washington recognized the fact that from Staten Island, British forces could march across New Jersey to attack Philadelphia. The Army of Observation was positioned to shield that city, eighty miles to the southwest. It would also keep the lines of communication open between Congress and the various military forces around New York and the New England states.

In Europe, according to one contemporary military dictionary, a "Flying-Camp, or army, is generally meant a strong body of horse and foot, commanded for the most part by a lieutenant-general, which is always in motion, both to cover its own garrisons, and to keep the enemy's army in a continual alarm."[1] Within a week after the United States declared independence, units for the Flying Camp began gathering at Perth Amboy, the capital of East Jersey. Here a few weeks earlier, the royal governor, William Franklin, had been arrested at the Proprietor's House and taken away to Connecticut. His wife Elizabeth and son William Temple Franklin remained behind at the mansion, little knowing that the town would soon turn into a military camp.

Brig. Gen. Hugh Mercer, a Scottish physician from Virginia, was appointed commander of the Flying Camp. At first, he thought New

The Proprietary-Royal Governor's House at 149 Kearny Avenue in Perth Amboy, New Jersey, was built in the 1760s in the hope of making Perth Amboy the permanent capital of New Jersey. The mansion was the onetime home of Gov. William Franklin, Loyalist son of Benjamin Franklin. The governor was arrested here in June 1776, and three months later, Ben Franklin suggested it as a place to meet Lord Howe. PHOTO BY KYLE R. WEAVER

Brunswick would be a good central rendezvous point, but upon further consideration, Mercer established headquarters at Perth Amboy, which sits on a hill overlooking the Arthur Kill, the river separating Staten Island from New Jersey.[2] Opposite Amboy is Billopp's Point, the westernmost tip of Staten Island. "When I formerly mentioned Brunswick as a proper place for that Camp, my idea of the Intention of raising & collecting an Army here, was the Security of Philadelphia only," he explained to Washington, "but as I find the design is equally to secure this Colony—and Pennsylvania, or assist in the operations on the N. York side—I am well satisfy'd that Amboy will in every view best fullfil that Intention."[3]

There was another good reason to occupy Perth Amboy: William Franklin was not the only Loyalist in town. "The known Dissafection of the People of Amboy & the Treachery of those of Staten Island who after the fairest Professions have shewn themselves our invetirate Enemies," a disgusted Washington wrote to Gen. William Livingston, commander of the New Jersey militia, "induces me to give Directions that all Persons of known Enmity or doubtful Character should be removed from Places where they might enter into a Correspondence with the Enemy & aid them in their Schemes." Washington authorized the discretionary use of force if necessary, for he told Livingston, "my Tenderness has been often abused & I have had Reason to repent the Indulgence shewn them," especially in light of the recent exposure of a Tory plot to assassinate him in New York. While insisting that they be treated humanely, he added that "Matters are now too far advanced to sacrifice any Thing to Punctilio."[4]

The few troops present in town were New Jersey militia who were eager to get home for the harvest, but units of Pennsylvania Associators and Pennsylvania state regulars soon began arriving. "About four Hundred of the pennsyl. Rifle Battalion have joind us," Mercer informed Washington on July 14, "and another Party of the Same Regiment is on its way; from this last I have ordered One hundred Men to take post at the Ferries of Pasiac and Hackensack." As they arrived, the troops were positioned up the shoreline towards Newark, covering crossing places in between. The New Jersey militia was supposed to gather at Elizabethtown (now Elizabeth), ten miles above Perth Amboy.

"When the two Battalions of Rifle men and one of Musketry from Pennsyl., are posted from hence to the Ferries towards N. York a favourable opportunity may probably offer to surprize the Enemies Small posts," Mercer optimistically told the commander in chief. "Boats may I think be procured—and the Rifle Men would be happy to be so employed," he said, knowing full well from his time spent living in frontier Pennsylvania and Virginia that these frontiersmen were restless souls who did not go off to war just to sit around New Jersey. Besides, he felt, the British could be surprised, for "Such an enterprize is not suspected by the Enemy, nor believed to be under consideration."[5]

That same day, July 14, Washington sent a message to "The Commanding Officer of the pensylvania Troops at Trenton or Elsewhere New Jersey," telling him, "As I do not see any Advantage which can arise from your continuance there & the Honble Continental Congress have Committed the Disposition of them to me untill the Flying Camp is formed you will on Receipt of this proceed to Amboy in New Jersey where General Mercer is appointed to command and their [*sic*] putting yourself under his Direction & Obey such Orders as he may give."[6] Washington was extremely careful in telling that officer (whoever he was—even Washington did not know) that Congress had "committed the disposition of them" to him because of the jurisdiction conflicts already rampant in the numerous military organizations.

Over the next two weeks, reports of hundreds, and then thousands, of eager, patriotic volunteers arriving in North Jersey circulated through the countryside. The tales echoed in the letters of congressmen, and since news traveled by horse, the information quickly disseminated from point to point. Often it was then repeated for weeks by word of mouth long after it was no longer valid (if ever), eventually ending up in newspapers, many of which copied news from other papers.

"I continued at Phila. till Thursday last when I returned homeward, We having first Obtained of Congress all the Assistance they could afford for our Province," Congressman Abraham Clark of New Jersey wrote from Elizabethtown on July 14. "Near half the Militia of Pennsyla. Chearfully offered to March to the Aid of this Province and indeed, their Ardour was such Congress was Obliged to stop part of the Militia of Phila. or the City would have been left wholly defenseless," he told Col. Elias Dayton, also from Elizabethtown, noting that "Part of the Pennsylvanians are at Amboy, and Many on the road this way." With great enthusiasm the congressman reported that "more than 10,000 of them it is expected will in a few days be here, and are to stay till a flying Camp of 10,000 men, now raising in Pennsyla., Maryland & Delaware Counties, take their place."[7] Samuel Adams told Richard Henry Lee the next day, "General Mercer commands the flying Camp in the Jerseys. We have just now appointed a Committee to bring in a Plan for a Reinforcement to compleat the Number of 20,000 Men to be posted in that Colony."[8] The numbers were increasing by the sentence.

Exactly who was in command of which types of troops became a growing source of contention. At Perth Amboy, "This night we joined Gen. Mercer's brigade," Lt. James McMichael of Samuel Miles's Pennsylvania Rifle Battalion entered in his diary on July 18. The Pennsylvanians were "no longer to take orders from under a Brigadier General," McMichael explained, "for we now act as Continental troops, tho' raised for the defense of Pennsylvania."[9]

Congressman Josiah Bartlett noted that among the Pennsylvania volunteers, "Col Roberdeau is appointed a Provincial Brigadier General," an appointment that was already causing dissention among the Pennsylvanians. Because Daniel Roberdeau was elected by the convention of Associator officers in Lancaster, the commanders of the state battalions in Philadelphia ignored his presumed authority because they were not consulted. "Col Dickinson, Col McKean and Col Cadwallader are gone with their regiments to the Jersies," Bartlett eagerly went on about the three battalions of Philadelphia Associators, Dickinson having just left Congress to take command the 1st Battalion. Additionally, "1200 Maryland militia are hourly expected in this city to join the army in the Jersies," he continued. "Col Miles with 1000 provincial riflemen and with him our friend Major Patton have joined the army in New Jersey." The outpouring of support seemed to be endless. "In short," the congressman glowingly reported, "Maryland and Pennsylvania are all in motion."[10]

Even John Adams allowed himself to be caught up in the moment, impressed by the local enthusiasm. "There is a most amiable, lawdable, and gallant Spirit prevailing, in these middle Colonies," he told Abigail on July 15. "The Militia turn out in great Numbers and in high Spirits, in New Jersey, Pensilvania, Maryland, and Delaware, so that We hope to resist Howe and his Mirimidons." To boot, the New York congressional delegation, which had abstained from voting on the issue of independence, finally received its instructions. "Independence is at last unanimously agreed to in the New York Convention," John was pleased to report. "You will see by the Newspapers inclosed what is going forward in Virginia, and Maryland and New Jersey." It was now unanimous; to Great Britain, Adams exclaimed, "Farewell! farewell, infatuated, besotted Stepdame."[11]

Meanwhile, across the Arthur Kill, small parties of Howe's "myrmidons" took up positions at the crossings.[12] At Elizabethtown Point, the river was several hundred yards across, and some militiamen tried their skills at long-distance shooting. "A young officer in the Army, Mr. Blennerhasset, was shot at by a large Party of the Rebels concealed on the opposite Shore, & mortally wounded," Ambrose Serle reported, the militia no doubt letting out huzzas when the redcoat fell, shot in the head. "They are fond of carrying on this unmanly and infamous kind of War, which no civilized Nation will allow," he wrote with revulsion. "An uncommon Spirit of Murder & Cruelty seems to actuate them in all their Proceedings."[13]

Serle's account gives the impression that the officer was shot at randomly for sport; in fact, Blennerhasset was head of a patrol to capture two Americans in a boat, and his troops opened fire first. "The Enemy opposite to the Point do not appear in such Numbers since our Skirmish with them last Saturday Night when they expended about 300 shot at a Pettiauger [a small boat]," General Livingston wrote a few days later, "& our Men in the Entrenchments at last returning the fire, dropt one of them & I since hear wounded three."[14] Lt. Col. Stephen Kemble of General Howe's staff confirmed that "Lieut. Blennerhasset, 10th Regt., was sent from the Quarters of that Regt. near Elizabeth Town Point, to endeavour to cut off one of the Rebel Boats, but, going too near, was fired upon from the Redoubt and

breast Work with small Arms and Cannon, by which the Lieut. was danger-ously Wounded in the head."[15]

The exchanges continued. A few weeks later, while walking near Bil-lopp's Point opposite Amboy, where the river widens from four hundred to one thousand yards, Serle himself came under sniper fire. "Some of the Riflemen we could see moroding [marauding] about on the opposite side of the Stream, some of whom had just discharged their pieces at two men a little before us, without Effect," he reported. "We expected that the next Charge, which we saw them preparing, would be directed to us." This brought to mind the demise of Lieutenant Blennerhasset, who was "lately killed at as great or greater Distance; and yet the Shot was so much spent, that if it had not struck him in a tender Part of the Head, it would scarce have occasioned a Wound."[16]

Mercer reported to Washington on July 16 that the British had "No Encampment—but the men Scattered all over the Island—no considerable Encampment."[17] As the Flying Camp began to materialize and other troops arrived, Mercer formulated ideas to raid the British outposts. With the help of Staten Island resident John Mersereau, he obtained information about British dispositions on the western side. From Elizabethtown that day he notified Washington, "I have reconnoitered the Enemies posts and last night had the Assistance of Capt. John Mercerau to bring some Intelligence from Staten Island—He undertook the Service very cheerfully." Mersereau managed to get to his brother's house, who informed him that "there were Soldiers in every house near the Shore—the Numbers rather uncertain." Mercer laid out a plan for a proposed attack, which seemed well organized.

And then, a single line in the letter revealed why the Pennsylvania troops were so necessary at that moment. "The Clamour of the Militia to get to their Harvest have obliged me to discharge many," Mercer told Washington.[18] It was the major flaw in the Flying Camp, a flaw that was going to result not only in the ultimate failure of the organization, but strangely enough would become part of the popular lore of the American Revolution. The irony of the mythology lay in the fact that, at this point of the war, the complexities of the American military would be continuously oversimplified decades and even centuries later into *everyone* in the Continental forces coming and going, confirming the idea that Washington was running an army of militiamen without any discipline or organization. Even more ironic was the creation of the "militia myth," that somehow the War for Independence was won by militiamen, virtuous citizen-soldiers destroying the king's forces between planting and harvesting. The myth couldn't be further from the reality.

There was already trouble with the actual numbers. Just a week later, on July 22, John Hancock notified the New Jersey Convention, meeting in New Brunswick to create a new state government, "The Congress, taking into Consideration the Strength of our Enemies, and the Force destined for the Attack of New York, have come to a Resolution to increase the Flying Camp. For this Purpose, I have it in Charge to request, you will immediately augment your Quota for the Flying Camp, with three Battalions of Militia, in Addition to those formerly desired by Congress, and send them with all possible Dispatch to join the Flying Camp."[19]

Numbers were not the only problem. Supply shortages, especially of ammunition, made it necessary for Congress to send out a desperate call for lead. With a continental army of somewhere between 15,000 and 20,000 men immediately in and around New York City, supplies were already tight but adequate at the moment. To create a Flying Camp of 10,000 additional troops ten or more miles away in north Jersey and supply them with the standard amount of cartridges—forty rounds per man—would require a minimum of 400,000 musket balls. Each ball weighed about an ounce, so to have just the basic amount of musket ammunition handy required more than ten tons of lead. And that was only the beginning.

But simply doing the math belies reality; considerably more than that would be needed to supply the troops adequately over an extended period of time. Taking into account the wastage through the very real but often unseen hands of carelessness, theft, and incompetence, the American forces found themselves almost perpetually short of supplies during much of the war. This condition was especially bad in the early days of independence, when organization and jurisdiction were rudimentary at best.

In Philadelphia, the Committee of Safety collected lead window weights and clock weights to melt into musket balls. Calls for lead went out to other states. "The Flying camp now forming in the Jersies and which will be immediately in the face of a powerful enemy, is likely to be in great want of that article," Thomas Jefferson wrote to a Virginia state armaments official on July 16. The situation required such immediate action, he explained, that there was not time to get newly chosen governor Patrick Henry's permission, though Jefferson had no doubt he would approve it. The lead, "tho not under our immediate charge, [is] within our reach," he told the official. "We therefore take the liberty of desiring you to stop so many of the powder wagons now on their way to Williamsburg as may be necessary and return them immediately with this lead, and whatever more you can collect."[20]

Mercer's letter to Washington on July 16 reflected the Flying Camp commander's ambivalence in the face of chaos. After mentioning the clamor of the militia for discharges, he said, "We have at Amboy 750 Rifle men—We expect 250 from Powles Hook—and depend on 400 of the Pennsyl. Light Infantry or Militia to be at Woodbridge tomorrow." Mercer hastened to add, "but should their march be so slow as to disappoint us—I shall have that Number of militia prepared on this Quarter, without weakening too much the Several Posts we occupy on the Jersey Shore."[21]

Down in Philadelphia, more troops were arriving each day. "Our city continues to furnish the most agreeable Scenes of public virtue," Dr. Benjamin Rush, a newly seated Pennsylvania delegate to Congress, exclaimed. "The general cry here is the flying camp." He couldn't help but share a heartwarming story with his wife Julia, the daughter of Congressman Richard Stockton of New Jersey, who lived in Princeton. "I saw a boy of between 13 and 14 yesterday Morning trudging Along upon the heels of his father in the uniform of his company with a heavy musquet upon his

Shoulder," Rush wrote. "He belongs to Capt Loxley's Artillery company," a Philadelphia Associator unit, whose muster roll of July 24 lists "Weaver, Michael" and "Weaver, Henry, son of Michael Weaver" under the list of wagoners. "Perhaps you may see him march thr'o Princetown," Ben told Julia, wistfully adding, "I would have given the world to have been the father of such a Son."

Others in town also shared the spirit. "Mr Dunlap called upon me yesterday, & told me that the troop of horse to which he belonged was ordered to remain in Philada. but that he was going as a volunteer in the foot service," Rush continued. "His zeal in the cause make him miserable at home while so many of his fellow citizens were in the field. 'Should I fall (said he) in fighting against the enemies of our country, I have only to beg of you as my last request to remember my Wife & my little Sally.' Here his eyes filled with tears," the doctor choked. "I was hardly Able to answer him."[22]

In a letter to the Continental Army's second senior commander, Maj. Gen. Charles Lee, Rush further described the euphoria. "The declaration of independence has produced a new era in this part of America," he told Lee, who was at Charleston, South Carolina, basking in the glow of the successful repulse of a British naval squadron. "The Militia of Pennsylvania seem to be actuated with a spirit more than Roman. Near 2000 citizens of Philada have lately marched towards New-York in order to prevent an incursion being made by our enemies upon the state of New-Jersey," he wrote, proclaiming, "The cry of them all is for BATTLE."

Also in town, "The tories are quiet—but very surly," he relayed. "Lord Howes proclamation leaves them not a single filament of their cobweb doctrine of reconciliation," Rush confidently affirmed. "The spirit of liberty reigns triumphant in Pennsylvania." As for the former Pennsylvania government officials, "The Proprietary gentry have retired to their Country Seats, and honest men have taken the Seats they abused so much in the government of our State."[23] Beginning with John Penn, the proprietor-governor, the list of suspect leaders also included Joseph Galloway, former Speaker of the Pennsylvania Assembly and author of the "Plan of Union," proposed at the First Continental Congress. Galloway, one of Ben Franklin's old political cronies and perhaps his most trusted friend before independence, left his fine townhouse on Market Street and retired for the summer to his Bucks County estate, Trevose, about twenty miles north of Philadelphia, to await the course of events.

Despite Rush's emotional and patriotic enthusiasm, the cracks in the façade were starting to show. "When I wrote you last, we were deceived in

General Washington's numbers," Thomas Jefferson bluntly told Francis Eppes on July 23. "By a return which came to hand a day or two after, he then had but 15,000 effective men. His reinforcements have come in pretty well since." As for the situation at Perth Amboy, "The flying camp in the Jerseys under General Mercer begins to form, but not as fast as exigencies require," he wrote. "The Congress have, therefore, been obliged to send for two of our battalions from Virginia."

Like many others, Jefferson worried about the imminent arrival of the rest of the British fleet with massive reinforcements. Concerning General Howe, "I do not expect his army will be here and fit for action till the middle or last of August," he surmised, but time was running out. "In the meantime, if Mercer's camp could be formed with the expedition it merits, it might be possible to attack the present force from the Jersey side of Staten Island, and get rid of that beforehand." He was amazed that from Pennsylvania, "the militia go in freely, considering they leave their harvest to rot in the field."[24]

The reality was another issue. "The Returns of the Troops are not so accurate as I could wish," an alarmed General Mercer informed Washington on July 24. Their lack of equipment was disturbing. "Of the Troops who joined yesterday—the 4th Battalion—Twenty of the Men had no Muskets, they were furnished with Pikes about 12 feet long." His concern was understandable, for across the Arthur Kill from Perth Amboy, "The Enemy have reinforced their Guards on this part of the Island—three Battalions appeared on the point opposite this Place yesterday—with four Peices of feild Artillery—probably this Arises from their perceiving our force daylie encreasing here."[25] The British were starting to take serious notice of the Flying Camp.

Opposite Perth Amboy was Billopp's Point, a thousand or so yards across the water. It was named for the Billopp family, English settlers who received a grant for a manor from King Charles II shortly after the area was taken from the Dutch a century before. A sandy beach ran along the shore, beyond which a gentle knoll rose gradually, crowned by a substantial, two-story manor house dating from the 1670s. Built in a plain, Anglo-Dutch colonial style, the dwelling's steep gables of thick fieldstone trimmed with brick gave it a rustic, old-fashioned appearance. The manor house was roomy and comfortable, featuring a wide center hall and two ample parlors finished with fine paneling on the first floor, four bedrooms and a garret upstairs, and a large basement kitchen and cold room for food storage. The estate was owned by Christopher Billopp, a prominent New York Loyalist and colonel of Loyalist militia from Staten Island. The point was now occupied by three British regiments supported by four fieldpieces, and they began to build gun emplacements.

No sooner was the British artillery emplaced than it was employed. *The New York Gazette and Weekly Mercury* reported that on Thursday afternoon, July 25, "Several Cannon were fired from our Battery at Amboy, at a Number of Boats from Staten Island, bound to Sandy-Hook, supposed to join the Ministerial Fleet there."[26] Five small sailing vessels called *shallops* came out of the Fresh Kills on Staten Island about three miles above Billopp's Point and headed down the Arthur Kill. General Mercer notified Washington the next morning that the shallops "that passed us yesterday from Fresh Kill were full of soldiers, who appeared on deck after getting round Billop's point into Prince's Bay." Mercer remarked that as the ships passed Perth Amboy, "our Field Pieces played on them but with little effect."[27]

Across the water, British drums beat the call to arms and "brought on a Cannonade from the Encampment of the Regulars at Billopp's Point, on the Island, which continued very hot on both Sides for near an Hour."[28] Mercer confirmed that "the Enemy returned the Cannonade briskly during the Space of one hour with four, six, and Twelve pounders." As for casualties, "One of our militia was killed and two wounded, though not dangerously."[29] According to the paper, "the Boats got clear, but many of the Regulars were seen to fall, and several carried off, supposed to be wounded," an observation unconfirmed from British sources. "On our Side, a Soldier belonging to one of the Philadelphia Battalions was Killed, and one wounded." The streets of Perth Amboy witnessed some sanguine drama as "a Horse in a Carriage had his Head shot off in the Street, and some Damage was done [to] the Houses."[30] The shooting war had come to Perth Amboy and Billopp's Point.

By the end of July, the situation of the Flying Camp had not improved, and Mercer's plan to raid Staten Island was foiled by bad weather. The window of opportunity to take action was steadily closing. "There is nothing new here," a disappointed Thomas Jefferson wrote on July 30. "Washington's and Mercer's camps recruit with amazing slowness. Had they been reinforced more readily something might have been attempted on Staten island. The enemy there are not more than 8, or 10,000 strong." As for the rumored reinforcements coming from England, "Ld. Howe has received none of his fleet, unless some Highlanders (about 8, or 10 vessels) were of it."[31]

At Elizabethtown, ten miles north of Perth Amboy, the situation had been even more chaotic, for New Jersey militia were supposed to be on duty. When General Howe's troops landed on Staten Island on July 2, many of the inhabitants fled. "A Number of the Enemy . . . proceeded within sight of our point, & expected to advance to Elizabeth Town, I immediately gave orders to beat to arms," Gen. William Livingston had informed Joseph Reed, Washington's adjutant general, on July 3. Livingston gathered a handful of militiamen and marched them to the point, only to have the British troops withdraw. "When I left E Town our People were in such Confusion that I left the Town with Reluctance, but thinking it my duty to proceed, I met Major Burr passing this town." From Maj. Aaron Burr, a native of New Jersey who had recently been transferred from Washington's staff to General Putnam's staff, he learned the seriousness of the situation and that the immediate defense of New Jersey was imperative.[32]

Elizabethtown was also the home of Congressman Abraham Clark and Col. Elias Dayton, commander of a Continental regiment. "From your feeling for your Town & family when you first received this News, you can form some Judgment of mine tho' I was much nearer to them," Clark told Dayton. "I expected nothing less from this event, than Eliza. Town long Obnoxious to the Enemy, would be laid in Ashes, and indeed, had they come over they would have met with no Opposition as our Militia a few days before had Marched to New York by request of the General."[33] The few militiamen Livingston had scraped together were the bottom of the barrel.

By the first week of August, the problems with discipline and desertion were mounting daily in the Flying Camp. Because the men were mostly young volunteers with no military experience, their initial enthusiasm was dulled by the routines of camp life. They were itchy to get into action, and the sight of redcoats across the water just out of range made them all the more unruly.

The weather was hot and humid, the limited food available was lousy, and mosquitoes from the swamps swarmed unchecked. The camps stank: the daily, mundane camp duties—digging entrenchments, digging "vaults" or latrines, "covering" or filling the vaults daily, carrying wood, digging more vaults, fetching water—was not what these men signed up to do. The officers, most of who were as inexperienced as the men and were in many cases elected by them, now had to give unpopular orders. The overall mood turned sour. Further, the New Jersey militiamen dismissed to go home to the harvest were showing no signs of returning. The Pennsylvanians became more resentful; they, too, had harvests to get in, as Rev. Henry Muhlenberg had pointed out. "A Cowardly, infamous Spirit of Desertion, prevails here too much," Mercer reported to Washington in early August.[34]

Reports of the situation made their way down to Congress. "I see We shall never get a regular, permanent Army, but must go on patching up an Army every 3 Months, with fresh Militia, at double the Expence," John Adams wrote in frustration on August 3. "Reason and Experience are sometimes lost upon the wisest and the best of Men."[35] Abraham Clark quickly sent a message through the congressional Committee of Secret Correspondence to the New Jersey Convention meeting at New Brunswick. "It was with the utmost Concern our Congress recd. information by Letter from Genl. Merser yesterday, that none of the Jersey Militia had joined him, & that the Phila. battalions were almost mutinous to return home," he wrote on August 7. "It is possible you may be unacquainted with the Strength of the Enemy—; And the Number of our Forces at New York & Jersey to Oppose them—; Or it may not be in your Power to call out our Militia," the congressman wondered. "If the latter is the Case we are in a most deplorable state," Clark stated emphatically, "and as to the Number of our Forces I dare say they are not half and I believe not one third, what is generally Supposed."

The danger was real and it was immediate. "It is in the Power of the Enemy to March through New Jersey & Pennsylvania or to go where they Please did they know our Strength," the congressman reminded them, "but happy for us I believe they are Ignorant of it and I dare not even mention the true state of our Army to you, least by some Accident it might Transpire by some of the members being over heard in speaking of it as I am persuaded none would designedly publish it." Loyalist ears were everywhere, and Clark did not mince words. "We are indeed in a most Critical Situation," he reiterated. "Danger Stands thick Around us, And Unless Our Militia Almost Universally take the field, nothing but ruin can be our Portion."

The situation was so urgent that his fellow Jersey delegates pressed him to make the report to the Convention in person, "but upon inquiry this Evening I find the Stage [wagon] is full." Clark was afraid that the Convention would break up before he could get there, as the ride to New Brunswick took two days and "you will probably rise the last of this Week." He again told the delegates, "If ever the utmost resistance was Necessary, Now is the Time; let me Conjure you with a feeling Sense of Present danger to Our New States but just brought into existence and to appearance Almost breathing their last, to use every possible Endeavour to call out all our Militia." Clark was sympathetic to the militiamen, saying, "I know it will be difficult for them, but without this All seems to be gone."[36] The "summer soldiers" were desperately needed.

The frustrations were endless. By the end of August, General Livingston was utterly fed up with his own militia, the Pennsylvania Associators, and soldiering in general. "I received yours of yesterday's date just after I got into my new Habitation which is a Marquee Tent in our Incampment here," he told Congressman Will Hooper of New Jersey. "You wou'd really be astonished to see how grand I look, while at the same time I can assure you I was never more sensible (to use a New-England Phrase) of my own *nothingness* in military affairs. I removed my Quarters from Town hither to be with the men, & to enure [inure] them to discipline, which by my distance from the Camp before, considering what scurvy Subalterns we are ever like to have while they are in the appointment of the mobility, I found it impossible to introduce." His fellow Jerseyans were difficult enough to discipline, but the Philadelphia Associators were, in his opinion, beneath contempt. "And the worst men (was there a degree above the superlative) would be still perjorated by having been fellow-soldiers with that discipline-hating good-living-loving too eternal-fam'd damn'd coxcomatical crew we lately had here from Philadelphia," he spat. Worn out with the daily rounds of idiocy and continuously harassed by a thousand nitpicky problems, Livingston melodramatically sighed, "My antient corporeal fabric is almost tottering under the fatigue I have lately undergone."[37]

Great changes were about to take place for the harassed militia commander. A few days later, Livingston was relieved of his military duties and handed another challenge. At the New Jersey Convention in New Brunswick, he was chosen governor of the state in place of royal governor William Franklin, the disowned son of Ben Franklin.

CHAPTER 7
The Lord and the Sage

⚜

As the Flying Camp was materializing, the wheels of reconciliation continued to spin. On July 13, the same day that Admiral Howe wrote his letter to Washington, a boat dispatched from the *Eagle* sailed around Staten Island carrying letters to the governors of the middle and southern colonies and "persons of influence" who might be helpful in achieving a peaceful settlement. "This was a prudent and decent Way of acquainting the People of America, that the Door was yet open for Reconciliation," Ambrose Serle explained.[1] The courier was 1st Lt. Samuel Reeve, who headed to Perth Amboy, the capital of East Jersey and late seat of the royal governor, William Franklin, son of Benjamin Franklin and a die-hard Loyalist, who was under arrest and being held in Connecticut. Amboy was also the headquarters of Gen. Hugh Mercer, commander of the American Flying Camp.

The weather turned foul and the rain pelted down; where Reeve spent the night is uncertain, because he did not arrive at Amboy until the next day. "This Morning Lord Howe sent Lt Reeve of the Eagle Man of War, with a flag of Truce to this Post," General Mercer notified Washington. "He delivered me the Letters which accompany this."[2] Following the punctilio of courtesy to military personnel under a flag of truce, Mercer was kind enough to invite the lieutenant to have a bite to eat. "Mr. Reeve breakfasted with *Mercer*, the American Commander, who behaved civilly, yet rather dryly," Serle noted. Gen. Hugh Mercer, a fifty-one-year-old Scottish physician who had served in the Jacobite forces under Bonnie Prince Charlie back in "the

'45" (1745–46 Scottish Rebellion), had only recently been appointed commander of the newly organized Flying Camp. "They had very coarse Fare, which the American noticed, but added, they had Plenty of Necessaries, and did not wish for Luxuries," Serle commented. "The Lieutenant very properly replied, that it was very happy for those who had not them not to wish for them."[3]

The letters were immediately forwarded to Washington in New York. When he received them on July 15, he promptly sent them to Congress. This was part of Lord Howe's plan to disseminate the information: send important dispatches under loose seals, knowing that prying eyes will open and read them, and then spread the news. Congress's foil to this was to publish all of the public correspondence in the newspapers so that the people would know what "the insidious court of Britain" was scheming to do next.

Reports of all of this eventually made their way back to Lord Howe, confirming the success of his circulation plan. "The inclosed printed Paper No. 3, which accidentally came to my Hands, will inform Your Lordship of the Resolution of the General Congress, upon their receipt of the above mentioned Packets," he wrote to Lord Germain a month later, "which it seemed were transmitted by Mr (called General) Mercier, the Commanding Officer at Amboy, to Mr. Washington at New York, and by him to Congress."[4]

Among the pieces of correspondence was a personal letter from Lord Howe to Benjamin Franklin, dated June 20, when the *Eagle* was about to make landfall. "I cannot my Worthy Friend, permit the Letters and Parcels which I have sent in the State I receiv'd them, to be landed without adding a word upon the subject of the injurious Extremities in which our unhappy Disputes have engaged us," the admiral told the doctor.[5] He wanted to meet with Franklin and, based on a number of previous conversations they had had more a year before, try to find some way to begin working out an accommodation.

During his long stay in London before the war, Franklin had become friends with Howe's widowed sister Caroline. The old doctor visited her house regularly to socialize and play chess. As the situation in the colonies deteriorated, the admiral expressed an interest in meeting Franklin, so through Caroline, the lord met the sage at dinner on Christmas Day 1774. The two developed a cordial relationship based on mutual respect and began exchanging letters with ideas for reconciliation.

Over the next few weeks, Howe and Franklin discussed the growing crisis and the ways in which war might be averted. They talked at length about the idea of a peace commission and how it could benefit everyone—Britain, America, and those individuals who made the commission happen. Franklin cautiously suggested how "a Person of Rank and Dignity, who had a Character of Candour, Integrity, and Wisdom, might possibly, if employed in that Service, be of great Use."[6] But a few months later, an embittered Franklin returned to America and took his seat as a Pennsylvania delegate in the Second Continental Congress, determined to push for independence.

Now that he had finally arrived in America, Lord Howe wished to enlist the doctor's help in effecting reconciliation. "You will learn the Nature of my Mission from the Official Dispatches which I have recommended to be forwarded by the same Conveyance," he told Franklin. "Retaining all the Earnestness I ever express'd to see our Differences accomodated, I shall conceive, if I meet with the same Disposition in the Colonies which I was once taught to expect, the most flattering Hopes of proving serviceable in the Objects of the King's paternal Sollicitude, by promoting the re-establishment of lasting Peace and Union with the Colonies." The admiral remained optimistic that he could build on the good personal rapport he and Franklin had developed in London.

At the same time, Lord Howe also knew that this was going to be an uphill battle, especially trying to win back the goodwill of the Americans. "But if the deep rooted Prejudices of America and the necessity of preventing her Trade from passing into foreign Channells, must keep us still a divided People," he added, knowing that his mission was a bit of a reach, especially with New England radicals like John and Sam Adams poisoning the wells of good faith. "I shall from every private as well as public motive, most heartily lament, that this is not the moment wherein those great Objects of my Ambition are to be attain'd."[7] Whatever the outcome, Howe went on to reassure Franklin that his personal regard for the doctor would remain the same.

Howe's letters arrived in Philadelphia on July 18 and were delivered to Congress. In addition to the proclamations were "a number of Letters principally from Friends in London to Friends here placing the Character of the Howes in the most amiable point of View, & recommending Reconciliation with G. Britain," William Ellery of Rhode Island informed Rev. Dr. Ezra Stiles. "Among the Letters were some to Dr Franklin, one to the Farmer"— John Dickinson, author of *Letters from a Farmer in Pennsylvania*—"and one to Mr Stockton," delegate Richard Stockton from New Jersey, who had advocated reconciliation for years before the war.

Benjamin Franklin by David Rent Etter, after an original by David Martin.
INDEPENDENCE NATIONAL HISTORIC PARK

"Dr Franklin was not in Congress when the Letters were bro't in, but was sent for," Ellery noted. Franklin was president of the Pennsylvania Convention, which was also meeting in the State House, drawing up a constitution for the new state government. "When he entered, his Letters were delivered to him sealed. He opened them, looked over them, and handed them to the President desiring him to read them." John Hancock read the letters to the Congress; Ellery said that they "contained much the same Sentiments with those to Friends, as did that to Mr Stockton, who is a Member of Congress, and who was treated and behaved in the same manner that Dr Franklin did."

John Dickinson was no longer present; he had left Congress two weeks earlier to go to the Flying Camp. "As the Farmer is in the Jersey at the Head of his Battalion, his Letter is kept sealed by the President until he shall return & receive it in Congress," Ellery told Stiles.[8] Dickinson was later notified about the letters and asked John Hancock to open and read them too, but for unknown reasons they were not.

"The Letters to the late Governors & the Declarations are ordered to be printed to let the People see upon what Terms Reconciliation is proposed to them," Ellery continued. "*Odi Danaos, etiam Dona ferentes*" ("I despise the Greeks, even bearing gifts"), he snarled to his learned friend Dr. Stiles, "but when what some People, Tories, may call the Olive-plant is handed to us at the point of the Bayonet, or is hurled to us from the Mouths of Canon, if possible I should more than hate it."[9] He was not the only one.

"The Truth is the Door is shut," the congressman exclaimed, "& it would now be in vain, to talk of any sort of Alliance with Britain but a Commercial One. We have been driven into a Declara[tion] of Independency & must forget our former Love for our British Brethren. The Sword must Determine our Quarrel," even though the military picture was far from rosy. "Our Repulse from Canada is disagreeable, but we must expect repeated Defeats," he admitted, reminding Reverend Stiles, "The Road to Liberty, like the Road to Heaven is strewed with Thorns."[10]

The next day, Congress resolved to publish the proclamation of the peace mission, which clearly stated that the Howes were invested with the powers to only grant pardons. This "has let the cat out of the bag," John Adams wrote to Abigail on July 20.[11] Congress also passed a resolution that day stating "that Dr. Franklin may, if he thinks proper, send an answer to the letter he received from Lord Howe."[12]

Franklin immediately wrote an elegant reply, first thanking the admiral for sending the letters, then cutting to the heart of the matter. According to the proclamation, the only power granted the admiral was to offer pardon to those Americans who submitted to the authority of Parliament, "which I was sorry to find, as it must give your Lordship Pain to be sent so far on so hopeless a Business."

Politely, yet with a keen edge of bitterness, Franklin explained to Lord Howe the American position. "Directing Pardons to be offered the Colonies, who are the very Parties injured, expresses indeed that Opinion of our Ignorance, Baseness, and Insensibility which your uninform'd and proud Nation has long been pleased to entertain of us," he told the admiral bluntly, "but it can have no other Effect than that of increasing our Resentment," essentially the same response which Washington gave to Colonel Paterson that very day in New York. Further, Franklin said, that it was impossible to believe that Americans would submit to a government "that has with the most wanton Barbarity and Cruelty, burnt our defenceless Towns in the midst of Winter, excited the Savages to massacre our Farmers, and our Slaves to murder their Masters, and is even now bringing foreign Mercenaries to deluge our Settlements with Blood." From the American Whig perspective, this was total war; from the British Tory perspective, this was how to handle treason and rebellion.

"These atrocious Injuries have extinguished every remaining Spark of Affection for that Parent Country we once held so dear," the sage told the lord. The damage on both sides of the relationship was permanent, Franklin wrote, for "were it possible for *us* to forget and forgive them, it is not possible for *you* (I mean the British Nation) to forgive the People you have so heavily injured." The British Empire was not created with charity in mind, but for Britain's gain, and from that perspective, the Americans were not being dutiful subjects.

"You can never confide again in those as Fellow Subjects, and permit them to enjoy equal Freedom, to whom you know you have given such just Cause of lasting Enmity," Franklin stated with regret. "And this must impel you, were we again under your Government, to endeavour the breaking our Spirit by the severest Tyranny, and obstructing by every means in your Power our growing Strength and Prosperity." Force was the only method seen by the ministry to compel obedience, bringing home the meaning of Charles James Fox's remark in Parliament two years earlier about whether it would be wiser to govern America by force or management.

"But your Lordship mentions 'the Kings paternal Solicitude for promoting the Establishment of lasting *Peace* and Union with the Colonies,'" Franklin observed. "If by *Peace* is here meant, a Peace to be entered into between Britain and America as distinct States now at War, and his Majesty has given your Lordship Powers to treat with us of such a Peace, I may venture to say, tho' without Authority, that I think a Treaty for that purpose not yet quite impracticable, before we enter into Foreign Alliances." Franklin was holding out his own straws here, for he knew that while Howe really had nothing of substance to offer, by the same token, there was no guarantee of foreign support for the American rebellion at this early and very uncertain stage of the game.

"But I am persuaded you have no such Powers," he admitted. "Your Nation, tho' by punishing those American Governors who have created and fomented the Discord, rebuilding our burnt Towns, and repairing as far as possible the Mischiefs done us, She might yet recover a great Share of our Regard and the greatest part of our growing Commerce, with all the Advantage of that additional Strength to be derived from a Friendship with us; I know too well her abounding Pride and deficient Wisdom, to believe she will ever take such Salutary Measures." Britain's empire was the hallmark of the national character: "Her Fondness for Conquest as a Warlike Nation, her Lust of Dominion as an Ambitious one, and her Thirst for a gainful Monopoly as a Commercial one, (none of them legitimate Causes of War) will all join to hide from her Eyes every View of her true Interests; and continually goad her on in these ruinous distant Expeditions, so destructive both of Lives and Treasure, that must prove as perrnicious to her in the End as the Croisades formerly were to most of the Nations of Europe."·

Franklin then inserted a personal note, as heartfelt as it was bitter. "Long did I endeavour with unfeigned and unwearied Zeal, to preserve from breaking, that fine and noble China Vase the British Empire: for I knew that being once broken, the separate Parts could not retain even their Share of the Strength or Value that existed in the Whole, and that a perfect Re-Union of those Parts could scarce even be hoped for." He then reached back to the time around Christmas in London nearly two years before, when they first met and began discussions. "Your Lordship may possibly remember the Tears of Joy that wet my Cheek, when, at your good Sister's in London, you once gave me Expectations that a Reconciliation might soon take place." But through the course of events, "I had the Misfortune to find those Expectations disappointed, and to be treated as the Cause of the Mischief I was labouring to prevent." Franklin's role in publishing private letters of Massachusetts governor Thomas Hutchinson had led to his censure by the Privy Council in 1774, where he was berated and ridiculed for two hours by Lord Wedderburn. It was said that Franklin walked into that chamber a loyal subject of the crown, and walked out a diehard rebel.

"My Consolation under that groundless and malevolent Treatment was, that I retained the Friendship of many Wise and Good Men in that Country, and among the rest some Share in the Regard of Lord Howe," Franklin told the admiral. "The well founded Esteem, and permit me to say Affection, which I shall always have for your Lordship, makes it painful to me to see you engag'd in conducting a War, the great Ground of which, as expressed in your Letter, is, 'the Necessity of preventing the American Trade from passing into foreign Channels.'" Franklin suggested that war for trade was unjust; "that the true and sure means of extending and securing Commerce is the goodness and cheapness of Commodities," a radical idea published in 1776 by the Scottish economist Adam Smith in his book commonly called *The Wealth of Nations*. Franklin added a fact which the British government already knew that year, "that the profits of no Trade can ever be equal to the Expence of compelling it, and of holding it, by Fleets and Armies."

"I consider this War against us therefore, as both unjust, and unwise; and I am persuaded cool dispassionate Posterity will condemn to Infamy those who advised it," the doctor told the admiral, "and that even Success will not save from some degree of Dishonour, those who voluntarily engag'd to conduct it."

Franklin finished his letter with a double-edged conclusion. "I know your great Motive in coming hither was the Hope of being instrumental in a Reconciliation," he told Lord Howe, "and I believe when you find *that* impossible on any Terms given you to propose, you will relinquish so odious a Command, and return to a more honourable private Station."[13] He closed with the greatest and most sincere respect to the admiral.

A week went by with no response from Lord Howe. August came: one week, two weeks, with no further communication. For the moment, the door was shut, and the issue seemed to fade into the background.

Then, a letter from the admiral to the doctor written on August 16 arrived in Philadelphia.[14] "I am sorry my worthy friend, that it is only on the assurances you give me of my having still preserved a place in your esteem, that I can now found a pretension to trouble you with a reply," Lord Howe began. "I can have no difficulty to acknowledge that the powers I am invested with, were never calculated to negociate a reunion with America, under any other description than as subject to the crown of Great Britain." The admiral went on to say that it was his intention to confer with "gentlemen of influence" to establish peace on the basis of the Olive Branch Petition, "were the temper of the Colonies such as professed in the last petition of the Congress to the King." So with the temper of the colonies now changed from resistance to independence—somehow the admiral omitted any reference to what might have changed that temper—the fault lay entirely with the rebels.

"But as I perceive from the tenor of your letter, how little I am to reckon upon the advantage of your assistance for restoring that permanent union which has long been the object of my endeavours, and which I flattered myself when I left England would be in the compass of my power," Howe again placed the blame on Franklin and the Americans. On a personal note, responding to Franklin's polite but stinging rebuff of the admiral's position, Lord Howe said, "I will only add, that as the dishonour to which you deem me exposed by my military situation in this country, has effected no change in your sentiments of personal regard towards me; so shall no difference in political points alter my desire of proving how much I am your sincere and obedient humble Servant."[15]

Having passed Howe's letter on to Franklin, Washington commented about the strange turn of events. "There is something exceedingly misterious in the conduct of the Enemy," he wrote on August 19. "Lord Howe takes pains to throw out, upon every occasion, that he is the Messenger of Peace—that he wants to accommodate matters—nay, has Insinuated, that he thinks himself authorized to do it upon the terms mentioned in the last petition to the King." The situation made little sense to him, Washington admitted. "Has the Nation got to that, that the King, or his Ministers will openly dispense with Acts of Parliament?" he wondered. "And if they durst attempt it, how is it to be accounted for that after running the Nation to some Millions of Pounds Sterling to hire and Transport Foreigners, and before a blow is struck, they are willing to give the terms proposed by Congress before they, or we, had encountered the enormous expence that both of us are now run to?" The whole business was extremely puzzling: either massive mismanagement or serious infighting was paralyzing the British high command, or something major was developing in Europe. "I say, how is this to be accounted for but from their having received some disagreeable intelligence from Europe; or, by having some Manouvre in view which is to be effected by procrastination?" The delay had given the American forces more time to gather and prepare, though they too had more than enough mysteries, mismanagements, and uncertainties with which to contend.

"What this can be the lord knows," Washington wrote in frustration. "We are now past the middle of August and they are in possession of an Island only, which it never was in our power; or Intention to dispute their Landing on." He noted the obvious, that "this is but a small step towards the Conquest of this Continent."[16]

CHAPTER 8

The Girl, the Generals, and the Toasts

❧

The month of July in 1776 saw more dramatic changes in America more rapidly than any other single month up to that time. Beyond the political spectrum, the sheer shift of population alone was incredible, with thousands of all types of soldiers flocking to the New York area and thousands of civilians fleeing the region. For many soldiers, it was exciting in that it was the first time they had been more than a few miles from home. The majority of them were young men in their teens and early twenties, enthusiastic to experience adventure through defiance of imperial governmental authority and confrontation with royal troops. In Philadelphia, "The influence of the declaration of independence upon the senate & the field is inconceivable," Benjamin Rush wrote on July 30. "The militia of our state pant for nothing more than to avenge the blood of our brave countrymen upon our enemies on Staten Island."[1]

Not surprisingly, some of the troops were panting for something more. A young girl, Miss Margaret Moncrieffe, years later related her experience with some of the Flying Camp at Elizabethtown. Her father was Maj. Thomas Moncrieffe, a British officer who had served in America for two decades under Lord Amherst and Gen. Thomas Gage. Except for brief schooling in Ireland, Margaret spent most of her childhood in America with her brother, Edward Cornwallis Moncrieffe, who attended King's College (now Columbia University) in New York. Her mother, who died before the age of twenty, was supplanted by two American stepmothers, both of whom also died shortly after marriage. Her first stepmother was a sister of former congressman William Livingston, now commander of the New Jersey militia and soon-to-be governor of New Jersey. Her second stepmother was the sister-in-law of Frederick Jay, brother of Congressman John Jay of New York. The result was an interesting and extraordinary complication of friends and relatives on both sides of the question.

Margaret's loyalties, though, were mostly with her father at this time, and "thus I found myself in the midst of republicans in war against the crown of Great-Britain, persecuted on every side because my father was fighting for the cause of *a king!*" she wrote shortly after the war. "At the age of thirteen I was sent to board at Elizabeth-Town, New Jersey, with the family of an American Colonel, where I was forced to hear my nearest and dearest relations continually traduced."[2] When the British army landed on Staten Island on July 2, Elizabethtown, opposite the northwestern tip of the island, was transformed overnight into an armed camp.

Dr. James Clitherall of South Carolina, a friend of Congressman Edward Rutledge, passed through the area on July 3, en route to New York. "When we arrived at Elizabethtown, we found the people much alarmed, and the women, children, and baggage were hurried out of town," the doctor confirmed, "occasioned by the appearance of the British Troops at the Point."[3] In the flurry of the panic, sprightly, precocious young Margaret Moncrieffe was evacuated to a village ten miles inland. But, "grieved with the gloomy scene before me," she ran away one Sunday while the family was at church, made her way back to Elizabethtown sometime in mid-July, and "placed myself *immediately* under the care of a lady (Mrs. De Hart) whose family loved me from my tenderest infancy."[4]

Mrs. Sarah Dagworthy De Hart was the wife of lawyer John De Hart, who had been a delegate to the First and Second Continental Congresses. Sarah was the mother of several children, and now, at age forty-five, was six months along in her twelfth pregnancy. Forty-nine-year-old John De Hart (not to be confused with John Hart, another congressman from New Jersey) was away at that moment, attending the New Jersey Convention in New Brunswick. The arrival of feisty young Margaret as a fugitive in the midst of all the panic must have been a less-than-welcome surprise for Mrs. De Hart.

The De Hart house stood in the center of Elizabethtown near the Barracks and had a fine garden around it. The town was occupied by a harum-scarum assortment of New Jersey militiamen. In mid-July, some Associators and riflemen, fresh from the hills and hinterlands of Pennsylvania, also appeared in town. "Walking one sultry day in the garden of my protectress," she recalled, "I was beset by a party of riflemen, just arrived from Pennsylvania." Margaret presumed they were riflemen, for like most of the Flying Camp and much of the Continental army, they were dressed in linen hunting shirts. But some of them must have been from one of the musket battalions, for according to her account, they were equipped with bayonets, which rifles did not usually carry.

Margaret's good looks attracted a lot of attention, especially in a garden on a sultry summer day, and her behavior, no doubt, was provocative. Exactly what she said or did to provoke them, she neglected to say. "Presenting their bayonets to my breast," the sassy young girl believed that they "would certainly have killed me, had not one of the men took compassion on my youth, discovering in my features something which conquered his savage purpose."[5]

Margaret then "applied for protection to Mr. William Livingston, my first stepmother's brother, who was [shortly after] the governor of New Jersey." At that moment, General Livingston had his hands more than full. As commander of the New Jersey militia, he had spent the past week desperately trying to shore up the local defenses. Letter after letter, many of them to Washington, poured from his quill—forty or more letters before the end of July, filled with rumors of attack, loyalists to be arrested, complaints of no supplies, no money, no flints, no ammunition. Undisciplined troops were all over the place, coming and going; some of them were turning on their officers, while others deserted in groups. The harassed general had no time to put up with the nonsense caused by a coquettish thirteen-year-old in the bloom of adolescence, especially since she had been taken out of harm's way once already. "He behaved to me with harshness, and even added insult to his reproaches," Margaret fatuously whined.[6]

While this was unfolding at Elizabethtown, across the water on Staten Island, Maj. Thomas Moncrieffe was becoming more and more concerned about his daughter's safety and well-being. The wrangling between the commanders over how to address letters to Washington was in full cry, and as the flags of truce and couriers passed up and down New York harbor, the major sent a letter to his daughter. *The Pennsylvania Gazette* reported that on Friday, July 19, "a third flag from the fleet appeared, which we hear brought only an open letter directed to Miss Margaret Moncrieffe."[7] This letter was carried by General Howe's aide Capt. Nisbet Balfour, who came up to arrange Colonel Paterson's meeting with Washington to straighten out the title issue.

After receiving her father's letter, and having been rebuffed by her uncle, in desperation Margaret turned to one of her father's old comrades from the French and Indian War, asking him to intervene on her behalf. "Thus destitute of friends, I wrote to General Putnam, who instantly answered my letter by a very kind invitation to his house, assuring me, that he respected my father, and was only his enemy in the field of battle; but that in private life, he himself, or any part of his family, might always command his services."[8]

Fifty-eight-year-old Gen. Israel Putnam, "Old Put" as he was called, was a legend in his own time. A crusty, rough-hewn New Englander, standing tall at five feet, six inches, Putnam performed hard service in the French and Indian War, surviving Indian captivity, shipwreck, and incredibly harsh wilderness expeditions. After the war, he opened a tavern named The General Wolfe in honor of Britain's fallen hero at Quebec. Active in the early protests against Parliament's taxes, he became a militia general for Connecticut after the war broke out. In New York in 1776, he was temporarily in command until Washington arrived, and served essentially as a deputy commander in the mercurial days after independence.[9]

Putnam responded to Margaret on July 26; as with Washington, evidently her father's letter referred to him without the title *general*, which did not bother "Old Put" at all, since it was a personal letter. "The omission of my title in Major *Moncrieffe's* letter is a matter I regard not in the least," the old hero began, "nor does it, in any way, influence my conduct in this affair, as you seem to imagine. Any political difference alters him not to me in a private capacity." The general explained to Margaret that, "As an officer, he is my enemy, and obliged to act as such, be his private sentiments what they will. As a man, I owe him no enmity; but far from it will, with pleasure, do any kind office in my power for him or any of his connexions."

Putnam went on to say that he spoke with Washington about her situation and asked his permission for her to go to Staten Island. "He informs me that Lieutenant Colonel Paterson, who came with the last flag, said he was empowered to offer the exchange of Mr. Lowell for Governor Skene. As the Congress have reserved to themselves the right of exchanging prisoners, the General has sent to know their pleasure, and doubts not they will give their consent." The old general promised her that "if this exchange is made, you will have the liberty to pass out with Governor Skene; but that no flag will be sent solely for that purpose."

In the meantime, Putnam felt that it would be best to have her come to New York. "Major William Livingston," probably Major William Smith Livingston of Lasher's New York Militia, "was lately here, and informed me that you had an inclination to live in this city, and that all the ladies of your acquaintance having left town, and Mrs. Putnam and two daughters being here, proposed your staying with them. If agreeable to you, be assured, Miss, you shall be sincerely welcome," he told her. "You will here, I think, be in a more probable way of accomplishing the end you wish, that of seeing your father; and may depend on every civility from, Miss, your obedient servant, Israel Putnam."[10]

The young girl was delighted. The following day, Putnam's former aide-de-camp, Lt. Col. Samuel Webb, now on Washington's staff, went over to Elizabethtown to escort Margaret to New York. "When I arrived in Broadway (a street so called) where General Putnam resided, I was received with the greatest tenderness both by Mrs. Putnam and her daughters," she recalled, "and on the following day I was introduced by them to General and Mrs. Washington, who likewise made it their study to shew me every mark of regard."[11] Being the daughter of a British officer and somewhat strong-headed and precocious, "I seldom was allowed to be alone," Margaret stated, "although sometimes indeed I found an opportunity to escape to a gallery on the top of the house (Almost every gentleman's house in New-York has a gallery, with a summer-house, on top), where my chief delight was to view with a telescope our fleet and army at Staten Island." Mrs. Putnam tried to keep Margaret and her own daughters busy by having them spin flax to make shirts for the soldiers.

With his main headquarters on the outskirts of New York, Washington was in and out of town and often dined at Putnam's quarters. "One day after dinner, the congress was the toast," Margaret wrote. She evidently did not conduct herself properly, for "General Washington viewed me very attentively, and sarcastically said, 'Miss Moncrieffe, you don't drink your wine.'"

Embarrassed at first, Margaret took her glass and replied, "General Howe *is* the toast."

Washington was not amused. "Vexed at my temerity," she recounted, "the whole company, especially General Washington, censured me."

Putnam came to the rescue, apologizing for her conduct and assuring the officers that she meant no offense. "Besides," he said, "everything said or done by such a child ought rather to amuse than affront you." According to Margaret, Washington was "piqued" at this, but then said, "Well, Miss, I will overlook your indiscretion, on condition that you drink my health, or General Putnam's, the first time you dine at Sir William Howe's table, on the other side of the water." The young girl was thrilled, taking it to mean that she would soon see her father. "I promised General Washington to do anything which he required, provided he would permit me to return to him," she replied.[12]

Margaret stated that more letters soon arrived from her father, demanding her return, "for he now considered me a prisoner." She claimed that Washington had tried to "seduce" her father from the British army by holding her as "a hostage for my 'father's good behaviour'," a claim which seems not only far-fetched but completely out of Washington's character. The girl added, "I must here observe, that when General Washington refused to deliver me up, the noble-minded Putnam, as if it were by instinct, laid his hand on his sword, and with a violent oath swore, 'that my father's request *should* be granted'," which also seems hard to believe.[13]

Asserting that she was then sent for safekeeping to Kingsbridge at the northern end of Manhattan Island, where some Pennsylvania battalions commanded by Gen. Thomas Mifflin were engaged in building fortifications, she wrote, "Here my heart received its first impression,—an impression, that amidst the subsequent shocks which it has received, has never been effaced."[14] The young girl met twenty-year-old Maj. Aaron Burr, a volunteer aide who had recently left Washington's staff and joined General Putnam's staff in exchange for Colonel Webb.[15]

Burr, a grandson of Rev. Jonathan Edwards, was born in Newark, New Jersey, and grew up in Elizabethtown. Brilliant, charming, and one of the most enigmatic figures of the day, Burr, at age thirteen, entered the College of New Jersey (now Princeton University, where his father had been the second president) and graduated at age sixteen with a B. A., followed up by law studies. He left college to join the Continental forces in 1775 and served as a volunteer aide with Gen. Richard Montgomery in the arduous invasion of Canada, where he narrowly escaped being killed with his commander at the gates of Quebec. Returning to New York, the hot-blooded young man joined Washington's staff, but lasted only a few weeks; some scholars have suggested that certain character flaws caused Washington to dislike and distrust Burr.[16]

Margaret Moncrieffe was instantly infatuated by the dashing young aide. "*My conquerer* was engaged in another cause, he was ambitious to obtain other laurels: he fought to liberate, not to enslave nations," she wrote ecstatically years later, the glow of admiration still evident. "He was a Colonel in the American army, and high in the estimation of his country: *his* victories were never accompanied with one gloomy, relenting thought; they shone as bright as the cause which achieved them!"[17]

What (if anything) happened between them can only be inferred from Margaret's writings long after the fact and after she was forced by her father's arrangement to marry an abusive British officer. "Oh! May these pages one day meet the eye of him who subdued my virgin heart, whom the immutable, unerring laws of nature had pointed out for my husband, but whose sacred decree the barbarous customs of society fatally violated," she cried. As for Major Burr, "To him I plighted my virgin vow, and I shall never cease to lament, that obedience to a *father* left it incomplete."[18] According to Margaret, she wanted to marry Burr immediately, so she wrote a letter asking General Putnam's advice.

"I was embarrassed by the answer which the General returned," she wrote. He reminded her that due to the political situation, Burr would be "obnoxious" to her father, and that she "surely would not unite [herself] with a man who, in his zeal for the cause of his country, would not hesitate to drench his sword in the blood of my nearest relation, should he be opposed to him in battle." Putnam regretted this feature of the situation, Margaret said, "since, in every other respect, he considered the match as unexceptionable."[19]

Suspicious of her behavior, Old Put kept his eye on Margaret afterwards and was somewhat less friendly to her. Though she claimed that he never "cease[d] to make me the object of his concern to congress," no reference to Margaret Moncrieffe has been found in the known papers and correspondence to Congress or its members. "After various applications," she asserted that "he succeeded in obtaining leave for my departure, when, in order that I should go to Staten-Island with the respect due to my sex and family, the barge belonging to the continental congress was ordered with twelve oars, and a general officer [Henry Knox], together with his suite, was dispatched to see me safe across the bay of New-York."[20]

Stephen Kemble of New Jersey, General Howe's deputy adjutant general, confirmed that on "Wednesday, August 7: Miss Moncrieffe was permitted to come to her Father's from New York."[21] Margaret recalled, "The day was so very tempestuous, that I was half drowned with the waves dashing against me." The group headed towards Admiral Howe's flagship, anchored in the bay near the Watering Place on Staten Island.

"When we came within hail of the Eagle man of war, which was Lord Howe's ship, a flag of truce was sent to meet us," Margaret wrote. "The officer dispatched on this occasion was Lieutenant Brown," Philip Brown, the same officer who carried Lord Howe's first letter to Washington on July 13 and had been turned back by Knox and Reed. "General Knox told him that he had received orders to see me safe to headquarters," Miss Moncrieffe said.

Brown replied that "it was impossible, as no person from the enemy could approach nearer the English fleet." He further told Margaret "that if I would place myself under his protection, he would certainly attend me thither." The young girl climbed out of the barge, "and bidding an eternal farewell to my dear American friends, turned MY BACK ON LIBERTY!" she wrote.[22]

"We first rowed alongside the Eagle, and Mr. Brown afterwards conveyed me to headquarters," Margaret went on. Once at headquarters, Lt. Col. William Sheriff, the deputy quartermaster general and a good friend of Margaret's father, presented her with an invitation to dine with General Howe, which she accepted.[23]

She desperately wanted to see her father. The events of the day and the dinner were overwhelming, and Margaret felt like she wanted to disappear. "Judge the distress of a girl not fourteen, obliged to encounter the curious, inquisitive eyes of at least forty or fifty people, who were at dinner with the General," she wrote. The thirteen-year-old quickly grew weary of the stiff, formal manners of the officers, the "fastidious" compliments such as, "She is a sweet girl, she is divinely handsome," and so on. Margaret was relieved somewhat to be seated next to Mrs. Frances Tucker Montrésor, who was born in New York and "had known me from my infancy," now the wife of Capt. John Montrésor, chief engineer of the British army. "Owing to this circumstance, I recovered a degree of confidence" the young girl admitted, "but being unfortunately asked, agreeably to military etiquette, for a *toast*, I gave General Putnam."

She had done it again. A shocked silence momentarily ensued, a pause during which Colonel Sheriff said to her in a low voice, "You must not give him here."

General Howe broke the tension and replied with a smile, "O! by all means; if he be the lady's *sweetheart*, I can have no objection to drink his health." The table rumbled with chuckles and smirks all around.

Having fulfilled the promise she had made to Washington, Margaret was now even more embarrassed. "I wished myself a thousand miles distant," she wrote, so in an attempt to divert their attention from her, she handed Howe a brief, personal note written by Putnam to her father. In her memoirs, she apologized for Putnam's wretched spelling, saying that "the bad orthography was amply compensated by the magnanimity of the man who wrote it." It read: "*Ginrole* Putnam's compliments to Major Moncrieffe, has made him a present of a fine daughter, if he don't lick her he must send her back again, and he will provide her with a fine good *twig* husband." Margaret commented that "The substitution of 'twig' for 'whig' husband, served as a fund of entertainment to the company."[24]

A fund of entertainment for the British officers indeed! In striking contrast to Washington's polished, formal reception of Paterson, Putnam's abysmal writing, his rough and rustic sense of humor, not to mention his facetious suggestion of a marriage which he had earlier condemned, furnished the company with no small amount of mockery of their bumpkin opponents. Confirming much of the tale, Lord Howe's secretary Ambrose Serle was so struck by Putnam's letter that he copied it into his journal: "Putnam . . . now I mention him, it may be a curiosity, if I preserve a Copy of the Note, which this great Commander sent to Major Moncrieffe, when he sent the Major his Daughter lately by a Flag of Truce. It is *verbatim* & *literatim*, in the Form & with the Interlineation as follows:

New York 7 of Agust 1776

Ginrol Putnams Compliments to Majir Moncref hoping this wil find you wel have maid a present to you this day of a fine Daughtour if you don't lik hur you send hur back & I will take cear of hur and Provid hur a fine Whig husband pray let me know how it is with mir berrow as his Lady is much Destrest to know

I am Sir yours to sarve, Israel Putnam.[25]

It was embarrassing for some on the other side. "I think a General Officer ought to be a Man of Letters, Taste and Sense," John Adams had commented privately to another officer a few days earlier in a letter naming some new candidates for generals' commissions. "But then you know that old officers would tare up the ground, if such Youths, and inexperienced People, as they would express themselves were put over their Heads," he added wistfully, most likely with Old Put foremost in his mind.[26]

Once the merriment had subsided, General Howe told Margaret that her father was with Lord Percy and that a carriage would be provided to take her to him. Further, "Amongst so many gentlemen a *beautiful young lady* certainly could not want a *cecisbeo* to conduct her," Howe added with a gallant flourish, *cecisbeo* being fashionable Italian for a handsome male escort with a noble lady. She asked a brigade major, John Small, whom she knew from childhood, to be her escort.

When they arrived at Lord Percy's, "My father was walking on the lawn with his Lordship," Margaret recalled. Not wanting to shock Moncrieffe, Major Small discreetly pulled Percy aside and hinted to him that Margaret was at headquarters. "Heaven be praised!" Percy exclaimed. "Major, let us instantly go and conduct her hither." Rather than make the nine-mile trek back, the officers decided to gently introduce Margaret to her father, "when, overcome by the emotions of filial tenderness, I fainted in my father's arms, where I remained in a state of insensibility during half an hour." Percy was kind enough to furnish father and daughter with private space in his headquarters rather than have her sleep in a marquee tent with the rest of the staff.[27]

In the midst of war, a small spark of humanity was rekindled.

CHAPTER 9

All the King's Horses and All the King's Men

ᢒᡱᢩᢇᡖᢅ

T he first two weeks of August 1776 were the busiest in New York Harbor's history up to that point. August 1 saw the arrival of a British naval squadron with Gen. Henry Clinton's forces, which had been repulsed from Charleston, South Carolina. "This morning between 40 and 50 Sail appeared in sight, which proved to be Sir Peter Parker's Fleet, with Generals Clinton & Lord Cornwallis, and the Troops under their command, on board," Ambrose Serle wrote. Though disappointed with the result, "the Reinforcement of 2900 Men is an agreeable Circumstance," he commented, "and especially as they are in very good health." This increased the size of Howe's army on Staten Island by thirty percent, which boded well for the royal forces; he now had about 12,000 British troops at his disposal. As a boost for morale, "The Ships, in coming in, made a very fine Appearance."[1]

Three days later, two more warships, including the fifty-gun *Reknown*, escorted twenty-two more vessels into the harbor. "We have had so many Arrivals of late," Serle commented, "that the Rebel commanders, we learn, give out to their People, that we send Ships down in the Night, which come up in the Course of the next Day, as a Manoeuvre to intimidate them."[2] A fine explanation to try and calm jittery nerves in New York and New Jersey! "Some Hessions and a pretty many of the Scotish Laddies have got in," Washington informed Gen. Charles Lee, "and the residue of the Fleet (parted with off the Banks of Newfoundland) hourly expected—When the whole arrive, matters will soon come to a decision."[3]

A week and a half later, on August 12, exactly one month to the day when Admiral Lord Howe's flagship *Eagle* made its grand entry into New York Harbor, Commodore Hotham's fleet from England finally arrived after three months at sea and began sailing through the Narrows. "This morning, as soon as it was light, we were gladdened with the sight of the grand Flight in the offing," an ecstatic Ambrose Serle wrote in his journal as dozens of ships came over the horizon with the sun. "The Joy of the Navy & the Army was almost like that of a Victory."[4]

From the shores of Long Island that morning, Gen. Nathanael Greene reported to Washington that "Twenty five Sail of ships are seen at a great distance at Sea coming in."[5] By the evening, there were more than a hundred cruising into the harbor. "So large a Fleet made a fine Appearance upon entering the Harbor, with the Sails crouded, Colors flying, Guns saluting, and the Soldiers both in the Ships and on the Shore continually shouting," Serle wrote. He couldn't help but glance up the harbor at New York City, watching "the Rebels (as we perceived by the Glasses) flocked out of their lurking Holes to see a Picture, by no means agreeable to them."[6]

The same day that "the grand Flight" sailed in, Gen. William Livingston wrote to Washington from New Jersey, "The 2000 Men for the flying Camp under General Dickinson"—troops that were posted at Elizabethtown—"are in great forwardness and (altho' very little acquainted with their duty) might answer a valuable Purpose in New York on the present Emergency." Despite this flicker of optimism, most of the Flying Camp was proving to be a disappointment. "A Considerable Body of Militia must be kept here to supply the Place of the Pennsylvania Associators who are deserting their Post in Considerable Numbers notwithstanding the most spirited exertions of their Officers, and particularly their Colonel whose Behaviour does honor to his Province in particular and America in general," Livingston continued ruefully.[7] The colonel was William Atlee of Lancaster, commander of the Pennsylvania State Battalion of Musketry. Gen. Hugh Mercer concurred, telling the commander in chief, "Give me leave to Introduce to your Excellencys notice—Colo. Attlee of the Pennsylva. Troops—His experience and Attention to every part of the service entrusted to his direction—will I am perswaded secure him to your Regard."[8] Shortly after, Atlee's and Miles's Pennsylvania state battalions were sent to Long Island.

The situation had grown critical, with desertions increasing and hints of mutiny. "We have taken such measures as I hope will put a stop to any further behavior of this kind," Livingston informed Washington. "This Corps since our Militia were dismissed have not carried on any of the works"—earthworks, meaning fortifications and entrenchments—"at the Point, which as soon as they are relieved by any Men under my Command, I shall order to be prosecuted with all possible Vigour."[9]

Meanwhile, on the far eastern side of Staten Island, the debarkation of the royal reinforcements began, swelling Howe's army to more than 30,000 men. In addition to more British regiments, including one thousand men in the Brigade of Guards, the bulk of the Hessians—seven thousand troops— were with this fleet, and another five thousand were on the way. As Washington noted, a shipload or two of Hessians had arrived about two weeks earlier, getting separated from the fleet in fog off Newfoundland, and others would continue arriving over the next few days.[10]

The complexion of the redcoat forces began changing as thousands of blue-coated German soldiers landed, glad to be ashore after more than three months at sea. "August 14th: At 9 AM we suddenly saw the praised America again and arrived the same day at Sandy Hook," Lt. Wilhelm Freyenhagen of the Hessian Musketeer Regiment von Donop exclaimed, praising the continent they had seen weeks before at Nova Scotia but were not allowed to touch. Coming from the central western part of Germany along the Rhine and Main Rivers, few (if any) of these soldiers had ever seen the sea before. After marching overland from Hesse-Cassel, this regiment boarded transport ships at Geestendorf near Bremerlehe on the Weser River on April 9 and did not set foot on land again until August 15, one hundred and twenty-nine days and nearly four thousand miles later.

"We arrived at 1 PM off Staten Island on the 15th where we were disembarked," the lieutenant continued. "The joy of getting off the ships was indescribable, but this island is not beautiful, it is full of hills but it was still very pleasant." A few days later, after getting their land legs back, these Hessians marched across Staten Island, and some of them were posted at Billopp's Point. "Maj. Gen. Stirn's brigade, consisting of the Leib, Prinz Carl and Dittfurth Regiments, broke camp and set up a new camp near Amboy, a small town across the Arthur Kill in New Jersey."[11]

The Leib Regiment, or Regiment du Corps, was an elite unit chosen from the Landgraf of Hesse-Cassel's Household Guards.[12] They had boarded the ships in Bremerlehe two weeks before the Regiment von Donop. "The 24th March was embarked at Bremerlehe on the following British transports: 1. *Lord Sandwich*; 2. *Fame*; 3. *Unanimity*; 4. *Mallaga*," the staff secretary, Regimental Quartermaster Lotheisen, of the Leib Regiment dutifully recorded.[13] They set sail on April 17 and arrived off Spithead near Portsmouth nine days later. Here, by remarkable coincidence, "the Regiment received another transport, named *Lord Howe*, to which Captain von Motz with Major von Wurmb's Company and a proportionate number of men taken from each of the other four ships were transferred." Along with the rest of Commodore Hotham's fleet, they set sail on May 6.

"The 11th August we first sighted the coast of New Jersey, and anchored on the 12th off Sandy Hook not far from the Light House," Lotheisen noted. "On the 14th and 15th August the Regiment was disembarked on Staten Island and encamped one English mile from the Flagstaff, where there is a fort which protects New York harbor." This fort, an earthen redoubt, had been constructed by British troops in early July.

"After the troops had recovered from the effects of the long sea voyage, preparations were secretly made to attack the rebels on Long Island with full force," the Hessian quartermaster wrote. But a sizeable portion of the army had to remain behind to hold Staten Island. "As Colonel von Lossberg's Brigade was appointed, along with another English Regiment, to occupy Staten Island, it left its camp on the 19th of August and was distributed round the island in nine separate detachments, which however maintained communications with each other, the island having a circumference of nearly sixteen English miles."[14]

One of the most important posts on the island was the one farthest west and most exposed to the Flying Camp, the position at Billopp's Point, opposite Perth Amboy. To man this, "The Leib Regiment then marched to Amboy Ferry where two companies and the staff under command of Colonel von Wurmb encamped, two companies under command of Major von Wurmb being $1^1/2$ miles away to the right, and the 5th company a mile further still on the right," Lotheisen recorded. These companies were further up the Arthur Kill towards the Fresh Kills. He noted, "By special order the camp of these three detachments was not pitched according to regulations, but in two lines close to the shore, in order to present a great front to the enemy lying exactly opposite in the province of New Jersey." This would make the Flying Camp think twice about any sort of attack, especially once the bulk of Howe's forces crossed the Narrows to Staten Island. To further discourage a rebel attack, "About one mile from the left wing of the Regiment, an English sloop-of-war lay at anchor in the river, and two miles further to the left, another armed ship." He observed that "this river which separates us from the enemy is about $^3/4$ of a mile wide," which put the troops almost out of rifle range.[15]

But still there were some close calls. "The enemy, who were posted on the opposite shore at Amboy, the capital of the province of New Jersey, harassed us frequently by shooting over the water into our camp with their long rifles, which compelled us to move our front back twenty paces," Lotheisen reported. At first, the Hessians were reluctant to fire back, but "as they, however, continued to fire upon our detachment posted in a small house close by the waters' edge, Artillery-Lieutenant Goercke *was ordered to discharge* some grape-shot upon the town of Amboy with the effect that the enemy no longer troubled us with their rifle-firing."[16] The desultory harassment sniping stopped for the time being.

The main scene soon shifted over to Long Island, and Billopp's Point became a backwater of the war. "Nothing of any importance happened except that once a small vessel belonging to the enemy, containing no men, however, accidentally got adrift, and floated towards the shore on this side, when the sloop-of-war lying at anchor on the left wing of the regiment put out a boat with armed sailors, in order to seize the said vessel," the Hessian quartermaster dutifully noted. He watched as "the rebels brought up some guns onto the height near the shore on that side and fired both upon the boat and our camp, without any effect however." Compared with the situation on Long Island, this was negligible; still, "we fired some twenty shots from our regimental guns, one ball falling into the town of Amboy and according to report, a rebel is said to have had his leg shot off; then the firing ceased on both sides and the hostile vessel was secured by the sloop of war without further resistance."

In another instance, "the rebels manned a large transport exactly opposite Major von Wurmb's detachment, presumably to make a descent upon Staten Island," Quartermaster Lotheisen wrote. "As soon as Colonel von Wurmb received information of this he ordered Artillery Lieutenant Goercke to proceed to the said camp with a regimental gun and bombard the ship." A couple of shots from this small gun were fired to find the range; "the third shot crashed through the cabin and was so well directed that the enemy were compelled to drive the ship ashore and give up their plan," Lotheisen noted with satisfaction.[17]

Between these episodes, some propaganda and psychological warfare was conducted by the American forces on these newly arrived German troops, hoping to entice them to desert. "It may be still further remarked, re.: Staten Island, that the rebels used to sometimes bring over printed papers secretly by boat at night not far from our Camp, in which with many promises they incited and encouraged our men to desert," Lotheisen stated.

The papers, printed in German, were suggested to Congress by Benjamin Franklin and discussed by him in a letter written in late August to Thomas McKean. "I send you herewith some of the Resolutions of the Congress translated into their Language, as possibly you may find some Opportunity of conveying them over the Water, to those people," Franklin told McKean, who was stationed at Elizabethtown. A little bait in the form of one type of "soldier's friend" would help, the wily doctor suggested. "Some of the papers have Tobacco Marks on the Back, it being suppos'd by the Committee, that if a little Tobacco were put up in each as the Tobacconists used to do, and a Quantity made to fall into the Hands of that Soldiery, by being put into a Drift Canoe among some other little Things, it would be divided among them as Plunder before the Officers could know the Contents of the Paper & prevent it."[18] To further encourage desertion, Christopher Ludwick, a large, gregarious Hessian gingerbread baker from Philadelphia, went over to Staten Island, risking his life to spread the word among the soldiers, hoping to entice them with promises of free land.

Few, if any, of the Hessians deserted at that time; the same could not be said for the men across the river in the Flying Camp. Already tired of army life, too many who had enthusiastically volunteered to fight for liberty a few weeks earlier were heading home on their own, and the roads to Pennsylvania began to throng with stragglers. The situation grew so bad that the officers were forced to publish deserter descriptions in the Philadelphia papers, such as this ad in *The Pennsylvania Packet*:

> Perth Amboy, August 29, 1776. THIRTY-SIX POUNDS REWARD. DESERTED from Capt. John Edwards' company, in the 5th Battalion of Philadelphia County Militia commanded by Col. John Bull, now lying at Perth-Amboy, in New Jersey, the following persons, viz. THOMAS VANDERSLICE, CADWALADER JONES, JOSEPH SHAMBOUGH, ANDREW BELL, ABRAM SKEEN, WILLIAM GROVES, and JOHN SHRACK, all well made strait young men, about (or pretty near) six feet high. Also John Bryan, a thick well set fellow; JOHN BATHURST, of a swarthy complexion; JACOB TANEY, a well set fellow; DANIEL TANEY, a fresh coloured young fellow; and GEORGE HIGH, **all formerly Associators, and living in New providence township, where it is suspected they are now gone.** The two first mentioned deserted in Philadelphia three weeks ago, and the rest went all together last night. Whoever takes up and secures said deserters, so that they be brought back again, shall receive the above reward, or EIGHT DOLLARS for each, paid by JOHN EDWARDS, Captain.[19]

New Providence Township was the site of Augustus Lutheran Church and Rev. Henry Melchior Muhlenberg's home. Just three weeks earlier, Muhlenberg had been asked to "say a word of admonition in English and German in Augustus Church as a farewell to them." The troops had sung "*Auf Christen-Mensch, auf, auf, zum Streit,*" ("Up Christian Men, Up, Up to the Strife") and then Muhlenberg "preached in English on Ephesians 6:10 ff., about arming with divine weapons, and then in German on Deuteronomy 20: 1-4," verses containing the admonition, "When thou goest out to battle against thine enemies, and seest horses, and chariots, and a people more than thou, be not afraid of them."[20]

Evidently, these former Associators did not understand German.

CHAPTER 10

The Debacle

⟜⟜

The American Revolution had begun more than a year before with the battles of Lexington and Concord on April 19, 1775. But up until July 2, 1776, it was a war to defend the rights of Americans as Englishmen. Now it was a war for independence, and it began with a debacle.

The Battle of Long Island was the first major engagement between the Continental army and His Majesty's forces. It was a tactical masterpiece on the part of Lt. Gen. William Howe, utilizing feints and flank marches that outmaneuvered and baffled Washington's troops and all but annihilated them. It also clearly demonstrated the catastrophic effects of poor planning, lack of reconnaissance, and lack of coordination on the side of the Americans, who were strongly positioned but utterly outgeneraled by the British.

The amazing part is that the outcome wasn't worse for the Continentals. In this situation, Washington had a weaker force to begin with, both in numbers and quality of troops, and he had divided it, putting a wide river between their positions. The British and Hessians had a numerical advantage of nearly four to one and outclassed their opponents in just about every category. The situation had all the makings of a complete disaster for the Americans, and many wondered how Washington was able to extricate his troops from total destruction.

There was really only one answer to that question: Lt. Gen. William Howe.

Howe was a light infantry expert. At the start of the French and Indian War, he and his older brother Augustus had served together in Braddock's army at the Battle of the Monongahela in 1755 and were among the few surviving British officers of that disaster. Witnessing the devastating effects of ambush and sniping on regular troops attempting linear formations in a forest setting, the Howes promoted the development of *light infantry*, troops who could take cover and move quickly from point to point, adapting to conditions while maintaining the discipline of regular soldiers. Firepower and accuracy were limited with muskets, so massing infantry in open terrain and firing volleys made more sense there. In more wooded countryside, a swift attack at close quarters with the bayonet was a much more effective tactic against undisciplined opponents, especially riflemen who were not equipped with bayonets.

More recently, at Breed's Hill, under the direction of Gen. Thomas Gage (another Braddock survivor), Howe led a light infantry column into withering, point-blank musket fire from New England militia and watched his men fall in heaps. He was determined not to waste lives again launching frontal assaults against entrenched Americans. Instead, flanking maneuvers and swift bayonet attacks supported by musketry and artillery became his hallmark in this war. The Battle of Long Island was his first demonstration of this successful style of highly mobile, aggressive maneuvering.

Thursday, August 22, dawned clear and hot. At the Narrows, a great spectacle unfolded as the king's forces commenced their operations against the American rebels. "The whole Army got ready for landing on Long Island," wrote Sgt. Thomas Sullivan, an Irish soldier in the 49th Regiment of Foot. "Our Brigade i.e. the 2nd, was under cover of the *Eagle*, and *Centurion* of 50 Guns." On the shore of Staten Island, "The whole Army were ready together in Flat-boats; the sight of which was very beautiful and delightful to any *English* Soldier or *Subject*, to see near twenty four Thousand men ready to land in a moment." With General Howe overseeing the troops, "His Lordship Admiral Howe attended the embarkation and Landing of the Army with great attention; & when all things were ready, he hoisted the Union [Jack] and landing Flags on board his Boat," Sergeant Sullivan wrote. "And the whole Army landed then in a body, without opposition; on the South-east end of Long-Island, at a place called Gravesend, near the Narras," or Narrows.

On the beach at Long Island, "when the Rebels saw that our Army was landing, the advance guards they had at the water side fled with great precipitation, and joined their main Body, and ran to their works," the entrenchments near Brooklyn. These troops were some of Col. Edward Hand's Pennsylvania riflemen who, after sniping at the king's men, "were Pursued by the Grenadiers, Chasseurs [Hessian jägers] and Highlanders . . .

The Grand Army British and Hessian landed at Utrick," the little Dutch village of New Utrecht.[1]

Over the next few days, British and Hessian light troops skirmished with Hand's riflemen, reputed to be expert marksmen with deadly aim. Each side claimed victory, boasting of how they drove their opponents off in confusion. The news created euphoria in the American camp. "Washington discovers a confidence, which he usually does only on very good grounds," Thomas Jefferson remarked after hearing the reports sent to Congress. "He says his men are in high spirits. Those ordered to Long Island went with the eagerness of young men going to a dance."[2]

General Howe was about to call the tune. By August 26, Howe's force of twenty-four thousand was confronted by two divisions of Americans, about thirty-five hundred men, posted on the Heights of Guian, a long, wooded ridge bisected by several passes. The passes were held by small contingents of American light troops and riflemen. Behind this natural fortress, Washington had entrenched his main force of six thousand on the heights around the little village of Brooklyn, with their backs to the East River. The rest of the Continental Army, estimated at ten thousand, remained across the river on Manhattan Island in and above New York City, effectively cutting them off from direct involvement in the battle.

The only American commander who had had any substantial knowledge of the terrain on Long Island was Maj. Gen. Nathanael Greene, but he was ill and out of action. Greene had been replaced a week earlier by John Sullivan, who in turn was superseded by Israel Putnam, but neither Sullivan nor Putnam knew much about Long Island. Sullivan, now commanding one division on the left, and Gen. William Alexander, "Lord Stirling," leading the other on the right, expected the king's forces to make a frontal assault, as they had done at Breed's Hill.

The American command structure was poorly coordinated. "I lay here within cannon shot of the Hessian camp for four days without receiving a single order from Genl. Sullivan, who commanded on Long Island, out of the lines," an angry Col. Samuel Miles, commanding the Pennsylvania State Rifle Regiment posted on the far left flank, wrote afterwards. "The day before the action he came to the camp, and I then told him the situation of the British Army; that Gen'l Howe, with the main body, lay on my left, about a mile and a half or two miles, and I was convinced when the army moved that Gen'l Howe would fall into the Jamaica road, and I hoped there were troops there to watch them." Miles's hope was in vain; there were no substantial forces guarding the Jamaica Pass, only a patrol of five men.

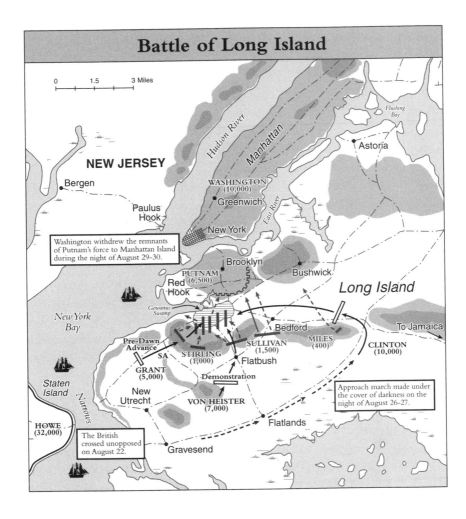

Battle of Long Island

0   1.5   3 Miles

Hudson River

NEW JERSEY

Manhattan

Flushing Bay

Astoria

Bergen

WASHINGTON
(10,000)

Greenwich

East River

Paulus Hook

New York

Washington withdrew the remnants of Putnam's force to Manhattan Island during the night of August 29-30.

Brooklyn

Bushwick

PUTNAM
(6,500)

Red Hook

Long Island

New York Bay

Gowanus Swamp

Bedford

To Jamaica

Pre-Dawn Advance

SA

SULLIVAN
(1,500)

MILES
(400)

CLINTON
(10,000)

STIRLING
(1,000)

Flatbush

GRANT
(5,000)

Demonstration

Narrows

Staten Island

New Utrecht

VON HEISTER
(7,000)

Approach march made under the cover of darkness on the night of August 26-27.

Flatlands

HOWE
(32,000)

The British crossed unopposed on August 22.

Gravesend

During the night, Howe's army began moving. Before dawn on August 27, five thousand troops under Gen. James Grant launched a diversionary attack against the American right along Gowanus Road, drawing the attention of Stirling's Continentals posted there. Shortly after sunup, Lt. Gen. Philip von Heister, commander of the Hessian forces, sent Col. Count Karl Emil von Donop's grenadier battalions towards the American center to attack Flatbush Pass, held by Sullivan's troops. Fanned out in front of the Hessian grenadiers were green-uniformed jägers, German marksmen armed with short rifles.

Meanwhile, the main body of Howe's forces, with the advance guard of light infantry commanded by Maj. Gen. Henry Clinton, made a wide, circuitous march during the night through the unguarded Jamaica Pass above

Sullivan's left flank, the very place Miles had warned the general that the attack might come. Clinton's force quickly moved into the area between the Americans' outer positions and the entrenchments on Brooklyn Heights, cutting off the entire left wing of Washington's advanced forces from the main body. By mid-morning, Sullivan's division was successfully enveloped.

Clinton's march was undetected by the American commanders until his troops were well behind their center. Despite his warning, Colonel Miles, holding the far left flank of the line, now found himself surrounded. Sullivan, "notwithstanding this information, which indeed he might have obtained from his own observation, if he had attended to his duty as a general ought to have done; no steps were taken," the Pennsylvanian seethed, adding that "there was a small redoubt in front of the village [of Flatbush] which seemed to take up the whole of his attention, and where he stayed until the principal part of the British army had gotten between him and the lines, by which means he was made prisoner, as well as myself." Furious, especially after hearing that he was being blamed for the debacle, Miles shot back, "If Gen'l Sullivan had taken the requisite precaution, and given his orders agreeably to the attention of the Commander-in-Chief, there would have been few if any prisoners taken."[3]

As Sullivan's troops—an agglomeration of Continentals, Pennsylvania state regulars, and selected Associator riflemen from the Flying Camp—realized that they were being cut off from behind, they fell back and tried to fight their way through Clinton's light infantrymen coming up behind them. "I led my Company into the very thick of them and had a most miraculous Escape," Capt. William Dansey, commander of the British 33rd Light Company, told his sweetheart. "In about three minuits I had three men kill'd & six Wounded out of thirty, Mr. Cotton my Lieut. got a graze upon the Shoulder, we were well supported by three Companies or there wou'd not have remain'd a man to tell the Story." The fighting was close and furious; "myself and five or Six of my men got into the Wood among them," Dansey wrote. "They jump'd up within Ten Yards and fir'd upon us, which did us no Harm; I order'd my Men to get behind the Trees and return it which they did and kill'd the Rebel Captain within twenty Yards of me."

Dansey's account gives an excellent description of light infantry tactics. "The Rebels gave us a second fire that came all round us, which knocked down my right and left hand men, the one dead," he recounted. Under the circumstances, the only sane course for the 33rd Light Company was to fall back and take cover—hardly the popular history image of red-clad automatons mindlessly advancing by ranks into gunfire. "Upon seeing us surrounded, I called to my Men to run to the first Wall they cou'd find," Dansey related, "and we all set off, some into some short Bushes, others strait across a Field about the Size of the Moat Meadow [a place on his family's estate] to a Wall we had come over." This was one important lesson learned from Braddock's defeat: taking cover as the situation required was not cowardice.

His company came close to being annihilated, for "in running across the field we [were] expos'd to the Fire of 300 Men we had literally run out at the midst of and they calling to me to surrender, I stop'd twice to look behind me and saw the Riflemen so thick and not one of my own men." Even officers, who were often targeted in these early days of the war by American riflemen, prudently if ingloriously headed for cover. Amid the gunfire, Dansey performed a strategic withdrawal. "I made for the Wall as hard as I cou'd drive and they peppering at me seeing very plain I was the officer, I was very much afraid they wou'd hit my Legs and then I cou'd not have run away from them; however at last I gain'd the Wall and threw myself headlong up."

So what was it like, being "peppered" by riflemen? "The only Idea I can give a person how the Balls flew about me whilst running over that small Field is: suppose Yourself under a large Apple Tree full of ripe Fruit and a person in the Tree Shaking it as hard as they can, how thick the Apples will drop about you and perhaps not one hit you." Once safely out of the gunfire, "when over the Wall I stop'd to collect my Company," Dansey reported. Realizing that nearly a third of his men were down, "that Scene was too affecting to be described with the Chearfulness of the foregoing Lines," he admitted. But, pulling himself and the survivors together, "suffice it to say there came up to my Assistance three more companies of Light Infantry supported by the Grenadiers." He lived to fight again, for "the Engagement was renew'd in that part: we gain'd the day, the Cheif Loss there falling on my brave but unfortunate Company," the captain concluded, adding, "I have not half described that Day's Work."[4]

The bayonets won the day. Across the field, with half of the Pennsylvania Rifle Regiment, "we fell in with a body of 7 or 800 light infantry, which we attacked without any hesitation," Colonel Miles recalled, "but their superiority of numbers encouraged them to march up with their bayonets, which we could not withstand, having none ourselves." Though accurate within a range of two to three hundred yards, the Pennsylvania long rifles were made for hunting or long-range sniping, not close warfare, and were not designed to hold bayonets. Forming an entire unit out of undisciplined riflemen was foolish; putting them in a battle line against highly mobile light troops well trained in the use of bayonets was disastrous.

Miles ordered his men to fall back towards the Brooklyn entrenchments. They ran into another large body of British troops, and "here we lost a number of men, but took Major Moncrieffe, their commanding officer, prisoner."[5] This was none other than Maj. Thomas Moncrieffe of Lord Percy's staff, the father of Margaret, the young girl who had toasted the generals three weeks before. "My father was taken prisoner at the battle of *Brooklyn,* and stripped of his regimentals," she recalled, meaning that his regimental coat was taken, and he "was forced to put on the *Red Ribbon* (a mark which the Americans wore, in order to distinguish their own staff officers)."[6] Why he was made to do this is unclear, but wearing white small-clothes (waistcoat and breeches) and with a red cockade in his hat would make him look like an American officer.

"The officers of the new levies wore cockades of different colors," Pvt. Joseph Plumb Martin of Connecticut explained. "The field officers [majors and colonels] wore red, the captains white, and the subaltern officers [lieutenants and ensigns] green." Watching the fighting in the distance, Martin witnessed his own officers do something that suggests an explanation regarding Moncrieffe's situation. Lt. Col. James Arnold and Maj. Phineas Porter "took the cockades from their hats; being asked the reason, the lieutenant colonel replied that he was willing to risk his life in the cause of his country, but unwilling to stand a particular mark for the enemy to fire at."[7] Having Moncrieffe do so would "hide him in plain view" as a prisoner and also make him a possible target for "friendly fire."

Despite their success in capturing the major, the situation for these Americans was all but hopeless. Moncrieffe was "a Scotch prize," or temporary award, Miles wrote, "for Ensign Brodhead, who took him and had him in possession for some hours, was obliged to surrender himself."[8] As it became clear that escape was impossible, Moncrieffe tried to convince his captors to give themselves up to British forces. "While he was endeavouring to persuade the men to surrender themselves to the Royal Army, they were surrounded by a party of Hessians, who mistaking my father, conceived him, from the badge he had on, to be a Colonel of the enemy," Margaret wrote. Moncrieffe tried to tell the Hessians who he was, but they paid no attention to him. Instead, with utter contempt, "they made him assist to draw the heavy cannon," a degrading activity for any officer, especially a British officer, "in which laborious exercise he was recognized by a Colonel in the British Army." The major was immediately released, and "the Hessian officer, confused on discovering his error, consequently made every due apology." Margaret recalled that for years afterward, "this event frequently caused us much entertainment."[9]

The Pennsylvania Rifle Regiment found nothing to entertain them. "Finding that the enemy had possession of the ground between us and our lines, and that it was impossible to cut our way through as a body, I directed the men to make the best of their way as well as they could," Colonel Miles stated. "Some few got away safe, but 159 were taken prisoners." The colonel himself and a small handful of men tried to conceal themselves in the woods, but were "discovered by a party of Hessians and obliged to surrender" later that afternoon. "Thus ended the career of that day," he bitterly recounted.[10]

Out in front of the heights, "the Hessian grenadiers moved forward through a woods in front of us," Lt. Wilhelm Freyenhagen of the Musketeer Regiment von Donop reported. "We followed them and positioned ourselves on a hill. The first took some enemy fire, but upon their arrival the rebels retreated." The grenadiers continued in their slow, steady pursuit, while the musketeers followed behind to mop up and collect the scattered pockets of Americans. "We searched the woods with several patrols and our regiment made prisoners of 13 officers and 87 privates, while we had one severely wounded," Freyenhagen noted.[11]

Von Heister's Hessians pushed through the pass in the center towards the confused and panicking American troops who were herding back on the British light infantry. Fanning out through the brush and sniping at their opponents, the green-coated Hessian jägers were more than a match for the American riflemen and light troops in Sullivan's center and promptly drove them in. Howe's pincers began to close as Count von Donop's grenadiers relentlessly pushed on with rows of gleaming bayonets.

The visual appearance of the Hessian grenadiers was absolutely terrifying, especially to raw troops who had never seen them before. Their dark blue uniforms, trimmed with wide lapels, cuffs, and collars in various colors, together with their disciplined drill and slow, deliberate motions, made them appear like a massive machine. The tall, polished miter caps of brass or tin glittered as they marched, and their hair, tightly curled and powdered white, made them all look alike. Strangest of all to see for the first time were the long, stiff mustaches worn by many of the grenadiers. At a time when men in the Anglo-American world were mostly clean-shaven, here were stiffly waxed, jet-black mustaches twirled into sharp points, giving the troops a ferocious, sinister look.

With the help of three cannons, Sullivan's men had almost broken through the British light infantry behind them when the main body of Howe's flanking column led by Lt. Gen. Hugh Lord Percy arrived. In front was the Brigade of Guards, followed by several British grenadier battalions. The grenadier and light infantry companies of the Guards, commanded by Lt. Col. Sir George Osborn, deployed and advanced eagerly, supported by two battalion companies. "I had however an Opportunity of sending the light Infantry of the Guards to attack a Party of the Rebels, but they ran away directly & only allow'd the Guards just Time to give them one Fire," Lord Percy told his father, the Duke of Northumberland. "Our loss on this Occasion is scarce to be mentioned," he wrote, emphasizing, "this was intirely owing to our Men attacking them the proper Way." Percy pointed out that "the moment the Rebels fired our Men rushed on them with their Bayonets & never gave them Time to load again."[12] Here was the main tactic that Howe had strongly encouraged his men to use: Get close quickly, fire one volley, then charge with bayonets into the woods without stopping to reload.

It worked brilliantly; not only were the riflemen driven away, the Guards captured the artillery. "The Light Infantry about that Time having been reinforced by the Light Company, the Grenadier Company, and two other Companies of the Guards, who joined them with the greatest Activity and Spirit, had taken three pieces of Cannon, and were warmly engaged with very superior Numbers in the woods," Howe reported to Lord Germain, "when on the Hessians advancing, the enemy gave Way and was entirely routed in that Quarter."[13]

The attack of the Guards drove Sullivan's men back into the trees from which they were trying to escape. Heavy fighting developed in the woods until the bayonets of von Donop's Hessian grenadiers blocked any further movement. Sullivan's force was effectively annihilated and Sullivan himself was captured, along with hundreds of his men.

"Our Men behaved themselves like British Troops fighting in a good Cause," Lord Percy reported, lauding their performance. "I cannot Omit mentioning the Guards at whose Head I had the Honor to be that Day. The Spirit & Alertness of both Officers & Men deserve the highest Encomiums. Their readiness & willingness to do whatever they were desired, has gained them the Esteem & Approbation of the whole Army." This special brigade of one thousand men, chosen from the three regiments of His Majesty's Foot Guards and commanded by Gen. Edward Mathew, had arrived from England only two weeks before and was eager for action. "In short they are not only the finest Body of Men that was ever seen, but it seems to be the

Study of every Officer & Man amongst them to be as distinguishable for Discipline, Spirit, & Conduct," he continued. "Nothing is a Hardship, nothing is a difficulty with Them," Percy enthusiastically told his father. "Whatever they are directed to do, they do with Chearfullness & Pleasure. I am happy to do them this Justice which they richly deserve & I am sure his Majesty must be pleased to hear that His Guards have proved themselves worthy of the Honor they enjoy of being near His Person when at Home, by their very proper & spirited Conduct when in the Field."[14]

Besides the strategy, the professional discipline and speed of Howe's British troops were the deciding factors. The Brigade of Guards served as a model for Howe's innovative light infantry tactics. The entire brigade, officers included, was dressed and equipped for field duty in light infantry-style campaign uniforms: cut-down regimental coats devoid of lace and decoration; hair cropped short, or "bobbed" (thus the light infantry nickname "light bobs"); and cocked hats converted into round hats or caps. Within the year, much of the British army in America appeared in the same campaign dress.

Howe did not dispense with European-style linear tactics or colorful uniforms; he adapted them to conditions in America and successfully worked them into an extraordinary fighting machine that would go on to win battle after battle. The ultimate failure of the British war effort seven years later lay in other areas.

Lord Stirling commanded the American right flank, which rested on a swamp at Gowanus Bay. This force included Smallwood's Maryland Battalion, commanded in the field by Maj. Mordecai Gist, and Haslet's Delaware Regiment, led by Maj. Thomas McDonough. The Marylanders were mostly young gentlemen volunteers from the Baltimore area, and the Delaware Regiment was composed mainly of young gentlemen from the area around Wilmington and New Castle. Also known as the "Delaware Blues," they were the only Continental regiment from tiny Delaware, troops so well drilled and well dressed in handsome blue uniforms faced with red that some British officers mistook them for Hessians. "Two companies suffered by an unfortunate mistake which might have created a good deal of confusion," Capt. Sir James Murray of the 57th Regiment told his sister Bessie. "They took a large body of rebels dressed in blue for the Hessians, and received a fire from them at a very small distance, before they discovered their mistake."[15] Reinforcing that impression was the fact that the Blues stood in disciplined ranks and maneuvered like veterans.

"The Delaware Battallion have been complimented as the finest in the Service," Col. John Haslet proudly informed Congressman Caesar Rodney of Delaware after the battle. "They stood unmoved in firm array four Hours exposed to the fire of the Enemy . . . then effected a most Noble Retreat up to the Middle thru a Marsh of Mud," the dreadful Gowanus Swamp near Brooklyn. Concerning the composition of the rest of the Continental forces, Haslet added, "I fear Genl. Washington has too heavy a task, Assisted mostly by Beardless Boys."[16]

Stirling's troops faced Gen. James Grant's Scottish Highlanders and Hessian musketeers in front, von Heister's Hessian grenadiers and jägers on the left, and Clinton's British light troops in the rear, and they, too, were annihilated. "Those two Battalions fought as Bravely as Men Could possibly do," Caesar Rodney wrote. "That the Marylanders lost 259 men missing, many of Whom were Killed. That it was owing cheifly to their being Seperated by which Means the Enemy got between them and oblidged them to fight in Small parties." As for the proud young gentlemen of Wilmington and New Castle, "The Delawares being well Trained kept and fought in a Compact Body the Whole Time, and when oblidged to retreat kept their Ranks and Entered the lines in that order, frequently while retreating obliged to fight their way through Bodies of the Enemy, Who had before made an attack on our lines, Where they were repulsed and were also retreating and Met each other. The Delawares in this retreat lost four or five Men, one or two killed and two or three drownd in Crossing a Creek . . . Greatest part of those were lost, either Killed or taken prisoners, but supposed Chiefly Killed. Upon the Whole the Delaware Battalion has now Missing thirty one."[17]

Despite the valor of units such as the Delaware Regiment and the Maryland Battalion, who sacrificed themselves to buy time for others to escape, the American forces out in front of Brooklyn Heights were utterly crushed: more than three hundred were killed, some of them drowning in Gowanus Swamp; hundreds more were wounded, and nearly one thousand were taken prisoner, including Lord Stirling, who handed his sword to General von Heister. Howe now had two Continental major generals as prisoners.

"Some of them made a very good stand that Day, perticularly their Rifle Men," Lt. Loftus Cliffe of His Majesty's 46th Regiment observed, "for Captn. Pain of 18th Regt. who is here on Staff Employ declares he buried 400 in one Pit himself, most of whom wore the Rifle dress, which is a frock & Trowsers of linnin, fringed with knotting which in warm weather is worn singly; in Cold, covers their Body Clothes & is very convenient for the Woods." Cliffe, an Anglo-Irish officer whose commander was Gen. Henry Clinton, noted a curious feature in the captured headquarters papers:

"In their returns we find almost every Name thats amongst us." With an unsettling sense of irony, he commented, "I was not a little surprised to find a Captain van Clift under the Command of General Clinton of theirs," bringing home to him the fact that this was truly a civil war.[18]

British losses in the battle were reported as 61 killed and 288 wounded, and the Hessians had only two killed and 26 wounded.[19] The Hessians established a reputation for ruthless terror in this battle. Having been told (among other things) that the Americans would kill them and eat them if captured, they combined their Prussian tactics, which included baring their teeth during a bayonet charge, with refusal at times to take prisoners (some of whom when caught were reportedly pinned to trees with bayonets and left behind).

The green-clad Hessian jägers, German foresters equipped with short-barreled, accurate rifles, were able to match the American frontiersmen with marksmanship and beat them with military discipline and ferocity. "They are a brave People," Lieutenant Cliffe commented about the Hessians, "and their Yaugers or Marksmen are the best opponents in the World to the Rifles to whom they shew no mercy."[20] In the same vein, "The Hessians, it is said, behaved with great Inhumanity," Congressman James Wilson of Pennsylvania reported to Judge Jasper Yeates, a patriot leader in Lancaster. "They even knocked on the Head the Men that were lying wounded on the Field of Battle."[21]

The Germans had been terrified by stories told by the British of American savagery. When some captured Hessians were later asked why they were so brutal at Long Island, they answered, "The English officers had told them that the Americans were savage cannibals, especially those who were shaggily clad, whom they must exterminate first of all if they were not to be tortured and eaten alive by them," Rev. Henry Muhlenberg related, "for the American chasseurs or sharpshooters, who shoot with rifles and are called *riflemen*, have a peculiar form of dress, much like that of the savage Indians, shaggy like the pictures of ancient fauns and satyrs."

The old pastor had described some of these very troops from Berks County in the area around Reading passing his house in Trappe a few weeks before. He noted then that their war cries and overall appearance were similar to those of Native Americans. "Hence the Hessians, etc. were, and are still being, incited to set upon men of their own race and blood," Muhlenberg wrote in disgust at the whole business, "for the crafty British would rather fill the graves with hired, foreign fascines than with their own native and lordly flesh."[22]

"The militia from Berks County [were] almost cut off," Lt. Jasper Ewing also told Jasper Yeates, his uncle. "The inhuman wretches thrust their bayonets through our wounded men and refused that mercy to us, which we granted to them." Ewing admitted that "The Idea which we at first conceived of the Hessian Riflemen was truly ridiculous but sad experience convinces our people that they are an Enemy not to [be] despised."[23]

"We took care to tell the Hessians that the Rebels had resolved to give no quarters to them in particular, which made them fight desperately and put to death all that fell in their hands," a Scottish officer of the 71st Highlanders confirmed. "You know all stratagems are lawful in war, especially against such vile enemies to their King and country," he wrote from Long Island. "The island is all ours, and we shall soon take New-York, for the Rebels dare not look us in the face."

The Scottish Highlanders, too, hacked their way through this battle on the American right flank and lived up to their reputation as savage fighters. They were especially out for blood because a few months earlier, several companies of Highlanders had sailed into Boston by mistake and were taken prisoner. One of their officers, Maj. Robert Menzies, was killed in a brief struggle, and Col. Archibald Campbell of the 71st Regiment was taken captive. "The Hessians and our brave Highlanders gave no quarters," the same officer bragged, "and it was a fine sight to see with what alacrity they despatched the Rebels with their bayonets after we had surrounded them so that they could not resist." With no qualms and a great deal of satisfaction, he wrote, "Multitudes were drowned and suffocated in morasses— a proper punishment for all Rebels."[24]

After this experience, over the next few months, the skirl of bagpipes or the appearance of Hessian grenadiers was often enough to send many American troops stampeding to the rear. "If they are all as bad as they were on that day, this will be more of a hunt than a war," Col. Johann von Loos reported to Col. Karl von Jungkenn back in Hesse-Cassel. "It will still be too bad for many an honest fellow who can be killed by these knaves," he sneered. "Several days after the battle which frightened them so, they still shiver at the word 'Hessians'."[25]

The few American survivors streamed back to the entrenchments on Brooklyn Heights. "Upon the whole, less Generalship never was shown in any Army since the Art of War was understood," Lt. Col. Daniel Brodhead of Pennsylvania wrote in disgust. With the three Pennsylvania state battalions shattered and their colonels all prisoners, Washington ordered the remnants to form into a unit under Brodhead's command. "I understand that

Gen. Sullivan has taken the Liberty to charge our brave and good Col. Miles with the ill success of the Day," Brodhead was astonished to learn, "but give me leave to say, that if Gen. Sullivan & the rest of the Gen'ls on Long Island, had been as vigilant and prudent as him, we might, & in all probability would have cut off Clinton's Brigade; our officers & men in general, considering the confusion, behaved as well as men could do." He added in postscript, with no little frustration, "The Great Gen'l Putnam could not, tho' requested, send out one Reg't to cover our retreat."[26] A dispassionate examination of the battle validates many of Brodhead's observations.

The victors were elated. "The enemy thought they were invincible in the woods," Col. Charles Stuart of the 1st Grenadier Battalion told his father, Lord Bute, "and they were amazed to see that we were bold enough to attack them in their own way, in defiance of redoubts, woods or anything."[27] The legends of eagle-eyed frontiersmen secure in the forests and sniping at will were dispelled in the British forces, replaced by tales of cowardice and contempt for their opponents. "You will be glad, & Gentlemen in Office will not be displeased that we have had the Field Day, I talked of in my last Letter," Gen. James Grant smugly informed Gen. Edward Harvey, the commander in chief of the British Army at headquarters in London. "If a good Bleeding can bring those Bible faced Yankees to their senses," he scoffed, "the Fever of Independency should soon abate."[28]

Contempt for the rebels extended into army nicknames. Camp fevers, including the "bloody flux" (amoebic dysentery), an especially painful and disgusting condition, afflicted both armies, especially in the hot summer weather. "Just now getting the better of the Yanky as they call the flux here," Lt. Loftus Cliffe of the 46th Regiment told his brother Bartholomew, "which indeed has reduced my Thigh to the thickness of my Leg, and my Leg to a Grenadiers Musquett Barrel." Describing the battle and its stinking aftermath, he said, "Well, about the Wars, to tell you the truth I have seen more things to shock me than affright me, Friends & Foes lying Dead and dying, Scalps & Limbs scatterd about, Rebels with clubbed firelocks"—muskets turned upside down as a token of surrender—"pale as Death & tottering every Limb, surrendring themselves prisoners, expecting instant Death as the reward for their iniquitous temerity." Even worse, there was "a beautiful Country layd waste: one part ravaged by Rebels, the other by their opponents, in short the Horrours of a Civil War are every Day before my Eyes."[29]

With six British warships hovering just down the East River, the military end of the American Revolution was in sight. The remaining six thousand Continentals on Long Island were strongly entrenched, but the sights and sounds of the battle in front, together with the reports of the survivors who streamed back to the earthworks, had deflated morale. Their opponents had the numbers, the skills, the momentum, and the will to keep going; the king's forces that afternoon were unstoppable by anything that Washington had at his disposal.

They were stopped, almost inexplicably, by General Howe.

Perhaps it was the sight of the entrenchments on Brooklyn Heights that made Howe hesitate. He already had a smashing victory here, so why risk a disaster such as Breed's Hill? Perhaps he chose not to lose any more men, and that having taught the Americans a lesson would cost them more losses through desertion than gunfire. With the warships so close, the British might even cut this force off completely and compel it to surrender.

Whatever the reasons, the royal army set up camp in the area around Bedford and began preparations for a siege of Brooklyn Heights. Many British officers were incredulous: The momentum of the day would probably have carried the heights, and Washington would have been driven into the East River.

As it was, Howe's decision allowed Washington time to escape. Three days later, on August 30, Ensign Thomas Glyn of the Guards Brigade observed, "In the course of this Night the Enemy retreated unobserved from the Forts of Brooklyn & crossed the Ferry to New York."[30] Wind from the northeast kept British warships out of the East River and brought in a thick fog from Long Island Sound. In absolute silence, Washington abandoned his entrenchments and managed to rescue several thousand men and most of his supplies from Brooklyn, successfully transferring them across the East River to the temporary safety of Manhattan. Howe's first grand opportunity for ending the American war was lost.

"Upon that Day I immagined we had an Enemy of some Spirit to contend with, as Strategm and I believe Numbers were on our Side," Lieutenant Cliffe commented about the American forces, "but ever since, they have shewn the greatest pusilinamity that can be immagined from Men who pretend to fight for Liberty & independance." He was astonished by how quickly the American positions fell apart. "We had been scarce two Days at work at our approaches to their Lines of Brookland (which were amazing strong and constructed with great Labour) than they quit them & their Battery of red Hook which commanded the Entrance into the Sound, and Governors Island where they had also works." It didn't make sense to the British officer, for "if a Spirited resistence had been made at those works they would have cost us a good deal of Time & Men." Cliffe wasn't complaining; he was puzzled, unlike many others, who saw it as further confirmation of the weakness of the American cause. "They had now taken refuge in York Island & Town," meaning Manhattan and New York City.[31]

Across the East River, "in the morning, unexpectedly and to the surprise of the city, it was found that all that could come back was come back," Rev. Mr. Shewkirk of the Moravian congregation said of the returning American troops. Before the battle, "Many had thought to surround the king's troops, and make them prisoners with little trouble," the usual trash-talk associated with inexperience. After the debacle and withdrawal, "The language was now otherwise," he noticed, and the change was striking. "The merry tones on drums and fifes had ceased, and they were hardly heard for a couple of days." To him, "it seemed a general damp had spread; and the sight of the scattered people up and down the streets was indeed moving." This war was going to be long and difficult.

Though lucky to have escaped, the troops were understandably in the dumps. "Many looked sickly, emaciated, cast down, &c.," Shewkirk observed with pity, "the wet clothes, tents—as many as they had brought away—and other things, were lying about before the houses and in the streets to dry." The scene in the streets was one of wretchedness. "In general," he wrote, "everything seemed to be in confusion." As for the casualties, "The loss in killed, wounded, and taken has certainly been great, and more so than it ever will be known."[32]

Washington tried to put on as good a face as possible. "I am sensible a retreating Army is encircled with difficulties, that the declining an Engagement subjects a General to reproach and that the Common cause may be affected by the discouragement It may throw over the minds of many," the commander in chief of the Continental Army told the president of Congress about the first major battle of the American War for Independence and its aftermath. "But when the Fate of America may be at Stake on the Issue, when the wisdom of Cooler moments & experienced men have decided that we should protract the War, if possible," he reasoned, "I cannot think it safe or wise to adopt a different System when the Season for Action draws so near a Close."[33]

In this letter, George Washington reported to John Hancock and the Congress the long view of his army's defeat at Long Island and withdrawal to Manhattan. It was well that he did, for the short view was beyond "discouragement." It was catastrophic.

CHAPTER II

"Sgnik Sdneirf"

~~~

Down in Virginia during the same week that the New York campaign finally got underway, "the stranded Englishman" Nicholas Cresswell was making his getaway, hoping to reach the British army and return to England. Cresswell managed to escape from Virginia using one of the oldest tricks in the book, that of a fugitive "hidden in plain view." Leaving Leesburg on Friday, August 23, with Alexander Cooper, "a Storekeeper in town," he paused to see his friend Thomson Mason, who gave him letters to carry to several Virginia congressmen: "Messrs. Francis Lightfoot Lee, Thos. Stone, Thos. Jefferson, and John Rogers Esq."[1] This trust would provide him with enough cover to get to Philadelphia safely, and he hoped it would help secure him a pass from Congress to go to New York. He also acquired a letter of introduction to Messrs. Warder & Sons, long-established Philadelphia merchants.

Borrowing a horse from his friend Mr. Kirk, Cresswell set out with Cooper for Philadelphia, a journey of nearly two hundred miles. Riding north through Frederick, Maryland, they covered forty miles the first day, a good pace maintained through the trip, and by Saturday evening they were in York, Pennsylvania, nearly eighty miles from Leesburg. "Pleasant and well laid out," Cresswell said of York, a town less than thirty years old, "the inhabitants Dutch [Deutsch: German] and Irish." They lodged at the Sign of the Brewhouse, where "The Landlord is a Dutchman with a confounded hard name and a Damn dirty house."[2]

The next morning, the pair headed east, crossing the wide, rocky Susquehanna River, "about $1^1/_4$ miles broad," at Wright's Ferry [now

Wrightsville/Columbia], passing from York County into Lancaster County. They were now leaving the back edge of the frontier and entering the more settled region of southeastern Pennsylvania, a major center of agriculture, ironworking, and firearms manufacturing, in particular the famously accurate Pennsylvania long rifles, made at numerous shops in the vicinity.

A few miles ahead, they could see the spires of Lancaster, the largest inland town in America. Situated on the Conestoga Creek in the middle of some of the richest, most productive farmland on the continent, Lancaster contained between two thousand and three thousand inhabitants. The oldest dwellings were rustic, constructed of log, stone, or German-style half-timber, but many of the newer buildings in the center of town were built of brick in elegant Georgian style. The streets were laid out in a grid pattern, and a handsome brick courthouse crowned the hill in the center square. "This is a large town, but the situation is disagreeable between two hills," Nicholas observed as they arrived in the early afternoon. He described Lancaster as having "several good buildings and some manufactories of Guns and Woollen, but no navigation." The travelers dined at the Sign of the Two Highlandmen, a respectable tavern kept by William Ross near the market square.[3]

Cresswell also tersely noted "Four hundred English prisoners here." These were soldiers of the 7th Royal Fusiliers and the 26th Regiment, the "Old Cameronians," a Scottish lowland unit. The men, along with the women and children belonging to both regiments, had been taken prisoner in late 1775 at Fort Ticonderoga and Fort St. Johns in upper New York and were now quartered in the old barracks.

A drummer of the 26th, seventeen-year-old Daniel St. Clair, had recently deserted the regiment and was now the drummer of Capt. Jasper Yeates's Company of the 7th Battalion Lancaster County Associators. This militia unit was in town, drilling and preparing to march towards New York when Cresswell passed through. Months earlier, the British officers had protested any encouragement for their men to enlist with the rebels and demanded the return of all deserters. Congress agreed to forbid prisoners to enlist, but Daniel somehow managed to evade this, perhaps by joining the Associators rather than the Continental forces.

It was difficult to make sure that the agreement was kept, for by the summer, most of the British officers were lodged out of town, some of them miles away. One of the captives was Lt. John André of the Royal Fusiliers, who had spent two months in Lancaster in early 1776. He was now eighty miles away at Carlisle, a frontier town in Cumberland County, "inhabited by a stubborn, illiberal crew called the Scotch-Irish, sticklers for the [Presbyterian] Covenant, and utter enemies to the abomination of curled hair, regal government, minced pies, and other heathenish vanities," André told his mother.[4] A large percentage of Pennsylvania's soldiers fit this description, and hundreds of them were armed with rifles made in Lancaster, weapons so accurate that they could pick off British officers at three hundred yards—or so the legends went.

Many of the Scots-Irish had left Northern Ireland in recent years, bitter and angry, feeling betrayed by the British government. Their ancestors had defeated the Catholic Irish in the previous century and were rewarded with land seized from the natives. Despite this, as non-Anglican Presbyterian "Dissenters," they were not permitted to vote but were still burdened with crippling property taxes. Mercantile laws favoring England completed the cycle of economic exclusion, so thousands of the ruined came to the American middle colonies to settle, mainly in the rural and frontier areas, well beyond the reach of established church and state. When war against England came, the Scots-Irish were eager to join.

Having already butted heads with some of the Presbyterians in Virginia, including a Rev. Mr. Thomson, Cresswell was about to encounter them again, this time armed and on the march. He did not tarry in Lancaster; continuing east towards Philadelphia, he and his companion "Crossed Conistogo Creek." Ten miles from Lancaster they "Lodged at *The Sign of the Duke of Cumberland*" in Leacock Township, a tavern kept by James Mercer, a captain in the 5th Battalion Lancaster County Associators.[5] "The Landlord is a Scotch-Irish Rebel Colonial," Nicholas grumbled, "and his house is dirty as a Hog's stye." Nearby stood the Leacock Presbyterian Church, a plain, solid structure built of rough, gray stone, as hard and flinty as its congregation. "Land good in general," Cresswell did notice, remembering his original purpose in coming to America, "farmers rich and industrious. Irish and Dutch inhabitants."

Though the innkeeper might well have been slovenly, much of the dirt came from hard usage, as Associator companies were constantly passing by on their way to and from New York. Cresswell and Cooper lodged there on a Sunday night, a day when no work was supposed to be done. Early the next morning, Monday, August 26, they happily "left *The Duke of Cumberland*, which is one of the dirtiest houses I ever put my foot in," Nicholas wrote with revulsion.

The travelers rode sixteen miles and "Breakfasted at *The Waggon*" in West Caln Township, Chester County, noting that Caleb Way Jr., "the Landlord [is] a rigid Irish Presbyterian." Fifteen miles ahead, in the mid-afternoon,

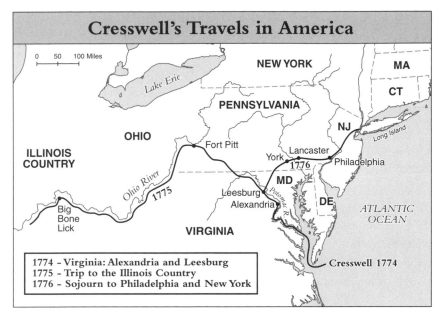

Cresswell's Travels in America

0 50 100 Miles

NEW YORK

MA

CT

Lake Erie

PENNSYLVANIA

OHIO

Fort Pitt

NJ

Long Island

ILLINOIS
COUNTRY

York Lancaster

Philadelphia

1776

Ohio River

1775

MD

Leesburg

Alexandria

Potomac R.

DE

ATLANTIC
OCEAN

Big
Bone
Lick

VIRGINIA

Cresswell 1774

1774 - Virginia: Alexandria and Leesburg
1775 - Trip to the Illinois Country
1776 - Sojourn to Philadelphia and New York

Nicholas Cresswell made the two-hundred-mile overland trip from Leesburg, Virginia, to Philadelphia in five days, averaging forty miles per day. His journal provides a rare day-by-day glimpse of the nation at war.

they "dined at *The Cross Keys*" in East Whiteland Township, down in the Great Valley of the old Welsh Tract, where Richard Jacobs was tavern keeper, but warranted no remark.[6] Ten miles on up the long, gradual climb of the South Valley Hill, they "lodged at *The Spread Eagle*, a clean Dutchman's house" in Radnor Township, kept by Jacob Hinkle near the 16th milestone. "Land broken and hilly," Nicholas commented, "but the Farmers seem rich, good stock, and their land well cultivated."

The Lancaster Road was busy with troop movements. "Passed 5 companies going to camp," he observed, mostly from Lancaster Associator battalions. They, too, were headed for New York via Philadelphia.

At dawn the following day, Tuesday, August 27, they "Left *The Spread Eagle*. Crossed Schulkill Ferry, got to Philadelphia to breakfast" after a sixteen-mile ride. Passing numerous taverns on the way, Cresswell noticed, "In our journey from Leesburg I have seen only 3 signs hanging, the rest pulled down by Soldiers." The vandalism from undisciplined and sometimes rowdy volunteers was becoming more and more evident.

Once in Philadelphia, Cresswell spent the day wandering the streets. "Making my observations," he wrote. "Lodged at *The Black Horse* in Market

Street," a tavern kept by William Graham on the northwest corner of Market and 4th, catercornered to The Indian Queen, the most famous tavern on this busy street.[7] He was fortunate in getting lodgings, for the city was buzzing with activity.

Officially called High Street, the main thoroughfare in Philadelphia was commonly called Market Street because the main city market ran down the middle of it for three blocks, ending at 4th Street just opposite The Black Horse. "The streets are sixty foot wide, except Market Street which is an hundred," Nicholas astutely observed, "but the Market house is set in the middle of this street which entirely spoils the beauty of it." Each of the three block-long sheds of the market house consisted of an arcaded roof set on rows of square brick piers, under which the stand holders set up their stalls each Wednesday and Saturday. The streets "are paved with brick and kept very clean with walks on each side for the foot people."[8]

That afternoon and evening, as the market people began arriving to set up for the Wednesday market, the already bustling street became clogged with herds of livestock and scores of wagons from the surrounding countryside, all bursting with harvest bounty to feed the forty thousand or so inhabitants of North America's largest city. Market days were always an event, and the clamor of horses and wagons coming in soon rose to a din as animals were slaughtered, barrels unloaded, and wheels of cheese and firkins of butter were displayed, while on the waterfront, fish, fruit, produce, and assorted preserved meat from across the Delaware River was carted up to the Jersey Market between Front and Second Streets. "Here is a large and plentiful Market," Cresswell noted, "but chiefly supplied from the Jerseys."[9] Vendors squabbled and gabbed in German, English, and Dutch (Welsh and Swedish could also be heard at times), while deep-toned African voices resonated in a variety of Caribbean accents as spicy as the pepper pot soup hawked by turbaned women screeching, "Peppa Pot! Smokin' hot!" On Second Street, two blocks down from The Black Horse, the chimes in the steeple of Christ Church pealed merrily into the night, welcoming the crowds.

All over Philadelphia, the taverns were jammed. In addition to the usual market throngs, troops were everywhere, hundreds of them. "Past 11, the 2nd Batalion came to town," Christopher Marshall of the Pennsylvania Board of War reported that day, "the 3rd & 5th Batalion come & coming to town from Camp," meaning that three battalions of Philadelphia Associators, somewhere between one thousand and fifteen hundred men, were returning from the camp in Perth Amboy, their two months of service having expired.[10] They were glad to be home, and New Jersey was glad to be rid of them. Excluding those battalions, *A Return of Troops Quartered In and Near the City* made the same day, August 27, counted just over twenty-one hundred troops from eight other Pennsylvania and two Maryland battalions.[11] They were nearly all Associators from the backcountry, undisciplined volunteers camped on the outskirts of town, strolling in and out unchecked and often unsupervised.

There were politicians galore, too. Not only was the Continental Congress in town, though its numbers were dwindling by the day, but the Pennsylvania Convention to create a new state government was in full session. Dozens of members, especially from the frontier counties, attended at the State House (now Independence Hall), while Congress continued to meet in the main chamber. "The State house is a good building but does not make a grand appearance," Nicholas commented. "Here all public business is done." He couldn't help but add, with a touch of bitter sarcasm, "Now the nest of the great and mighty Sanhedrim."[12]

Back at The Black Horse after an uneasy night, "Don't like my lodgings, full of Irish Colnls., Captns., and Convention men," Cresswell scribbled the next day, "most of them profoundly ignorant and as impertinent as any Skipkinnet [*skipkennel*: a lackey; a low-bred ignoramus]. These are here for the purpose of making a new code of Laws for the Province." Although Benjamin Franklin was the president of the Pennsylvania Convention, he divided his time between those meetings and Congress. Most of the convention members were chosen from the local Committees of Safety, where they were noted for their prominence as tavern keepers or mill owners rather than for polished manners or scholarship. "O, Happy people indeed that has such wise guides," Nicholas sniffed.

Despite his peevishness and general discomfort, overall Cresswell liked Philadelphia. "This is the most regular, neat and convenient city I was ever in and has made the most rapid progress to its present greatness," he wrote enthusiastically, the city being less than a century old. "Everything is kept in the greatest order." There was a college, a hospital, a "Bettering House" for the homeless, and a barracks, the last three establishments the largest in North America. In the shipyards along the Delaware, "they build as fine Ships here as any part of the World and with as great dispatch," including four Continental frigates. He noted twenty houses of worship of various denominations. Overall, "The Buildings are Brick, very plain, convenient and neat, no very grand edifices as the Quakers have the management of public affairs."[13]

After walking around town on this unseasonably cool and pleasant August morning, "so cool this day as to wear my winters coat & jacket, at night blanket & coverlet on the bed," Christopher Marshall noted, Cresswell took his letter of introduction and sought out Jeremiah Warder, a long-established importer of fine wines and assorted "India and European goods," who kept a store on Third Street just above Market.[14] "Delivered my letters to Mr. Warder, who received me very kindly and invited me to dine with him," he wrote. Warder "introduced me to several Gentlemen of his acquaintance. All Quakers. Spent the evening at The Sign of the Black Horse with Mr. Joseph Brewer—Clerk to Mr. Jeremiah Warder."

Cresswell's conversations with Joseph Brewer opened the door to another side of Philadelphia society in 1776: the Loyalists. After walking around town again the next morning, August 29, Cresswell "dined at Mr. Brewer's with Mr. Buchhannan, an Irish Gentleman. Find him a sensible, polite man. In the afternoon met with Phillip Morchington, who keeps a pretty large store here."[15]

Philip Marchinton was a very successful businessman operating in the heart of Philadelphia's commercial district. He was a clothier and fancy goods merchant who kept a large store downtown at No. 4 Market Street, on the north side between Front and Second, opposite the Jersey Market. As a secret Philadelphia Loyalist at this time and a contact for Cresswell during his stay in the city, his background and activities are of particular interest.

Marchinton was born in England in 1736 and came to Philadelphia in 1771.[16] By November 10, 1773, he was advertising his new store in *The Pennsylvania Gazette*. "*PHILIP MARCHINTON* Hath imported, by the last ships from LONDON, LIVERPOOL, and HULL, A LARGE and neat assortment of EUROPEAN and INDIA GOODS" including more than thirty types of fancy cloth "suitable to the season" such as shalloons, bombazeens, paduasoys, and peelongs, along with silk gloves, stockings, and caps. He also advertised jewelry and cutlery.[17]

Six months after the Boston Tea Party, despite the boycotts, Marchinton was bold enough to advertise in the *Gazette* "the best hyson, common green, souchong and bohea TEAS for sale."[18] It was in this same period, May of 1774, when Cresswell had attended Washington's election ball in Virginia and remarked that tea was in disfavor. Undaunted, Marchinton continued to import fancy goods, as evidenced by his advertisements in late 1774, when he expanded into a full line of haberdashery.[19]

Like many other merchants of all political persuasions, he was an opportunist who had no qualms about making money from the outbreak of revolutionary fervor. One year to the day after Congress authorized the formation of the Continental Army, Marchinton advertised that he was going into the woolen manufacturing business:

> Philadelphia, June 14, 1776. WHEREAS the subscriber hath fixed a connection to carry on the Woollen Manufactory in all its branches, as large as it can be made to answer, and *as it may be of very great service in the present situation*, NOTICE is hereby given to all Wool growers and Skinners, that may have Wool on hand to dispose of either for the purpose of cloths or stuffs, if they will either bring or send it by any conveniency that they can make agreeable according to their situation, they may depend on having the best price according to the quality, and ready money as soon as delivered, for any quantity great or small. *PHILIP MARCHINTON*, at his Store, No. 4, between Front and Second streets, in Market street.[20]

No sooner was independence declared than Marchinton intensified his double-dealing by opening the wool manufactory. With all of the army officers, Associators, navy people, and Continental quartermaster personnel scrambling to buy uniforms, Marchinton announced in mid-August that he "continues taking in all the wool he can possibly meet with, and he hath fixed his Manufacture in Moorecourt, between Market and Chestnut streets, in Front street, where scribblers, combers, spinners and weavers may have full employ." The advertisement was very particular in stating that "any person or persons that are in the Continental Service, either by land or sea, may have a supply; none else need apply, as they are for that use only."[21] This, too, is another example of "hiding in plain view," with great profits to boot.

Interestingly, as his woolen manufactory for the Continental service was getting under way, the secret activities of Marchinton and others came to light from an informant who was "examined" by local authorities. "Our first meeting was at the Widow Balls . . . some Time in Spring, 1775," Isaac Atwood, an English-born comb maker, revealed about local Loyalists to the Committee of Safety on July 11. "Their meetings are still held at the Widow Balls, where they have a private Room, into which they will admit no one. They also meet at Medcalf's. There are sometimes fifty of them." Most damning was the statement, "The Principal persons concerned are: Philip Marchinton, in the light Horse, whom I heard say that he would never fight against the English. He did not attend the Meetings, but I know him to be opposite to the Cause." Atwood also testified that "a clerk of Jeremiah Warder"—Joseph Brewer, with whom Cresswell spent an evening at the Black Horse—"is very busy, and attends the Meetings."[22]

After being introduced to Marchinton, Cresswell "spent the evening with him and one Thos. Thornbur from Skipton and one Gresswold [Joseph Griswold], a distiller in town, at the City Tavern," the newest, largest, and best tavern in town, where members of Congress regularly gathered between sessions. The tavern was located on the corner of south Second Street at Walnut, directly across from Mrs. Yard's boardinghouse, where John Adams and other congressmen lodged, and many congressional delegates boarded in nearby houses. Along with the Old London Coffee House at Front and Market Streets, Smith's City Tavern was the best place in town to gather news, gossip, and all sorts of information, for the new merchants' exchange was also located here.

"Thornbur and Gresswold two sensible men, but Morchington is an extravagant fop," Nicholas commented. Given his line of business—selling the fanciest sorts of silks and satins to have tailored into extravagant clothes—Philip Marchinton could afford to be his own best advertisement by wearing the latest flashy clothes. Cresswell also inadvertently mentioned Marchinton's growing source of wealth: "Great preparations for War, and great numbers of ragged soldiers come into town."

While at City Tavern on the evening of August 29, they heard "news that the English had defeated them on Long Island and taken a thousand prisoners" two days earlier. The news electrified the Loyalists, for now it seemed that the full might and wrath of the British army was coming home to roost. It certainly made them bolder, for the following day, "Mr. Buchhannan went with me to every place of note in town," Cresswell wrote. "Dined at Marchington's Lodgings. Spent the evening with Messrs. Brewer & Buchhannan. Both *Sgnik Sdneirf.*"

Sgnik Sdneirf—"king's friends" spelled backwards. Why Cresswell chose to write the words backwards is a mystery. Was it in case his journal was read by someone? Perhaps, though any literate person of average intelligence could figure it out without too much difficulty. He may have done it for his own edification, for in another entry, he wrote, "if I stay amongst the *Sleber*, I must go to *Liaj.*" He would have found a lot of company there, for after making his observations of the State House, he noted, "Near this is the New Jail, a good and large stone building now occupied with *Sgnik Sdneirf.*" On Monday, September 2, he again commented, "Great numbers—I believe half the people in town—are *Sgnik Sdneirf.* Some of the people have hung Washington, Putnam, and Mifflin on their sign post in public."[23]

Over the centuries, the popular history of Philadelphia as "the cradle of liberty" has projected the image of a quaint brick city, home to flag-sewing seamstresses, kite-flying philosophers, and enthusiastic, armed patri-ots attentively listening to the Declaration of Independence on the Fourth of July before marching off to the front, attended by fifes and drums tootling "Yankee Doodle" as the Liberty Bell peals in the background. While some elements of this image have some basis in reality, together they have created a selectively comfortable fantasy that never existed. John Adams, whose sharp eye and sharper tongue would brook no patience with such nonsense, wrote to Benjamin Rush in 1790, "The history of our Rev-olution will be one continued lie from one end to the other. The essence of the whole will be that Dr. Franklin's electrical rod smote the earth and out sprung General Washington. That Franklin electrized him with his rod—and henceforward these two conducted all the policy, negotiation, legisla-tion, and war." He grumbled peevishly, "These lines contain the whole fable, plot, and catastrophe."[24]

The reality was considerably more difficult. Back in July, "The decla-ration of independence, whose date will never be forgotten so long as lib-erty remains the fashion and demagogues continue to thrive upon it," was quickly dispatched and read to the army, wrote Capt. Alexander Graydon of Philadelphia, who grew up on Second Street across from City Tavern. "If it was not embraced with all the enthusiasm that has been ascribed to the event," he recalled vividly, "it was, at least, hailed with acclamations, as, no doubt, any other act of congress, not flagrantly improper, would at that time have been." This was hardly an enthusiastic endorsement of so impor-tant a document.

Graydon's unit, the 3rd Pennsylvania Battalion, raised largely in Philadel-phia, was busy digging entrenchments at Fort Washington, a massive fortifi-cation at the northern end of Manhattan Island, when they heard the Declaration read.[25] "The propriety of the measure had been little canvassed among us," he commented, meaning that the troops had little discussion among themselves about independence, "and perhaps it was to our honour, considered merely as soldiers, that we were so little of politicians."[26]

Cresswell went to meet the politicians on Saturday, August 31, at the State House. "Waited on Mr. Francis Lightfoot Lee and Mr. Thos. Jeffer-son with my letters," the letters given to him in Virginia by Thomson Mason. The young man struck paydirt, for both congressmen "behaved with the greatest complaisance and politeness," and "proferred to get me a pass from the Congress by virtue of which I may travel where I please."[27]

He would have to wait until Monday, September 2, however, for Congress's Saturday session was very short, and Jefferson himself was packing to leave for Virginia.

After all of the traveling, anxiety, close calls, and near-misses because of politics and the war, Cresswell could see light at the end of the tunnel. He had landed in Virginia more than two years earlier and spent the past year trying to get back to England. Now, his goal was finally within reach.

In his wildest dreams, Nicholas could never have imagined the irony that the one to give him his ticket to New York—and home—was not only a Virginia radical, but the author of the Declaration of Independence.

CHAPTER 12

The Decoy Duck

◆━━◆

W hat of the American generals captured at Long Island? On August 29, two days after the battle and only hours before the American evacuation of Brooklyn, "Ld. Stirling (so called) and Mr (called Genl.) Sullivan, late one of the Members of the Congress, were taken among other Prisoners" and brought on board Lord Howe's flagship. "They were admitted to dine with the Admiral, with whom they both, and particularly Sullivan, had much Conversation," Secretary Serle noted. The admiral was extending professional and personal courtesy—with an agenda.

Why was Lord Howe so affable with Sullivan? It may have been a combination of factors, but one answer is that the thirty-six-year-old Sullivan had been a member of Congress. He may also have been the more talkative of the two and appeared more eager to ingratiate himself with the fifty-year-old admiral, compared with fifty-year-old Lord Stirling of New Jersey, who maintained a dubious claim to a Scottish earldom. In Sullivan, Howe spotted someone who knew Congress and was willing to be in the limelight.

John Sullivan was born in Somerworth, New Hampshire in 1740, the son of Irish immigrants.[1] As an attorney, he had a reputation for being "litigious," or a lawyer who likes to quarrel. In 1772, he served in the local militia with the rank of major. A representative of New Hampshire at both the First and Second Continental Congresses, Sullivan was commissioned brigadier general in June 1775, one of the first in the Continental Army, and served in the siege of Boston. "He is active, spirited, and zealously attached to the Cause," Washington wrote in support of Sullivan in 1776. "That he does not want Abilities many members of Congress, as well as myself, can testify," an endorsement that tried to build on the positive.

"But," the commander in chief hastened to add, "he has his wants; and he has his foibles," Washington privately told John Hancock. "The latter are manifested in a little tincture of vanity, and in an over desire of being popular, which now and then leads him into some embarrassments."[2] Among Washington's leadership qualities was a gift for tact, a quality he shared with Lord Howe. They both recognized Sullivan's foibles, and each tried to work them to their advantage.

After the British evacuated Boston in early 1776, Washington sent Sullivan to Canada with a column of reinforcements for what was left of Montgomery's and Benedict Arnold's forces, which had barely survived the winter campaign. The New Hampshire general took command there on June 1, but the complicated circumstances of extremely harsh conditions, rampant sickness among the troops, and confusion in the command structure was a setup for disaster. A few days later, a large portion of his new contingent was nearly annihilated at Trois Rivières by British forces under Sir Guy Carleton, so Sullivan prudently ordered a withdrawal up Lake Champlain to Crown Point.

Shortly after his arrival, Sullivan learned that Congress had promoted Horatio Gates to major general and placed him in command. A British army veteran who had settled in Virginia before the war, Gates was supported by a largely southern faction in Congress. To the New England lawyer, not only did the appointment smack of sectional political chicanery, he felt his honor as an officer had been insulted.

Sullivan was outraged. "Surely my Honour Calls upon me to Leave the Service, after a person is put in over me without any Impeachment of my Conduct," he complained to Gen. Philip Schuyler, commander of the Northern Department.[3] Furious, the New Hampshire general stormed down to Philadelphia, threatening to resign. He submitted a letter to Congress to that effect on Friday, July 26.

It touched off a military storm in a political teacup. "Sullivan is here, and in a Miff, at the promotion of Gates, has asked Leave to resign his Commission," John Adams told Abigail the next day. "I am sorry for this inconsiderate step," he remarked, meaning that he wished Sullivan had given it careful consideration first, for "it will hurt him more than the Cause." To make matters worse, Adams got wind of a rumor going around military circles in New York that the general was ambitious to be the "first Man" in New Hampshire. "If this is really his Motive," Adams wrote, "he ought to be ashamed of it, and I hope he will be disappointed." Through his committee work on the Board of War, Adams was becoming more disenchanted with the wrangles over seniority among the officers. "The Ladies have not half the Zeal for Precedence, that We find every day among the Gentlemen," he groaned to his wife.[4]

The episode touched on a growing sore point between officers in the army and appointments by Congress based on experience, political pull, or both. "What shall we say of this phantom honour, the soldier's deity & object of worship?" Secretary Charles Thomson pondered as the Sullivan case distracted Congress for a few days. "I would not have a soldier devoid of it: But I think it a plant better suited for the gardens of monarchy than those of a republic." Thomson, a classics scholar born in northern Ireland, told his fellow Pennsylvanian John Dickinson, who was with the Flying Camp and dealing with those military woes, "Our minds are too much depraved with monarchical principles. For my part I am inclined to think it a weed, and am therefore ready to order it to be thrown over the fence, provided I could have enough of *amor patria* ["love of country"] to plant in its stead."[5]

Others in Congress were also annoyed by Sullivan's behavior. "Our army from Canada is now at Tyconderoga, but in a shattered condition," Thomas Jefferson informed fellow Virginian Richard Henry Lee. "General Sullivan left it and came here to resign on Gates's appointment." Unimpressed by the drama, Jefferson blithely remarked, "It was referred to this morning that a proper rap of the knuckles might be prepared, but on the advice of his friends he asked leave to withdraw it and repair to his duty."[6]

Whatever else transpired behind the scenes, John Hancock had a private talk with the dissatisfied general. "Upon conversing with Genl. Sullivan, and stating to him the Reasons of Congress promoting Genl. Gates over him, he desired Me to move for leave to withdraw his Application to resign—in which the Congress have acquiesced," Hancock notified Washington on July 31. "He has now Orders to repair to New York, where you will please to assign him such Post of Duty as you shall think proper."[7] Sullivan promptly went to New York City where, on August 9, he was promoted to major general.

Washington's right-hand man in New York was Maj. Gen. Nathanael Greene of Rhode Island. He commanded the troops on Long Island, who at that time were engaged in building fortifications on Brooklyn Heights in anticipation of a British attack on New York City via Long Island and Brooklyn Ferry. To prepare for this, Greene familiarized himself with the terrain by reconnoitering the island's rolling, wooded countryside and broad, flat plains, carefully examining roads, waterways, and passes through the hills. Thousands of men labored all summer on the heights around Brooklyn, constructing a formidable assortment of redoubts, redans, lunettes, and breastworks, all built of earth and wood.

The work was hard, the weather hot, and the local water supplies quickly turned foul with "effluvia," the runoff from the camps. Millions of flies and mosquitoes from the local marshes plagued the area. Disease swept through the army camps like wildfire, and thousands fell sick with deadly "camp fevers"—a generic name for diseases such as typhus, typhoid fever, dysentery, and cholera, all caused by poor sanitation and close living. Scores of men died miserably over the course of the summer; in mid-August, Greene himself was stricken with a raging fever. He was so ill that he was bedridden for five days, unable to function. With great reluctance Washington temporarily relieved the intrepid Rhode Islander until he recovered.

Sullivan was appointed in Greene's place. He crossed the East River on August 20 to take command of the nine thousand troops on Long Island and began viewing the works in progress near Brooklyn. Two days later, General Howe sent twenty-two thousand men across the Narrows; the campaign was now underway.

Sullivan's command did not last long. Based on seniority and experience, Israel Putnam superseded Sullivan on August 24. Neither Sullivan nor Putnam had any good knowledge of the island's topography, and three days later, that lack of reconnaissance played a major role in the defeat of Washington's army. Sullivan and Stirling were captured and were now conversing with Admiral Howe.

"I had also a great deal of discourse with them both," Serle noted, "in which, by the softest Words & manner I could, I labored to convince them of their Error, how the People in America had been duped by artful Insinuations, and what real Desire the Mother-Country had ever had of bringing matters to a pacific Conclusion." According to the secretary, "They both acknowledged they had either misconceived the affair, or were misinformed, and that they had ever understood that G. Britain had but one simple Idea, on the Subject, which was their absolute Submission." Serle proceeded to mention Lord Howe's role as peace commissioner and "the Intention of the Commission, which was peace & Settlement, and explained how necessary it was to their own Interest & Welfare to propose and even entreat an accommodation. To this they seemed to agree."

The New Hampshire lawyer-turned-general tried to argue the American position. "Sullivan, with great art but not with art sufficient to impose upon or delude any man acquainted with the subject, expatiated upon the internal Strengths and Resources of America, and of her Capability of maintaining the War for a long Time," Serle reported. "To all Discourse of this kind, I countermined with the Power & opulence of Great Britain, and argued the Incapacity of America from the Necessity of their running into Debt for 10 Years to come, in order to support the War of the present Year, and in order to support it another, they must run at least 15 Years further forward still, with the greater & increasing Improbability or Difficulty of Discharging it." Not surprisingly, Serle mentioned nothing about the British government's ever-growing debt from this war, nor the fact that the taxes spawned from the previous war's debt were major causes of the current conflict.

Besides, the secretary reasoned, from the British perspective, this entire rebellion had been engineered by radicals, in particular the Massachusetts crowd. "I dwelt a good deal upon the insidious Arts which designing men had employed to inflame the Americans, and upon the great Industry they had used to prevent the Circulation of the Truth," Serle replied. "I could not help saying (I told him) that such men, whoever they were, were not only Foes to Great Britain, but to America chiefly, and to all Humanity itself; that a good Cause needed no such bad means to support it; and that a true Cause always coveted, never avoided, the Light, in order that its Truth might appear."

"Lastly," the secretary told him, "I regretted that the Conduct of the matter was lodged in such intemperate Hands, and, that if ever affairs were adjusted, it must be placed with cooler minds & more considerate Heads." Though primarily aiming at the radical American Whigs, he was treading a narrow line between them and the Tory extremists in London.

"My whole Discourse was as soft as possible in its manner, and as strong as I could make it in the matter," Serle emphasized. "They seemed to feel a good Deal, and came down vastly in their Style & Air, which at first was rather lofty & warm. I engaged myself to them in this way, and am persuaded that if those, who meant well among them, were properly discoursed with, and singly, a good effect might be produced."[8] In that regard, the secretary was toeing the same line as Admiral Howe.

The admiral had a plan: send Sullivan to Philadelphia with a proposal to Congress for the exchange of himself and Lord Stirling for two captured

British generals (both minor characters) as a token of goodwill. He would then deliver Howe's personal message to Congress verbally, asking to meet privately with influential gentlemen to work out an accommodation.

Sullivan was willing to go, but needed to clear it with Washington. To this end, on the morning of August 30, Lord Howe permitted Sullivan to go to New York under a flag of truce to speak with his commander in chief.

The mood at headquarters must have been bittersweet, for the army had just evacuated Long Island under the cover of night and fog, enduring the added strain of enforced silence in slipping away. Though the operation was remarkably successful, it came on the heels of great losses in defeat and a long day and night of miserable, teeming rain, which soaked everyone thoroughly and turned the extensive Brooklyn entrenchments into stinking mud pits. Meeting with Sullivan that morning, Washington, though not pleased, saw no reason not to allow the hapless general to go to Congress with Howe's message.

From town, Sullivan informed the admiral, "Agreeable to your Lordships Request I have Conversed with General Washington, who says that he has no power to Treat upon the Subject your Lordship mentioned, but has not the least objection to my going to Philadelphia to Inform Congress of what your Lordship has been pleased to Communicate to me upon the Subject." Being under Howe's authority as a prisoner of war, Sullivan closed the letter by saying, "I shall wait your Lordships further Direction."[9] The letter was immediately dispatched to the admiral's flagship.

A few hours earlier, shortly after Sullivan left the *Eagle*, "we were most agreeably surprised to find, that the Rebels had entirely abandoned Long Island," Serle wrote with delight. "This hasty Evacuation surprised us the more, as they had constructed Forts, Redoubts and Intrenchments without End. Not a foot of Ground was unfortified," he commented with amazement. It would have taken a great deal of trouble and cost many men to have taken it all by force, the secretary remarked.[10]

Sensing the momentum, Lord Howe quickly responded to Sullivan that afternoon, saying, "Understanding by your Letter That the only Doubt of the propriety of your going to Philadelphia is, by your Conversation with General Washington, Removed, I do not see occasion to give you further Trouble but to Recommend the prosecuting of your Journey, as you were pleased on that Condition to propose."[11] His note went up to New York that evening under a flag of truce, "directed to Sullivan (who is to set out to-morrow morning for the Congress at Philadelphia)," Serle noted.[12]

News of the evacuation and of Sullivan's mission quickly reached Philadelphia. "We expect Sullivan here every hour," Congressman Will Hooper of New Jersey wrote to William Livingston, now governor of New Jersey, early on the morning of September 2. "We are told that he has a Message from Lord Howe to Congress." Hooper was uneasy about this; the man who had managed to acquire command of the British fleet and the peace commission through the convoluted maze of Parliament, Court, and Ministry was no mere courtesan. "I fear the Arts and address of Lord Howe, who by all Accts is a Politician, a Soldier and a Gentleman," the congressman confessed, "more than I dread the British Arms."[13]

Sullivan arrived in Philadelphia that same morning and went to the lodgings of Josiah Bartlett, his old New Hampshire colleague. "The Congress is at this time very thin," Bartlett told his other colleague William Whipple, urging him to come to Philadelphia as quickly as possible, since members were going home for a variety of legitimate reasons.[14] Among those departing was Thomas Jefferson, with Richard Henry Lee arriving to take his place. "Col Lee is arrived here, but several others have taken leave of absence, among them Mr. Jefferson and Mr. Haywood."[15] Jefferson did not return to Congress until the end of the war, six years later; Monday, September 2, 1776, was his last day, the same day that Nicholas Cresswell went to receive his pass to go to New York.

In the bustle of people in and around the State House, Cresswell might well have crossed paths with Bartlett and Sullivan as they went to Congress that morning, where the general delivered Howe's message. "He says he has a verbal message to Congress to propose himself and Lord Sterling in exchange for Generals Prescott and McDonald," Bartlett wrote. That proposal was acceptable; Gen. Richard Prescott had been captured in Canada in late 1775, and Gen. Donald MacDonald had led an uprising of loyalist Scottish highlanders in North Carolina, where he was badly defeated at Moore's Creek Bridge in February 1776. To arrange a "general-for-general" exchange was easily done.

The next part of the message was a bit more complicated. "Lord Howe expressed himself very desirous of an accommodation with America, without any more bloodshed; that he was very willing to meet, at almost any place, a number of the members of Congress (as private gentlemen, for he could not own any such body as Congress) to try if they could make any proposals for an accommodation; that he said he had waited near two months longer in England than he should have otherwise done, to procure proper powers for a final accommodation, with which he said he was now vested, &c, and he allowed General Sullivan to come here to propose the aforesaid conference to Congress."[16]

There was something else in the verbal message, John Adams later reported. According to Adams, Howe informed Sullivan "he would sett the Act of Parliament wholly aside, and that Parliament had no right to tax America or meddle with her internal Polity." If true, this extraordinary statement carried enormous political implications.

Having heard the general's oral report, Congress requested him to put it to writing, whereupon Sullivan withdrew. Strangely enough, the statement asserting that Parliament had no right to tax or meddle in American affairs did not appear in Sullivan's written version. "In this written Statement of the Message it ought to be observed that General Sullivan has not inserted, what he had reported verbally, that Lord Howe had told him 'he would sett the Act of Parliament wholly aside, and that Parliament had no right to tax America or meddle with her internal Polity'," Adams wrote in his autobiography.[17] Did Sullivan exaggerate, misconstrue, or fabricate what Lord Howe allegedly said about taxes? Did the foibles mentioned by Washington—a "tincture of vanity," the "overdesire of being popular"—lead the general to magnify the idea while in the limelight, and then retract it when ordered to put it in writing? Did Lord Howe hint or suggest the idea during his conversations with Sullivan, shrewdly calculating that the man's character flaws would create confusion or false hope in Congress?

When the general mentioned Howe's proposal for a meeting, John Adams nearly exploded. "I sat next to him while Genl. Sullivan was delivering a request to Congress from Lord Howe for an interview with a committee of the House in their private capacities," Benjamin Rush wrote. "Mr. Adams, under a sudden impression of the design, and dread of the consequences of the measure, whispered to me a wish 'that the first ball that had been fired on the day of the defeat of our army, had gone through his head.'" When Adams stood up to speak against the proposed interview, "he called Genl. Sullivan 'a decoy duck, whom Lord Howe has sent among us to seduce us into a renunciation of our independence,'" Rush recalled.[18]

Never shy in sharing what was on his mind, Adams minced no words. In a letter, he wrote the essence of what he said in Congress. "So! The Fishers have set a Seine, and a whole Schull, a whole Shoal of Fishes, have swam into it and been caught," he raged in disgust to a friend. "The Fowlers have set a Net, and a whole flock of Pidgeons have alighted on the bed, and the Net has been drawn over them," John tartly continued,

John Adams by Charles Willson Peale. INDEPENDENCE NATIONAL HISTORIC PARK

describing the defeat at Long Island and the capture of nearly a thousand American troops. "But the most insolent Thing of all, is sending one of those very Pidgeons, as a Flutterer to Philadelphia, in order to decoy the great flock of all," the Continental Congress. "Did you ever see a decoy-Duck?" he asked facetiously.[19]

Sullivan's checkered career in the War for Independence was already off to a bad start, with one threatened resignation and one capture within a month, and now, as an errand boy for Howe's peace commission. Within the next year he would threaten another resignation, face two courts-martial and one congressional recall, a near-duel with a wrongheaded congressman, and leave a trail of letters complaining of imagined slights and insults to honor. Later in the war, he was embroiled in further contention with French allies in Rhode Island. Sullivan survived it all, but such a record might well earn him the dubious award of "the hard-luck general" of the American Revolution.

But now he touched off a political typhoon which would engulf Congress in heated and impassioned debate over the next few days: to go or not to go?

CHAPTER 13

To Go or Not to Go

❧

"What will be done in the affair by Congress I know not, but think there are difficulties on both sides," Josiah Bartlett of New Hampshire observed after Sullivan delivered Howe's message. It was an understatement, to be sure, for "if the Congress should accept of the proposed conference, only on a verbal message, when at the same time Lord Howe declares he can consider them only as private gentlemen, especially when we are certain he can have no power to grant any terms we can possibly accept; this I fear will lessen the Congress in the eye of the public, and perhaps at this time intimidate people when they see us catching hold of so slender a thread to bring about a settlement." The New Hampshire congressman had caught the essence of the dilemma that was about to engross Congress.

But there were other, broader realities to consider. "On the other hand, General Sullivan's arrival from Lord Howe with proposals of an accommodation, with 30 falsehoods in addition, are now spread over this City, and 'twill soon be over the Continent," Bartlett revealed. Elated with the British victory at Long Island, the Philadelphia Loyalists were actively fueling the rumor mill, and wild exaggerations spread quickly. "If we should refuse the conference," he continued, "I fear the Tories, and moderate men, so called, will try to represent the Congress as obstinate, and so desirous of war and bloodshed that we would not so much as hear the proposals Lord Howe had to make."

The word on the street from Tory quarters was that Howe's proposals would be "highly advantageous for America, even that he would consent that we should be independent provided we would grant some advantages as

133

to trade." Where this came from is unknown, but "such an idea spread among the people, especially the soldiers at this time might be of the most fatal consequence," Bartlett worried.[1] Indeed it could be, for it sounded like Britain was offering America its own cake to eat, provided the mother country could have some of the icing.

Congressman Will Hooper of New Jersey concurred. "I am apprehensive of the effects this disappointment"—the loss at Long Island—"may produce upon Luke Warm whigs, men too indolent to think for themselves, or too phlegmatick hitherto to have taken an active part," he told Governor Livingston. Worse yet, "The Tories will assume a temporary Triumph."[2]

John Adams was even more vehement about who was fueling the fires of hope. "Lord Howe is surrounded with disaffected American Machiavillians, Exiles from Boston and elsewhere, who are instigating him to mingle Art with Force," he complained to James Warren on September 4. "He has sent Sullivan here, upon his Parol, with the most insidious, 'tho ridiculous Messages which you can conceive." Sullivan was being used as a cat's-paw, Adams felt, and "it has put Us rather in a delicate Situation, and gives Us much Trouble."[3]

The discussion of Howe's offer lasted for several days. On September 5, a motion introduced in Congress "Resolved, That General Sullivan be requested to inform Lord Howe that, this Congress, being the Representatives of the free and independent States of America, cannot with propriety send any of its members, to confer with his Lordship in their private Characters." However, Congress being "ever desirous of establishing peace, on reasonable terms . . . will send a Committee of their body, to know whether he has any authority to treat with persons, authorized by Congress for that purpose . . . and what that Authority is, and to hear such propositions as he shall think fit to make" respecting the issue of peace. In other words, since Congress could not send members directly to Lord Howe, because he did not recognize them, they would send a committee to find out exactly what authority he did have to speak with people *authorized* by Congress. It was a classic verbal waltz—to step through a political minefield—the same waltz that Lord Howe had danced with the Ministry.

As for Sullivan's peculiar role in the business, the resolution further recommended that John Hancock write to Washington and express the opinion that in the future, "no proposals for making peace . . . ought to be received or attended to, unless the same be made in Writing" and addressed to Congress.[4] This was not only in reference to Sullivan's verbal delivery but to another confused situation caused by Lord Drummond, a British officer on parole who had corresponded with Washington along the same lines a few weeks earlier. Washington tersely informed Drummond that engaging in such ad hoc, unauthorized political proposals was a parole violation.

John Adams was against the resolution; he was against even answering Howe's proposal, considering it contemptible. And he was not alone in being dead set against accepting Lord Howe's offer to meet members not as congressmen, but as private gentlemen only. George Ross of Pennsylvania, a lawyer from Lancaster, spoke against it, wondered how King George III would react if Congress proposed to negotiate with him as Elector of Hanover instead of King of Great Britain. The king would reject such a proposal as insulting, he asserted. "Let the American States act in the same manner," Ross stated. "We are bound to cherish the honour of our country which is now committed to our care. Nothing could dishonour the Sovereign of Britain that would not in equal circumstances dishonour us."

Dr. Benjamin Rush, also of Pennsylvania, spoke against the resolution, saying that "our country was far from being in a condition to make it necessary for us to humble ourselves at the feet of Great Britain." While it was true that America had lost a battle and an island, the rest of New York was still free. "But suppose that State had been conquered?" he asked. "Suppose half the States in the Union had been conquered; nay, suppose all the States in the Union except one had been conquered, still let that one not renounce her independence," Rush thundered eloquently. "But I will go further: should this solitary state, the last repository of our freedom, be invaded, let her not survive her precious birthright, but in yielding to superiour force, let her last breath be spent in uttering the word 'Independance'." Rush recalled that one of those in favor of the motion retorted that "he would much rather live with dependance than die with independance upon his lips."[5]

The most eloquent speech denouncing the proposed meeting came from Dr. John Witherspoon of New Jersey. A fifty-three-year-old, Scottish-born Presbyterian minister, Witherspoon became president of the College of New Jersey in 1768 at the behest of Richard Stockton and instituted major educational reforms there. He did not approve of clergymen getting involved in politics, but as the storm approached, the minister overcame his scruples and joined Congress in 1776 in time to swing votes in favor of independence. Witherspoon was also active in the arrest and imprisonment of Governor William Franklin.[6]

"The subject we are now upon, is felt and confessed by us all to be of the utmost consequence, and perhaps I may also say, of delicacy and difficulty," Witherspoon began. The variety of opinions expressed in Congress were proof of how important it was to study the proposal very carefully, for "it comes from the commander in chief of the forces of the king of Great Britain, and one who is said to carry a commission to give peace to America."[7]

Given the conduct of the Ministry, the acts of Parliament, and the contents of Howe's proclamation, it was clear "that absolute unconditional submission is what they require us to agree to, or mean to force us to." Further, Witherspoon pointed out, "the king has not laid aside his personal rancour; it is rather increasing every day." Although the admiral supposedly wishes to bring peace, "yet he has constantly avoided giving up the least punctilio on his side." For example, "he could never be induced to give General Washington his title." Lord Howe could not speak with Congress, "but he has allowed a prisoner of war to come and tell us he would be glad to see us as private gentlemen." Some have suggested that this is not meant as an insult or a disgrace to Congress, the doctor continued, but that it was difficult in getting over "the point of honour" of opening the door for peace overtures with rebels. "This, Sir, is mistaking the matter wholly," Witherspoon argued. "He has got over this point of honour; he has made the first overtures; he has told General Washington, by Colonel Putnam [*sic*: Paterson, the adjutant general] that he wished that message to be considered as making the first step. His renewed attempts by Lord Drummond, and now by General Sullivan, point out to all the world that he has made the first step." This was all part of a scheme laid in London, the Scottish minister insisted, "and I am of opinion it is already written and boasted of to the ministry at home, that he has taken such a part." As a result, "any evil or condescension that can attend seeking peace first, has been submitted to by him."[8] Howe's enemies in London would certainly concur.

Through it all, His Lordship has consistently refused to state or even imply that the Americans are anything but disloyal subjects in rebellion, he reminded Congress. If sincere in wanting reconciliation, why were the admiral's communications not kept secret, but instead delivered under flying seals to be opened by anyone? "If he meant only to communicate his mind to the Congress by private gentlemen, he might have done that many ways, and it needed not to have been known either to the public or the Congress, till these private gentlemen came here on purpose to reveal it." These circumstances convinced Witherspoon that this was all part of a scheme.[9]

"The question is, shall we comply with it in any degree, or not?" What good would be derived from it, Witherspoon wanted to know, since everyone in Congress who spoke declared that there was no thought of giving up independence, "and by the greatest part, if not the whole, that there is not the least reason to expect that any correspondence we can have with him will tend to peace." Some members suggested that it should be embraced as a means or step in that direction; the doctor disagreed. "We were told that it was easy for us to boast or be valiant here," Witherspoon stated, "but that our armies were running away before their enemies." Would the cause of independence be able to stand against such overwhelming and obvious evidence of futility?

The minister looked far beyond the immediate crisis of Long Island. "I found my hope of success in this cause, not in the valour of Americans, or the cowardice of Britons, but upon the justice of the cause, and still more upon the nature of things." He maintained that America was the injured party, and that the injuries were being continued by Britain. Besides, "If we take the whole events of the war since it commenced, we shall rather wonder at the uniformity of our success, than be surprised at some cross events," the success of building an army from scratch and maintaining it in the field, however awkward or incomplete. "We have seen bravery as well as cowardice in this country," the minister added, "and there are no consequences of either that are probable, that can be worth mentioning as ascertaining the event of the contest."[10]

Witherspoon recognized, as did John Adams and some others, that this war was going to be long and difficult. "Lord Howe speaks of a decisive blow not being yet struck," he stated, "as if this cause depended upon one battle, which could not be avoided. Sir, this is a prodigious mistake. We may fight no battle at all for a long time, or we may lose some battles." The Scottish preacher pointed out the fact that British troops had been routed early on in the 1745 Scottish rebellion, where, "at the battle of Preston, Sir, they broke to pieces, and ran away like sheep, before a few highlanders. I myself saw them do the same thing at Falkirk, with very little difference, a small part only of the army making a stand, and in a few hours the whole retreating with precipitation before their enemies." He asked rhetorically, "Did that make any difference in the cause? Not in the least." When Bonnie Prince Charlie's army marched towards London, "the militia in England there gathered together, behaved fifty times worse than that of America has done lately. They generally disbanded and ran off wholly" as the Scots came "within ten or twenty miles of them." It was through the determination of the leaders of the nation, Witherspoon insisted, that they ultimately prevailed.[11]

"In short, Sir, from anything that has happened, I see not the least reason for our attending to this delusive message," Witherspoon concluded.

"On the contrary, I think it is the very worst time that could be chosen for us; as it will be looked upon as the effect of fear, and diffuse the same spirit, in some degree, through different ranks of men." Because of the first defeat, some might be having second thoughts about independence; the Congress must stand firm.

Besides, "I beg you would observe, Sir, that Lord Howe himself was fully sensible that the declaration of independence precluded any treaty, in the character in which he appeared; as he is said to have lamented that he had not arrived ten days sooner, before that declaration was made," the doctor pointed out. "Hence it appears, that entering into any correspondence with him in the manner now proposed, is actually giving up, or at least subjecting to a new consideration, the independence which we have declared. If I may be allowed to say it without offense, it seems to me that some members have unawares admitted this, though they are not sensible of it; for when they say that it is refusing to treat, unless the whole be granted us, they must mean that some part of that whole must be left to be discussed and obtained, or yielded, by the treaty." This, of course, was out of the question for both parties under the circumstances.

But others in Congress were seeing this as much as a propaganda ploy for public consumption. "They have considered it as necessary in the eye of the public, to satisfy them that we are always ready to hear anything that will restore peace to the country," Witherspoon asserted, knowing that "in this view it is considered as a sort of trial of skill between Lord Howe and us, in the political art." To illustrate the political effect, Witherspoon proceeded to divide America into three parties: the Tories, the Whigs and friends of independence, and the army.

The reverend doctor pointed out that the Tories "are earnest for our treating. They are exulting in the prospect of it; they are spreading innumerable lies to forward it. They are treating the whigs already with insult and insolence upon it. It has brought them from their lurking holes: they have taken liberty to say things in consequence of it, which they durst not have said before." Witherspoon feared that it would further encourage them. "In one word, if we set this negotiation on foot, it will give new force and vigour to all their seditious machinations."

"But, Sir, shall their devices have any influence upon us at all?" he asked, wondering whether Congress should be driven by their actions. "If they have at all, it should be to make us suspect that side of the question which they embrace. In cases where the expediency of a measure is doubtful, if I had an opportunity of knowing what my enemies wished me to do, I would not be easily induced to follow their advice," he succinctly observed.

"As to the whigs and friends of independence, I am well persuaded that multitudes of them are already clear in their minds, that the conference should be utterly rejected," Witherspoon flatly stated, "and to those who are in doubt about its nature, nothing more will be requisite, than a clear and full information of the state of the case, which I hope will be granted them." Congress was already doing this by publishing all of the correspondence in the newspapers.[12]

"As to the army, I cannot help being of opinion, that nothing will more effectually deaden the operations of war, than what is proposed," the New Jersey congressman feared. "We do not ourselves expect any benefit from it, but they will." Witherspoon was concerned that army morale, already damaged by the loss at Long Island, would be further shaken and the remaining soldiers "will possibly impute our conduct to fear and jealousy as to the issue of the cause; which will add to their present little discouragement, and produce a timorous and despondent spirit."[13]

Despite the well-reasoned arguments, on Friday, September 6, the majority of Congress chose the middle course and adopted the resolution authorizing a committee to meet with Lord Howe and find out exactly what powers he had to negotiate with persons authorized by Congress. John Sullivan was instructed to return to Lord Howe with a certified copy of the resolution in hand. Later that day, the hapless general left for New York; three days later, "this Morning Sullivan returned upon his parole, in a Boat bearing a Flag of Truce," Howe's secretary Ambrose Serle noted.[14]

"This day, I think, has been the most remarkable of all," John Adams wrote to Abigail on the evening of September 6. "Sullivan came here from Lord Howe, five days ago with a Message that his Lordship desired a half an Hours Conversation with some of the Members of Congress, in their private Capacities." Having spent "three or four days in debating whether We should take any Notice of it. I have, to the Utmost of my Abilities during the whole Time, opposed our taking any Notice of it," he told his wife. But the majority prevailed and the resolution was adopted.

"It would fill this Letter Book, to give you all the Arguments, for and against this Measure," John wrote. Howe was "playing off a Number of Machiavillian Maneuvres, in order to throw upon Us the Odium of continuing this War," he was certain. "Those who had been Advocates for the Appointment of this Committee, are for opposing Maneuvre to Maneuvre, and are confident that the Consequence will be, that the Odium will fall upon him."

And then, the remarkable happened. "When the Committee came to be ballotted for, Dr. Franklin and your humble servant were unanimously chosen," John revealed. Adams would represent New England; Franklin, the middle states. For the South, Edward Rutledge of South Carolina, who was in favor of the resolution, and Richard Henry Lee of Virginia, who opposed it, were also chosen, but Lee adamantly refused to go. John Adams, too, requested to be excused from the duty; Congress deferred and asked him to think about it overnight.

"My Friends here Advise me to go," John explained to Abigail. "All the stanch and intrepid are very earnest with me to go, and the timid and wavering, if any such there are, agree in the request." They prevailed on him, "so I believe I shall undertake the Journey." Given the resolution, Adams doubted whether Howe would even agree to see them, but if not, since they would be in the New York area, the committee would inquire into the condition of the army, "so that there will be Business enough, if his Lordship makes none."

John felt that there was another, more peevish reason why he was chosen. Referring to Thomas Hutchinson, the former royal governor of Massachusetts, "An Idea has crept into many Minds here that his Lordship is such another as Mr. Hutchinson, and they may possibly think that a Man who has been accustomed to penetrate into the mazy Windings of Hutchinsons Heart, and the serpentine Wiles of his Head, may be tolerably qualified to converse with his Lordship." With his spleen now vented, John decided to behave and hold his tongue, telling Abigail, "However this may be, my Lesson is plain, to ask a few Questions, and take his Answers."[15]

Adams knew that his participation in the commission would be viewed with disdain by some of his friends and colleagues in Massachusetts. "I was totis Viribus, against it, from first to last," he wrote to Col. James Warren on September 8. "But, upon this Occasion, New Hampshire, Connecticut, and even Virginia, gave way . . . All sides agreed in sending me." Many members also felt that Lord Howe might not receive the committee anyway, but if he did, Adams thought that by being there, "as little Evil might come of it, as possible."

John was especially concerned about the reaction of his cousin Sam, who "will rip, about this measure, and well he may." He would feel that it was going into the lion's den and mouth, no doubt. "Nothing I assure you but the unanimous Vote of Congress, the pressing Solicitation of the firmest Men in Congress, and the particular Advice of my own Colleagues, at least of Mr. Hancock and Mr. Gerry, would have induced me to accept this Trust," he told Warren.

As for his hot-blooded cousin, "Tomorrow Morning Dr. Franklin, Mr. Edward Rutledge and your humble servant sett off to see that rare Curiosity, Lord Howe," he wrote to the elder Son of Liberty later that day. "Don't imagine from this that a Panick has spread in Philadelphia," John reassured Sam Adams, "only refinement in Policy!"[16]

Franklin wrote Lord Howe a personal letter that same day. He had not replied Howe's last letter in mid-August "because I found that my Corresponding with your Lordship was dislik'd by some Members of Congress." The doctor was looking forward to speaking with Howe "vivâ voce"—by word of mouth, or in person—"as I am with Mr. Adams and Mr. Rutledge appointed to wait on your Lordship in consequence of a Desire you exprest in some Conversation with Gen. Sullivan, and of a Resolution of Congress made thereupon which that Gentleman has probably before this time communicated to you." Franklin told the admiral that they would set out the next morning and hoped "to be at Amboy on Wednesday about 9 aClock, where we should be glad to meet a Line from your Lordship, appointing the Time and Place of Meeting." Franklin offered two suggestions for a meeting place: "If it would be agreable to your Lordship, we apprehend that either at the House on Staten Island, opposite to Amboy"—the Billopp manor house—"or at the Governor's House in Amboy, we might be accommodated with a Room for the purpose."[17] He would be happy to contact his grandson William Temple Franklin to make the arrangements at the Governor's House.

Franklin sent the note with a cover letter to General Washington, requesting him to immediately forward it to Lord Howe. He also asked the commander in chief that "if an Answer comes to your hands, that you would send it to meet us at Amboy." Travel was difficult enough for the old doctor, but "what we have heard of the Badness of the Roads between that Place and New York, makes us wish to be spar'd that part of the Journey."[18]

The letters went off as quickly as possible to make the hundred-mile trip, first to New York City, and then to the *Eagle*, now anchored off Bedloe's Island. It must have been a hard ride by couriers day and night over wretched roads, for some thirty or so hours later, on the evening of September 9, "I received Information that Doctor Franklin, Mr. (John) Adams, and Mr. Rutledge would meet me at any appointed Place on the Morning of the 11th," Lord Howe reported to Lord Germain. In a curious twist, "General Howe's Presence being that Day necessary with the Army, he could not accompany me to the Meeting, which I appointed should be on Staten Island, opposite to the Town of Amboy."[19]

The admiral was going alone; upon receiving Franklin's note, he replied:

Eagle off Bedlows Island

Sepr. 10: 1776.

Lord Howe presents his compliments to Dr. Franklin, and according to the tenor of his favour of the 8th. will attend to have the pleasure of meeting him and Messrs. Adams and Rutledge tomorrow morning at the house on Staten Island opposite to Amboy, as early as the few conveniencies for travelling by land on Staten Island will admit. Lord Howe upon his arrival at the place appointed, will send a boat (if he can procure it in time) with a flag of truce over to Amboy. And requests the Dr. and the other gentlemen will postpone their intended favour of passing over to meet him untill they are informed as above of his arrival to attend them there.

In case the weather should prove unfavourable for Lord Howe to pass in his boat to Staten Island tomorrow as from the present appearance there is some reason to suspect, he will take the next earliest opportunity that offers for that purpose. In this intention he may be farther retarded, having been an invalid lately; but will certainly give the most timely notice of that inability. He however flatters himself he shall not have occasion to make farther excuses on that account.[20]

Despite all of the roadblocks, machinations, and political hoop-dancing over the past two years, the time had come. Richard Lord Howe was going to single-handedly try to stop the American Revolution.

Chapter 14

"Between hawk and buzzard."

ᢗᡒᢩ

As the debate over an appropriate response to Admiral Howe's overtures began to heat up in Congress, Nicholas Cresswell was "determined to go to New York and make my escape to the English Army." On September 2, the same day that General Sullivan delivered Howe's message, Cresswell went to the State House and "waited on Mr. Jefferson, who gave me a pass written by Mr. John Hancock, Pres. of the Congress." A week or so earlier, having settled his accounts in Virginia, the young man had borrowed a horse from Mr. Kirk to get to Philadelphia. Since he would not be returning, his Loyalist friend "Marchington will send the horse to Leesburg." Cresswell was desperate, saying, "In short, I have no other alternative, if I stay amongst the *Sleber*, I must go to *Liaj*."[1] He had to get to New York as quickly as possible.

Cresswell's journey over the next few days provides an interesting view of the country at war and the difficulties of travel in the summer of 1776. Except for express riders, who rode alone on relays of swift horses and could average about six miles per hour in dry conditions, the fastest way to go between Philadelphia and New York in the 1770s was by Bessonett's Flying Machines. These were not aircraft but fast-moving "stage wagons," so named because the trip progressed in stages and the horses were changed every twenty or so miles, allowing travelers a few brief opportunities for meals and personal needs. The wagons could seat a dozen passengers more or less, who paid twenty shillings for a one-way trip before the war.[2] The price included meals, lodging for two nights, and allowed up to fifteen pounds of carry-on baggage per person.

This service had been introduced by Charles Bessonett of Bristol, Pennsylvania, with advertisements appearing in the *Pennsylvania Gazette* as early as 1771. Bessonett's ad in 1773 described his overland stage line as "the first attempt of its kind in America," promising the speed and safety of "four setts of excellent horses, with sober and good coachmen," a bonus in an era notorious for wagon drivers slaking their thirsts too frequently at roadside taverns.[3] Two decades later, when numerous stage lines plied their trade between the two cities, a traveler on this same route complained that "the carriages are very high, long and narrow, and the drivers, who are almost always slightly drunk, drive so fast that accidents are excessively common."[4]

The Flying Machine was scheduled to depart from the Cross Keys Tavern on the corner of Third and Chestnut Streets at 6 A.M. on Mondays and Thursdays, with earlier departures during the summer months. The wagon journeyed to Princeton, New Jersey, on the first day, a distance of forty-two miles, where it "meets the New York stage and exchanges passengers." This part of the trip, which included full stops for breakfast and dinner, would usually take about fourteen hours in good weather.

The travelers stayed overnight in Princeton and continued at daybreak on the New York stage another forty-two miles to Newark. Early on the third morning, the stage made the final two-to-three-hour leg on tortuous roads through flat meadowlands and around mosquito-infested salt marshes to Paulus (or Powles) Hook, across the Hudson River from New York City. From there, a ferry boat took the passengers to Manhattan, where they would arrive about 9 A.M., some fifty or so hours after leaving Philadelphia.

There were other routes before the war—via Elizabethtown or Perth Amboy to Staten Island—but the British presence on the island in 1776 required a shift of routes to Newark. The straight-line distance between Market Street and Wall Street is about ninety miles, but the actual journey covered nearly a hundred miles in little more than thirty hours of riding. The length of time varied largely depending on the weather, which significantly affected road conditions as well as stream crossings. There were no bridges over the Delaware or Hudson Rivers at that time, so travelers had to cross on ferry boats powered by oars, sails, or both, at the mercy of crosswinds and tides. Many of the creeks en route had to be forded, and rain could quickly make them impassable.

Outside the cities, none of the roads were paved, so they were dusty in dry weather, especially in the heat of summer, and frequently mired after rain. The soil in much of central New Jersey is sandy, which added its own peculiar conditions to travel. And, in the summer of 1776, with hundreds of wagons and thousands of men and horses continuously tramping up and back from the New York area week after week, the roads became severely rutted. Never before had this area seen so much concentrated, continuous traffic in such a short period of time.

Then there was the vehicle itself. The Flying Machine was a long wagon with a flat roof, open on the sides and fitted with button-down leather flaps in case of inclement weather or choking dust. "These stages are usually drawn by four horses and have nine or twelve places, on benches without backs, three people to each bench," a contemporary traveler wrote, adding, "the space is hardly ever sufficient for three." To get in and out of the vehicle, "The front is open, because the driver always sits on the first bench. It is through the front that one gets into the back of the carriage, by stepping over the benches." As for the fifteen pounds of baggage allowed each person, "the passengers are crowded in together, unable to stretch their legs because their baggage is placed beneath the benches."[5] Travelers had to hang on for dear life while the horses alternately trotted, cantered, or galloped at the whim of the driver, heedless of ruts, potholes and "plashes"—great big muddy puddles. But these travelers were spoiled, for springs had recently been added to the backless benches for comfort.

The sun rose at 5:33 A.M. on Thursday, September 5, ushering in a pleasant summer day with sunshine and clouds. It was a perfect day to travel: the temperature near Philadelphia was 65 degrees F. at 7 A.M. and a light, northwest breeze kept the area cool all day.[6] "Set out from Philadelphia about 5 o'clock this morning in a vehicle neither coach nor waggon but between both," Cresswell stated. "It holds 15 persons and is not uneasy travelling."[7]

Some four hours after setting off, the group "breakfasted at *The Wheatsheaf* 12 miles," stopping for about half an hour. Five miles on they "Crossed Shammory [Neshaminy] Ferry," where the wagon was carried across Neshaminy Creek on a large raft pulled with the aid of a rope. An hour later, around noon, "Stopped at Bristol, a small town opposite Burlington where we changed Horses, 20 miles from Philadelphia," probably at the Sign of King George III tavern, kept by stage line owner Charles Bessonett, who also operated a ferry crossing the Delaware River to Burlington.

Ten miles above Bristol, the Flying Machine "Crossed Delaware River at Trenton Ferry," a challenging undertaking because of the strong current above and below the Trenton falls. By this time it was mid-afternoon, and the stage paused for an hour. "Dined at Trenton," Cresswell remarked, "this is a small town and very little trade." Trenton had but two main streets and perhaps fifty houses. One of the largest buildings in town was a stone barracks capable of housing three hundred men, part of a chain of barracks built in New Jersey towns twenty years earlier during the French and Indian War.

About 4 P.M. they were back on the road for the last leg of the day's journey. Six miles, or two hours' riding brought them "through a small town or rather village called Maidenhead [now Lawrenceville]." The sun set shortly before half past six that day, but the moon, waning in its last quarter, did not rise until just before midnight, so the final miles were covered in ever-deepening dusk. Another six miles brought them to the end of the day in the dark, around 8 P.M., where they "lodged at Prince-town."

Before turning in for the night, Cresswell made a few observations about the village and the College of New Jersey (now Princeton University). "This is a neat Little town with an Elegant College for the education of Youth," he commented. The college's radical Presbyterian president, Rev. Dr. John Witherspoon, had delivered an eloquent, impassioned address denouncing Lord Howe's proposals that very day in Congress. Of Nassau Hall, the college building, Nicholas wrote, "I believe there are 60 rooms in it for the students, each room has two closets and two beds, a Chapel, Library and Schoolroom. Cellars and storerooms complete." He also viewed two of the scientific wonders of North America, which many visitors were proudly shown: David Rittenhouse's orrery, an extraordinary mechanical model of the solar system; and a device for making and storing electricity in glass Leyden jars. "Saw the Orrery and Electrical Machine made by the famous David Written-house. Electrical machine and apparatus not complete." Rittenhouse, an ingenious mathematician, scientist, and clockmaker, was an important leader of the Pennsylvania Board of War and chairman of the Philadelphia Council of Safety who devoted his talents in 1776 to establishing facilities for manufacturing gunpowder and muskets.

Cresswell noted that the passengers "Lodged at The Sign of Hudibras," a popular tavern standing on the corner of Nassau Street and College Lane, within a few yards of Nassau Hall. The tavern was a substantial, L-shaped stone building with a wide porch along its front. It was also fairly new; on a frigid January night in 1773, "the whole house was laid in ashes" by a catastrophic fire, but it was soon rebuilt and back in business.[8] In 1774, on his way to the First Continental Congress, John Adams stayed here, writing on August 27, "About 12 O Clock We arrived at the Tavern in Prince Town, which holds out the Sign of Hudibrass, near Nassau Hall Colledge." Adams

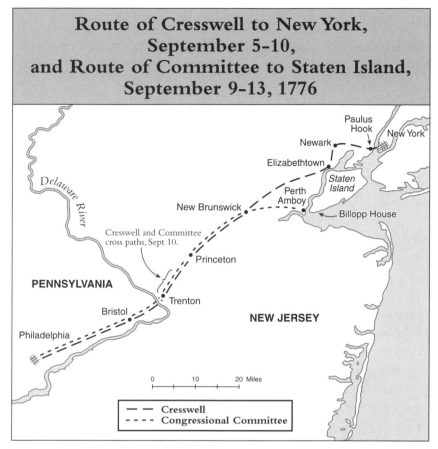

**Route of Cresswell to New York,
September 5–10,
and Route of Committee to Staten Island,
September 9–13, 1776**

The route between Philadelphia and New York, showing the journey of the congressmen to the Staten Island Conference. Nicholas Cresswell's trip to New York City followed the same route until he reached the area of New Brunswick.

lodged for two nights and noted, "The Tavern Keepers name is Hire." Jacob Hyer, like many tavern keepers, was now a militia officer, appointed lieutenant colonel of the 3rd Regiment Middlesex County Militia three weeks before Cresswell's arrival.[9]

The second stage of the journey resumed the next morning at daybreak when the Flying Machine "left Prince-town. Passed thro' Kingstown. Breakfasted at Brunswick," fifteen miles and four or five hours from Princeton. "This is a small trading town," Cresswell observed, "situated on Rareaton River, which is navigable to the town for small craft." Brunswick, or New Brunswick, had direct trade by water with New York, but only by small craft,

147

which had to wind down the Raritan River and around Staten Island to the Narrows at the mouth of New York harbor. Brunswick, too, had a stone barracks for three hundred troops, described by John Adams as "tolerably handsome."[10]

After breakfast, the stage wagon crossed the Raritan on a wooden bridge, the only long bridge on the route. Nicholas commented that the land was good and that there were "several pleasant seats along the Banks," meaning elegant country houses. Twelve miles on, around 1 P.M., "Changed horses at Woodbridge and paid the other half of the fare, 11s. here and 10s. at Philadelphia. This is a small, neat town." The stage drove another ten miles, and about 4, "Dined at Elizabeth town, this is a small town of some trade" and the main outpost for the New Jersey militia, along with units of the Flying Camp.

Six miles beyond Elizabethtown, as dusk settled in about 7 P.M., the travelers "lodged at Newark," which Cresswell described as "nothing more than a Village." He was now deep in the war zone and briefly noted, "Country populous in general but now in distraction," meaning in great turmoil and confusion. "Land along the Rivers good," but "hills rather poor," he keenly observed. With his personal predicament never far from his mind, Nicholas also mused, "Believe one of the company is a Spy upon my actions."

The day had been cloudy and cool, but the weather was about to change, as the wind shifted northeast. Rain in the night and early morning mist reduced visibility considerably. At daybreak, on the last leg of the trip, the stage wagon "left Newark. Crossed Passihack or Second River, then Hackensack River, then North River at Powlershook Ferry." Each of these crossings was slow and tedious as the road snaked through mosquito-infested salt marshes and the stage wagon had to cross the winding Passaic and Hackensack Rivers on flat ferry boats.

The North, or Hudson River, was the most difficult to navigate, with very strong currents and shifting tides. It required a large ferry boat with sails and oars, crossing at Paulus Hook. The weather conditions in New York harbor by mid-morning were "fresh Breezes & hazey" as recorded in the log book of the *Eagle*, anchored down the river at Bedloe's Island.[11] "River about $1^1/_2$ miles wide," Cresswell noted, "landed in New York about nine o'clock, when one Collins, an Irish merchant, and myself rambled about the town till three in the afternoon before we could get anything for breakfast."[12]

When the war broke out, New York had a population of about thirty thousand, concentrated in less than a square mile at the lower tip of Manhattan Island. On the day Cresswell arrived, the population was anybody's guess, for the city was essentially under siege at that moment, nearly surrounded by British forces and occupied by hundreds of Continental troops. "We may be properly said to be between hawk and buzzard," Washington's adjutant general Joseph Reed had written the day before. It was somewhat unsettling, Reed felt, for "I look around and see how few of the numbers who talked so largely of death and honour around me," he told his wife. "Your noisy Sons of Liberty I find are the quietest on the field."[13] Few things are more effective in silencing the loudmouths and emptying the bandwagons than a defeat, especially in war; real heroes do their duty without fanfare, despite the setbacks. The "summer soldiers and sunshine patriots," as Thomas Paine so aptly termed them a few months later, were already shrinking from the service.

Loyalists abounded in town, though not publicly at this time. The mayor of New York, David Matthews, was under arrest. Back in June, Washington received information "that a most horrid plot was on foot by the vile Torys of this place and the Adjacent Towns and Villages," Col. Samuel Webb noted. On Washington's orders, at 2 A.M. on June 21, "a number of Officers & Guards went to different places & took up many of their principles; among whom, was David Matthews, Esqr., Mayor of the City; and to our great astonishment we found five or more of the General's life Guard to be accomplices in this wicked plan." The plot called for the blowing up of the powder magazine, spiking the guns in the batteries, and assassinating Washington and other generals as soon as the British fleet appeared. "But thank God, they are discovered," Webb went on, relieved, "and many of them in close Custody; where, I hope, they will receive the punishment due such Infamous wretches." Matthews later managed to escape to the British, but at least one of the Life Guards, Thomas Hickey, "was hang'd, in presence of most of the Army—besides great numbers of others—spectators."[14]

By September, thousands of residents had left town, and with nearly all regular commerce at a standstill, food was scarce. "At length we found a little Dutch tippling house and persuaded the old woman to get us something to eat," Cresswell wrote. "It was a stew of pork bones and cabbage so full of Garlic, nothing but necessity would have compelled me to eat it, my companion would not taste another mouthful," he recalled with disgust, adding, "Nothing to be got here."[15]

The only thriving commercial operations in town involved military personnel, with high-ranking officers occupying some of the better taverns and houses, while troops billeted in all sorts of buildings. There were also the usual forms of entertainment found in ports and military towns: cheap taverns and taprooms, brothels, and black market operators. At the notorious "holy ground," New York's oldest "pick-up" spot not far from the Bowling Green, "The inhabitants of the holy ground has brought some of the officers and a number of the soldiers into difficulty," Col. Loammi Baldwin of Massachusetts wrote home. "The whores (by information)"—meaning "or so he heard," he hastened to tell his wife—"continue their imploy which is become very lucrative." Any modesty or virtue in a person must be lost to anyone associating with "these bitchfoxly jades, jills, haggs, strums, prostitutes and all these multiplyed into one another," Baldwin shuddered. His occasional duty as officer of the day required him to take a guard escort around town, where he "broke up the knots of men and women fighting, pulling caps, swearing, crying 'Murder', etc—hurried them off to the Provost dungeon by half dozens," at which place "some are punished and sum get off clear—Hell's work," to be sure.[16]

In late August, Washington had issued a proclamation from headquarters ordering "women, children, and infirm persons yet remaining in the city" to evacuate. By now, "all the inhabitants are moved out," Cresswell jotted in his journal, "the town full of Soldiers." He spent the remainder of September 7th "viewing the town and fortifications and contriving means to effect my escape." Roaming up one street and down another, he began to "despair of it, the Rivers are too well guarded."

While wandering the streets, Cresswell made astute observations about New York. "This town is the best situated for trade of any place I ever saw," he noted. "It is on a point of Land with wharfs two thirds of the way round the town and very near the Sea. The town is not so regular as Philadelphia, nor so extensive, neither has it so many good buildings, but more elegant ones both public and private." For the soul, "here are three English Churches, the old Trinity Church, St. Paul's and St. George's Chapel, two Dutch Churches, four dissenting [Calvinist] meeting houses, one Quaker Meeting, and a Jews' Synagogue and a French Church"; for the health of mind and body, "a College and Hospital, two elegant buildings." Recently, down at the Bowling Green, just after the Declaration of Independence was read, "there was a fine equestrian statute of his Majesty, but the *Sleber* has pulled it down and cast it into Bullets," forty-two thousand musket balls reportedly, the gilded royal figure being made of lead.

Further on, "the Statue of the Earl of Chatham is still standing unhurt in the attitude of an apple woman, dressed like a Roman Orator." Sir

William Pitt, Earl of Chatham, was a hero of the Whigs, so his statue was not defaced—yet. "I am not a judge, but don't think it clever," Nicholas commented. "The liberty pole, as they call it, is covered with Iron bars."

Washington's troops had built batteries in the city along the North and East Rivers, and many of the streets were barricaded. On the banks of the East River for several miles above the city, the Continentals were now frantically digging entrenchments opposite Long Island, where the British army was in plain view. "Streets fortified with small batteries towards the River," Cresswell observed. The town was so full of military personnel that "my fellow-traveller, Mr. Collins, and I should have lodged in the streets, had we not luckily met one Godard, Postmaster, who got us a sorry lodging at the Hull Tavern," the old City Arms Tavern kept by Robert Hull on the west side of Broadway at No. 18, on the corner of Stone Street (now Thames Street).[17]

Like many buildings in port cities, Hull Tavern had a viewing platform on the roof, a place where patrons and merchants could keep an eye out for ships in the harbor. "From the top of this house have a prospect of Long Island, Staten Island, Governor's Island, Bedlow's Island and Gilbert's [Ellis] Island, three last small ones," all within a mile or two. After months of anxiety and despair, together with the stress of having traveled more than three hundred miles in the past two weeks, Nicholas's goal was finally within sight.

The most powerful military force in the world at that moment was before his eyes. Through the haze to the south and east was Long Island, where the bulk of General Howe's army, nearly twenty-four thousand strong, stretched from Brooklyn to Hell Gate. To the southwest, the masts and rigging of over four hundred vessels—more than forty percent of the world's most powerful navy—appeared like a tangled gray forest across the horizon from the Narrows to Staten Island, where another six thousand royal troops were stationed. Closer was Governor's Island, recently evacuated by the Americans and now home to hundreds of royal troops within cannon shot of the city. Behind that, a little more than a mile out to the west, was Bedloe's Island (now Liberty Island). Here HMS *Eagle* rode at anchor, the large white ensign with the red cross of St. George fluttering from her foremast, where Admiral Howe awaited word from Philadelphia about his proposed meeting. Other large British ships-of-the-line, such as the sixty-four-gun *Asia*, and frigates like the forty-four-gun *Roebuck*, were anchored near the *Eagle*.

Almost unbelievably, Nicholas's escape was not to be. "All the British Fleet and part of the Army make a fine appearance," he scribbled with what must have been indescribable frustration, "but it is utterly out of my power to get to them. I never, till now, thought of it, but honour forbids it, as I am enabled to travel by the interest of Mr. Mason." After all he had been through, Nicholas abruptly gave this rather unconvincing explanation and left it at that for the moment, commenting only, "Was I to make my escape, he might be reflected on."[18]

As darkness fell across New York harbor on that Saturday night, September 7, 1776, few had any idea that an historic moment in naval warfare was about to begin. Over on the North River, from somewhere on the edge of the city not far from the little village of Greenwich, a dozen New England men unloaded two very large wooden kegs from some wagons and carefully eased them into the river. Three whaleboats towed the kegs out into the Hudson and began rowing them down towards Bedloe's Island.

On board the *Eagle*, Capt. Henry Duncan noted in the log book, "At $^1/_2$ past 10 the out Guard Boats made the alarm Signal, fired a Gun & made the signal for sending the Guard Boats to their Assistance." Lord Howe's secretary, Ambrose Serle, wrote in his journal, "A slight alarm happened to-night from the Enemy's Boats approaching too near: they were soon driven back by the Musketry in our Boats." The secretary guessed that "their Intention was, as we apprehended, to bring down 2 or 3 Fire-ships to set adrift in the Fleet."[19]

What was known only to the Americans in the whaleboats and a very few other people is that the first submarine attack in recorded history was underway. David Bushnell, a Yale undergraduate, had been tinkering for years with the idea of a submersible vessel capable of attaching an explosive device to the bottom of an enemy ship. The result of his curious idea was the *Turtle*, a one-man submarine propelled by hand and maneuvered by oars. The vessel resembled a large barrel and was able to submerge or surface with the aid of hand-operated pumps and a massive, detachable lead weight on the bottom as ballast. Towed behind it was an egg-shaped "powder magazine" or "torpedo" chiseled out of two massive pieces of solid oak and filled with one hundred and fifty pounds of gunpowder. This device would be attached to the bottom of an enemy hull by the operator using an auger and a large screw. Once attached, the operator could activate an ingenious flintlock timing mechanism invented by Bushnell and set off a massive underwater explosion.

After extensive testing in Connecticut and the training of Bushnell's brother as the operator, the *Turtle* was secretly moved down the coast of Connecticut to New Rochelle, New York, where it was carried overland in

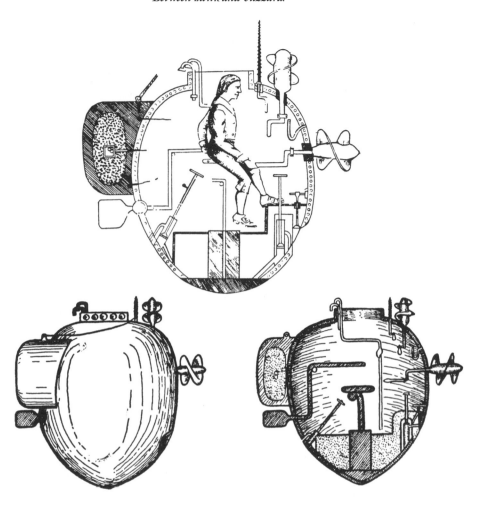

The Turtle, *as described by David Bushnell. The torpedo is mounted on the left above the*
rudder. DOVER PUBLICATIONS (FROM *THE AMERICAN REVOLUTION: A PICTURE SOURCEBOOK*)

wagons to the North River. Its mission: destroy the flagship of the British
fleet, the HMS *Eagle*, and in all probability eliminate one of the two most
powerful British commanders in America, Admiral Richard Lord Howe.

While waiting for calm tides on a night with minimum moonlight, the
operator fell ill, probably from camp fever, which was raging through the
American army. Sgt. Ezra Lee of Connecticut then volunteered to operate
the submarine. After some rudimentary training, the mission set off toward
Bedloe's Island on the hazy night of September 7 and went as close to the
British guard boats as they dared.

The outgoing tide carried the *Turtle* below Bedloe's Island, so Lee had to laboriously crank the propeller to get back up to the ship. Under a waning crescent moon, it was nearly 2 A.M. before he was able to get near his target.[20] He came under the stern of the *Eagle*, close enough to hear talking on the deck. The sergeant submerged into the pitch-black water and inched forward, hoping to find the keel, his only light being from some phosphorescent material called "foxfire" on the *Turtle's* compass. Then, disappointment: He could not get the bolt to screw into the keel. Later suggestions that it was because of the *Eagle's* copper-sheathed hull were erroneous; the hull wasn't sheathed at the time, and thin, soft copper plates could have been pierced by the auger anyway. The *Turtle* was under the stern, and a long, thick iron plate, which fixed the rudder to the keel, was the probable culprit. David Bushnell felt afterwards that a more skillful operator might have been able to shift several inches and find wood.

Whatever the cause, Lee was unable to attach the torpedo and the mission failed. The *Turtle* contained only enough air to remain submerged for half an hour, so the pilot was forced to surface. As the sky began to lighten, he began to furiously propel the submarine and torpedo across the harbor toward the East River with the incoming tide.

According to Lee, British soldiers on Governor's Island spotted the strange craft at a distance and sent out a rowboat to investigate, so he released the torpedo and submerged. The British saw only a large, floating piece of wood; fortunately for them, they turned back. An hour later, the torpedo, "after getting a little past the Island, went off with a tremendous explosion, throwing up large bodies of water to an immense height," Sergeant Lee recalled.[21] Had the *Turtle's* mission succeeded, it might well have killed Lord Howe and significantly changed the subsequent course of events.

It is not known for certain whether Cresswell heard the blast. "Left New York early this morning," he scribbled in his journal that day, "Crossed the North River to Powlershook." While on the Hudson, he "heard a smart cannonade crossing the Ferry this morning, *supposed* to be at Hellgate," a few miles up the East River.[22] Lt. Col. Stephen Kemble, General Howe's deputy adjutant general, confirmed that "Our Batteries opened early in the morning upon the Rebel Redoubt at Hornes Hook," not far from Hell Gate.[23] Whether what Cresswell heard in the distance was only the British batteries or also the *Turtle's* torpedo exploding in the East River (or possibly both) is not absolutely clear.

Once at Paulus Hook, "while we waited for the Stage," Cresswell "viewed the *Sleber* Fortifications here. They are made of earth, but what

number of Guns or what size I cannot tell. No admittance into the Fort."
As for the soldiers, "The Troops stationed here are Yankee men, the nastiest
Devils in creation." He gave a graphic description of the conditions found
in many of the American military camps: "It would be impossible for any
human creature whose organs of smelling was more delicate than that of a
hog to live one day under the Lee of this Camp, such a complication of
stinks." He also commented, "The Army here is numerous, but ragged,
dirty, sickly, and ill-disciplined. If my countrymen are beaten by these raga-
muffins I shall be much surprized."

The food combinations were disgusting. Army food was often scarce
and never epicurean, and regional American tastes were downright strange
to many Europeans. Much like ketchup in the contemporary American diet,
molasses was a common condiment, especially among New Englanders in
the army. Outside the fort at Paulus Hook, Cresswell almost gagged when
he "Saw a Yankee put a pint of molasses into about a gallon of Mutton
Broth." Later, concerning food available in New York, he commented,
"Some droll cookery here. Molasses in everything, even to Salt pork. They
are right Yankees."[24]

It being a Sunday, travel was somewhat slower. "Got to Newark to dinner," he wrote, only a few miles from Paulus Hook, "Great scarcity of provisions." He also noted, "the roads full of soldiers." After his night in New
York, he felt "Very uneasy. Must be obliged to go into Canada or stay in
this Damn'd Country."[25]

Some months later, Nicholas revealed why he had to head back to Virginia so suddenly. He was planning to escape from New York "by means of
a floating stage that was moored in the old Ship," probably referring to a
waterfront tavern. "No other thing, either Boat or Canoe, was to be found,"
he said. But then, he was spotted by "Mr. Thomson, a Presbyterian Parson
and Chaplain to one of the Virginia Regiments." Cresswell had had a quarrel with this "puritanic Priest" two years earlier, probably in Alexandria,
where he had been disgusted with the fire-and-brimstone political sermons
at the local Presbyterian meetings. Nicholas's friend Thomson Mason had
already bailed him out of political trouble on two occasions, but now he
bumped into this chaplain in New York, who "behaved with the greatest
politeness, only took care to put a guard over me."

Suspecting the young man's motives in coming to New York, the
preacher told Cresswell that he was going to hand him over to the provost
marshal unless he immediately returned to Virginia under escort. Nicholas
lied to the parson, saying he came to New York only out of curiosity, but

Reverend Thomson would have none of it. He sent a Lieutenant Noland along with Cresswell as an escort to guarantee his return to Virginia. "Had it not been for the thoughts of him being a guard over me," Nicholas said regrettably of Noland, he "would have been an excellent companion."[26]

On Monday, September 9, Cresswell and his guard "Left Newark. Breakfasted at Elizabeth town. Dined at Brunswick. Lodged at Prince-town." He again observed, "Great numbers of soldiers on the road. Our company chiefly Irishmen."[27] The next morning, September 10, the Flying Machine left Princeton and continued on its way to Philadelphia, stopping in Trenton for breakfast.

Somewhere that morning, among the crowds of soldiers and travelers on the road between Princeton and Trenton, or possibly in Trenton itself, Cresswell passed two small, horse-drawn "chairs" and a horseman heading in the opposite direction. They were on their way to Staten Island to meet with Lord Howe, who was looking for a way to change the course of history.

CHAPTER 15
September 11, 1776

━━◆◆◆━━

Exactly where on the road Cresswell passed the committee as they were heading to Staten Island on the morning of September 10 is unknown. John Adams gave the best description of the sojourn a quarter of a century later in his autobiography. Though his recollection of some minor details was faulty, in no way does it diminish the tale; rather, the particulars of the story are enhanced with support from other sources.

The excursion began on September 9, when, "On this day, Mr. Franklin, Mr. Edward Rutledge and Mr. John Adams proceeded on their Journey to Lord Howe on Staten Island, the two former in Chairs and the last on Horseback," Adams recalled. Franklin was seventy years old, the oldest member of Congress, and rode in a "chair," a light, two-wheeled carriage literally carrying a chair and drawn by a single horse. Rutledge, at age twenty-seven, was the youngest member; given his age, chances are good that it was Ned Rutledge who rode on horseback.

Did Adams go on horseback, as the autobiography says, or was he in a chair, as was Franklin? In the previous weeks, Adams had complained repeatedly about how exhausted he was from the endless work in Congress. He was forty-one years old, serving on multiple committees, living and working alone without an amuensis [secretary] to help with his voluminous correspondence. This, along with other health-related issues and comments he wrote at the time in his diary, makes it likely that he also rode in a chair.[1]

John's autobiography also states, "the first night We lodged at an Inn, in New Brunswick," suggesting that the delegation made the sixty-mile trip to New Brunswick in one day. This simply did not happen; given the weather, the road conditions, his own physical condition, and the fact that Dr. Franklin was seventy years old and suffering from gout, kidney stones, and old age, the delegation probably went no further than Trenton, halfway to Brunswick, on the first night.

The next morning, September 10, dawned gray and rainy in both Philadelphia and New York, so travel would have been slower than usual. "On the Road and at all the public Houses, We saw such Numbers of Officers and Soldiers, straggling and loytering, as gave me at least, but a poor Opinion of the Discipline of our forces and excited as much indignation as anxiety," John wrote, seeing many of the same men that Cresswell saw. "Such thoughtless dissipation at a time so critical, was not calculated to inspire very sanguine hopes or give great Courage to Ambassadors," he admitted, but "I was nevertheless determined that it should not dishearten me."

The congressmen would have arrived at New Brunswick in the evening, the distance being thirty miles from Trenton over badly mired roads. "The Taverns were so full We could with difficulty obtain Entertainment," John said. "At Brunswick, but one bed could be procured for Dr. Franklin and me, in a Chamber little larger than the bed, without a Chimney and with only one small Window." This was where their argument over opening or shutting the window took place, when John received a lecture from Franklin about the health benefits of fresh air.[2] Where and under what conditions Rutledge stayed that night is not presently known, but being a young man, he may well have 'roughed it' and stayed in the common room.

Before turning in for the night, Ben wrote a letter to his grandson, William Temple Franklin, who was still with his mother at the Proprietor's House in Perth Amboy:

Brunswick, Sept. 10, 1776.

Dear Grandson,

It is possible that a Line from Lord Howe may be left for me at your good Mother's, as I have appointed to be there to morrow Morning, in order to meet a Notice from his Lordship relating to the Time & Place of a proposed Interview. If it should come there to-night, or very early in the Morning I could wish you would set out with it on horseback so as to meet us on the Road not far from hence, that if N York should be the Place, we may not go so far out of our way as Amboy would be. Besides I should be glad to see you. My Love to your Mother. Mr

Adams & Mr Rutledge are with me. If Amboy or the House opposite to us on Staten Island is to be the Place of a Meeting we shall want private Lodgings there.

I am as ever, Your affectionate Grandfather,
B Franklin

[P.S.] If no Letter is come to your House enquire at Headquarters if any for me is come there: but do not mention from whom, or the Occasion.[3]

September 11, 1776, dawned cloudy and damp after the previous day's rain. "The first part [of the day] Moderate & fair, Middle & later light airs & Cloudy," Capt. Henry Duncan noted in his journal on the *Eagle*, anchored off Bedloe's Island.[4] The three congressmen rose early in the New Brunswick tavern and made their way to Perth Amboy, a three-to-four-hour journey over muddy, severely rutted roads. It was probably there that Franklin received Lord Howe's note informing him that the meeting would be held at the Billopp house. By 9 A.M. they were on the shore of the Arthur Kill, waiting for a boat to take them over the water.

Across the river, at the Hessian outpost by the Billopp House, "Admiral Lord Howe came to our camp in order to hold a private Conference with several members of the American Congress," Staff Secretary Lotheisen of the Leib Regiment wrote in the regimental journal. "A drummer of the Regiment was immediately dispatched by boat to Amboy under a flag of truce, with whom then the three Americans, including Franklin and Adams, returned to our camp."[5] Admiral Howe's gleaming red-and-gold barge, propelled by a dozen sailors rowing in perfect cadence, cast off from Staten Island and headed across the water with the German drummer and a British naval officer under a white flag. As the vessel approached the opposite shore, the Hessian musician, splendidly dressed in a blue-and-yellow coat heavily laced with red-and-white chevrons, stiffly and precisely beat a parley signal on his shining brass drum in accordance with prescribed military custom.

When the barge landed, the officer, spotlessly uniformed in Royal Navy blue and white, climbed out, uncovered his head, bowed courteously, and then stood aside as Franklin, Adams, and Rutledge climbed in. The officer did not climb in after them, but remained on the shore. Puzzled, John Adams asked him what he was doing. He politely informed the congressmen that he was "an Hostage for our Security." Adams, shocked by the very thought of such an arrangement, turned to Franklin and said, "It would be childish in us to depend upon such a Pledge and insisted on taking him over with us." Franklin and Rutledge heartily concurred. "We told the Officer, if he held himself under our direction he must go back with us," Adams related. The officer bowed, climbed in, and "we all embarked in His Lordship's Barge."[6]

Lord Howe was waiting for them on the other side, magnificently attired in an immaculate white and navy blue uniform trimmed with yards of thick gold lace. As the barge approached the shore, the admiral walked to the water's edge. Seeing the 'hostage' returning in the boat, Howe smiled ever so slightly and said, "Gentlemen, you make me a very high Compliment, and you may depend on it, I will consider it as the most sacred of Things."[7] The revolutionaries were in no danger of being placed under arrest.

With the admiral was one of his secretaries, Henry Strachey, who was there to take notes of the meeting. "Lord Howe received the Gentlemen on the Beach," Strachey wrote. "Dr. Franklin introduced Mr. Adams and Mr. Rutledge. Lord Howe very politely expressed the Sense he entertained of the Confidence they had placed in him, by thus putting themselves in his hands."[8] After the proper introductions, Howe escorted the men up to the house, chatting amiably.

Lining the path up the knoll were Hessian fusiliers of the Leib Regiment, who presented arms and saluted, following the complicated Prussian drill manual of a series of stiff motions and staccato commands barked in German. These soldiers wore fusilier caps, cone-shaped helmets fronted with a pointed tin plate embossed with the lion of Hesse-Cassel and backed with yellow wool trimmed with tin, all highly polished. The caps were similar to grenadier caps, but shorter. Many of these soldiers wore thick mustaches, blackened with wax and twirled into sharp points, making them look all the more ferocious. "We walked up to the House between Lines of Guards of Grenadiers, looking as fierce as ten furies," John Adams recalled, "and making all of the Grimaces and Gestures and motions of their Musquets with Bayonets fixed, which I suppose military Ettiquette requires but which We neither understood not regarded."[9] The blank stares and "war faces" of the Hessians could be intimidating, but John Adams and the others ignored them.

Admiral Howe had an unexpected surprise waiting for them in the house. Col. Friedrich von Wurmb was the commander of the Leib Regiment and had used the Billopp house for his headquarters. His staff secretary, Quartermaster Lotheisen, wrote, "Lord Howe met them with great condescension, entertained them at an elegant breakfast and shut himself in with them in a room which Colonel von Wurmb had placed at their dis-

Now called the Conference House, the Billopp House at 7455 Hylan Boulevard, Staten Island, was also known as the Manor of Bentley and is the oldest house in New York City. Constructed around 1680, it was almost a century old when Lord Howe met with Franklin, Adams, and Rutledge in his attempt to stop the revolution on September 11, 1776.
PHOTO BY KYLE R. WEAVER

posal, for nearly an hour."[10] Strachey noted that "A cold dinner was on the Table—[we] dined—the Hessian Colonel present."[11] John Adams was astonished: this sort of repast was called a "cold collation," and Howe "entertained Us with good Claret [red Bordeaux wine], good Bread, cold Ham, Tongues and Mutton."

It was the room decor, however, which made the event so striking and strange, even surreal. "The House had been the Habitation of military Guards, and was as dirty as a stable," Adams wrote. To cover the mess and keep down the stench, "his Lordship had prepared a large handsome Room, by spreading a Carpet of Moss and green Spriggs from Bushes and Shrubbs in the Neighbourhood, till he had made it not only wholesome but romantically elegant."[12] The sweet aroma of cut pine boughs masked the not-so-sweet stink of war.

Wanton destruction of property was a hallmark of this period and all of the armies were culpable, though the Hessians made a name for themselves in this regard. "I was very sorry to be informed (I think by Lord

Dunmore) that these People had committed already several Depredations, and even upon the Friends of Government," Strachey's counterpart Ambrose Serle had written in his journal shortly after the bulk of the Hessians had left Staten Island in late August. "I fear our Employment of these upon this Service will tend to irritate and inflame the Americans infinitely more than two or three British Armies." The Billopp family was Loyalist, yet their handsome manor house was now a foul-smelling wreck. The post had been occupied for seven weeks, first by British troops, then by the Hessians. "It is impossible to express the Devastations, which the Hessians have made upon the Houses & Country Seat of some of the Rebels," Serle continued on September 1, describing what he saw on Long Island. "All their Furniture, Glasses, Windows, and the very Hangings of the Rooms are demolished or defaced. This with the Filth deposited in them, make the Houses so offensive, that it is a penance to go into them."[13] Loyalist properties did not fare much better, first from the rebels, then from the Hessians.

Once the cold collation was finished and the table was cleared, Colonel von Wurmb left the room and closed the door. With Henry Strachey there to take notes, Lord Howe was now face-to-face alone with two of the key leaders of the American Revolution, Benjamin Franklin and John Adams, along with Edward Rutledge. It was an extraordinary moment in history.

Howe opened the discussion by saying that for a long time, "he had entertained an opinion that the Differences between the two Countries might be accommodated to the Satisfaction of both" and that "he was known to be a Well Wisher to America." As Boston had been the center of the rebellion, the admiral emphasized that he was especially endeared to the people of Massachusetts because of the monument they had erected in Westminster Abbey to the memory of his elder brother George Augustus, who was killed in the French and Indian War near Fort Ticonderoga.[14] "He lived respected and beloved," the inscription reads, "the Publick regretted his loss; to his family it is irreparable." The monument, a splendid marble allegory to the founder of British light infantry, remains prominently displayed inside the main door of the abbey. Admiral Howe "esteemed that Honour to his Family, *above all Things in this World,*" John Adams recalled him saying. "That such was his gratitude and affection to this Country, on that Account, that he felt for America, as for a Brother, and if America should fall, he should feel and lament it, like the Loss of a Brother."

In response, Franklin bowed to the admiral, and with "all that Naivetee which sometimes appeared in his Conversation and is often observed in his

Writings," smiled and said, "My Lord, We will do our Utmost Endeavours, to save your Lordship that mortification."

Adams observed that Howe "appeared to feel this, with more Sensibility, than I could expect." He looked hard at Franklin and said, "I suppose you will endeavour to give Us employment in Europe," meaning that the Americans would seek alliances there against Britain. No one answered; "not a Word nor a look from which he could draw any Inference, escaped any of the Committee," John wrote.[15]

The admiral told them that he had early on advocated reconciliation to the king, with himself as sole peace commissioner. He genuinely felt that his personal intervention might have been able to smooth the waters between the contending parties. When others suggested a joint commission, Howe protested, pressing to be sent alone and with a civil commission. His plan "was to have gone immediately to Philadelphia," he told the three Americans, and that "he had even objected to his Brother's being in the Commission, from the Delicacy of the Situation and his desire to take upon himself all the Reproach that might be the Consequence of it." After a great deal of politicking, "it was however thought necessary that the General should be joined in the Commission . . . having their hands upon the Two Services."[16]

Howe further stated "that he had hoped to reach America before the Army had moved." He alluded to the Olive Branch Petition, which had been sent to England by Congress in the summer of 1775, asking the king to intervene with Parliament on behalf of the colonies. Howe "did not doubt but if their Disposition had been the same as expressed in their Petition to the King," meaning that if they still regarded the king as their friend, "he should have been able to have brought about an Accomodation to the Satisfaction of both Countries—that he thought the Petition was a sufficient Basis to confer upon—that it contained Matter, which, with Candour & Discussion might be wrought into a Plan of Permanency." The admiral added that "he had however still flattered himself that upon the Grounds of the Petition, he should be able to do some good." What he neglected to mention was that the king had spurned the petition and declared the colonies out of his protection, asking Parliament to declare them in rebellion and to raise forces to subdue the rebellion. Those actions had changed the disposition of the colonies—permanently.

Lord Howe then told the congressmen "that they themselves had changed the ground since he left England by their Declaration of Independency." If the declaration could not be rescinded, then he could not proceed with further negotiation, as he had informed Franklin in his letter back in July. The admiral frankly told them that he did not have the power to treat with the colonies as anything but colonies; he could not acknowledge the legitimacy of the authority of Congress, nor "could he confer with these Gentlemen as a Committee of the Congress." This was a very important point, for "if they would not lay aside that Distinction, it would be improper for him to proceed." Howe softened the point by quickly adding that "he thought it an unessential Form, which might for the present lie dormant," and that they must allow him to consider them only as gentlemen of great ability and influence who were having a discussion to stop "the Calamities of War."

Howe emphasized the fact that he had gone out on a limb to do this, asking them to consider "the Delicacy of his Situation" and "the Reproach he was liable to, if he should be understood by any step of his, to acknowledge, or to treat with, the Congress." The admiral had to be very careful, as his enemies in the Ministry, Admiralty, and Parliament would scrutinize every syllable reported to them, hoping to find a misstep. His Lordship made it clear to the committee that "he hoped they would not by any Implication commit him upon that Point" and that "he was rather going beyond his Powers in the present Meeting."

Responding to the admiral's deep concern, Franklin interjected, "You may depend upon our taking care of that, my Lord," assuring him that he did not have to worry about the risk of speaking with them. The doctor said that the admiral may consider them as he chose so that "the Conversation might be held as amongst friends," but that the committee members were also free to consider themselves in their real character.[17]

John Adams was in agreement, with one caveat. "Your Lordship may consider me, in what light you please," the Massachusetts man quickly answered, looking the admiral in the eye, "and indeed I should be willing to consider myself, for a few moments, in any Character which would be agreeable to your Lordship, *except that of a British Subject.*"

Lord Howe paused, turned to Franklin and Rutledge and solemnly said, "Mr. Adams is a decided Character." John wasn't sure why Howe was so solemn at that moment. Years later, when ambassador to England, he was informed that the Privy Council had already "decided" that if and when the time came, he and a few others were not to be pardoned.[18]

Howe then advanced the point that "the Idea of a Congress might easily be thrown out of the Question at present," reasoning that "if Matters could be so settled that the King's Government should be reestablished, the Congress would of course cease to exist, and if they meant such Accommodation, they must see how unnecessary & useless it was to stand upon that Form which they knew they were to give up upon the Restoration of legal Government." While it certainly affirmed the British government's position, it essentially rendered the idea of Congress and all of its actions as meaningless. In many ways, it was an indication of how far apart the two sides were on the political field.

The Declaration of Independence "had since rendered him the more cautious of opening himself," he told the committee. Howe could not possibly negotiate with it in effect, but "if That were given up, there was still room for him to effect the King's Purposes." He went down the list of the king's purposes, which included the reform of Parliament's methods of interference in colonial legislation; the prompt redress of "real" grievances; the granting of pardons to most rebels; and a reunion established upon honorable terms. The congressmen well knew that Britain "expected Aid from America," meaning tax money, Howe cajoled them, and "that the Dispute seemed to be only concerning the Mode of obtaining it." Franklin replied, "That, we never refused, upon Requisition," meaning that the colonies had always contributed their fair share when asked, but not when imposed upon.[19] The tax money was the smallest part of the issue, the admiral countered, for it was America's "Commerce, her Strength, her Men, that we chiefly wanted."

This prompted a sneering laugh from the old doctor. "Aye, my Lord," Franklin chortled, "we have a pretty considerable Manufactory of Men," which Strachey took to mean "their numerous Army."[20]

The admiral was not amused. "It is desirable to put a stop to these ruinous Extremities, as well for the sake of our Country, as yours," Lord Howe pleaded. "When an American falls, England feels it. Is there no way of treading back this Step of Independency, and opening the door to a full discussion?"

Having stated his case, the admiral sat back to hear what the committee had to say. Franklin began by referring to the congressional resolution that allowed them to come to hear what powers the admiral actually had, and that if this conversation had no immediate good result, it might be useful in the future. He reiterated what Congress had discussed and what he had said to the admiral in his letters, that they could not expect happiness under British domination. "Forces had been sent out, and Towns destroyed," he told the admiral, and "all former Attachment was obliterated."[21]

John Adams went next, telling the admiral that "the Resolution of the Congress to declare the Independency was not taken up upon their own

Authority," but that it came from all of the states, "and that it was not in their power to treat otherwise than as independent States." On a personal note, John emphatically reiterated "his own Determination not to depart from the Idea of Independency." The "decided character" had been decided for a long time.

Edward Rutledge, whose personality John Adams unflatteringly described as "jejeune, inane and puerile," with bird-like mannerisms, such as shrugging shoulders, shifting eyes, and nodding head—"a perfect Bob-o'-Lincoln—a swallow, a sparrow," then spoke.[22] Although the youngest in age, "he had been one of the oldest Members of the Congress," a member since the beginning. Rutledge suggested that Britain would receive greater commercial advantages from an independent America, but "that it was impossible the People should consent to come again under the English Government." Speaking on behalf of South Carolina, he flatly told the admiral that even if Congress revoked independence, that South Carolina would never do so.[23] The others concurred.

Rutledge also brought up the controversial statement about taxation made by General Sullivan in his oral report to Congress, which did not appear in the written statement submitted by the general. "Sullivan had said, that his Lordship told him, he would sett the Act of Parliament wholly aside, and that Parliament had no right to tax America, or meddle with her internal Polity," Rutledge asserted. Admiral Howe answered that Sullivan "had misunderstood him, and extended his Words much beyond their import," leaving open the question of what Howe had actually said to the captive general on that topic.[24]

The two sides remained at loggerheads. Lord Howe then stated, "that if such were their Sentiments, he could only lament it was not in his Power to bring about the Accommodation he wished—that he had not Authority, nor did he expect he ever should have, to treat with the Colonies as States independent of the Crown of Great Britain—and that he was sorry the Gentlemen had had the trouble of coming so far, to so little purpose," echoing what Franklin had written to him back in July when he first arrived. The admiral admitted that "if the Colonies would not give up the System of Independency, it was impossible for him to enter into any Negotiation."

In a final grasp at straws, Franklin suggested that it would take as much time to float the ideas by their constituents as it would for Howe to get fresh instructions from London, about three months. The admiral responded that "it was in vain to think of his receiving Instructions to treat upon that ground." The room fell silent for a few moments.[25]

Then, Franklin suddenly broke the silence, saying, "Well my Lord, as America is to expect nothing but upon (total) unconditional Submission, and Your Lordship has no Proposition to make us, give me leave to ask whether, if we should make Propositions to Great Britain—not that I know, or am authorized to say we shall—you would receive and transmit them?"

When Franklin said the word "submission," Howe interrupted him, insisting that "Great Britain did not require unconditional Submission, that he thought what he had already said to them, proved the contrary, and desired the Gentlemen would not go away with such an Idea." Strachey noted to himself, "Perhaps Dr. Franklin meant Submission to the Crown, in opposition to their Principle of Independency." The admiral then said that he was not sure if he could avoid receiving "any Papers that might be put into his hands." He doubted the propriety of sending such papers to England, "but did not say that he would decline it."[26]

Further discussion was fruitless. "Their Arguments not meriting a serious Attention, the Conversation ended," Lord Howe wrote to Lord Germain. With cordial punctilio, the conference concluded, and "the Gentlemen returned to Amboy."[27]

CHAPTER 16

"They met, they talked, they parted."

⤳❧⤳

"They met, they talked, they parted," Lord Howe's secretary Ambrose Serle astringently remarked in his journal after learning the particulars of the Staten Island Conference. "And now, nothing remains but to fight it out against a Set of the most determined Hypocrites & Demagogues, compiled of the Refuse of the Colonies, that were ever permitted by Providence to be the Scourge of a Country."[1] Any lingering sparks of hope that America would willingly come back under British authority were finally extinguished.

The meeting to stop the revolution had lasted three hours, including the fine meal at the beginning. When it was over, Lord Howe's barge conducted the committee safely back to Perth Amboy and the congressmen then returned to New Brunswick, where they spent the night of September 11. From there at 10 P.M., Ned Rutledge wrote a letter to Washington, informing him "that our Conferrence with Lord Howe has been attended with no immediate Advantages. He declared that he had no Powers to consider us as Independent States, and we easily discover'd that were we still Dependent we would have nothing to expect from those with which he is vested." The admiral spoke only in general terms, Rutledge explained, but had no specific powers except to grant pardons upon submission. "This kind of Conversation lasted for several Hours & as I have already said without any Effect," he reported to the commander in chief. "Our Reliance continues therefore to be (under God) on your Wisdom & Fortitude & that of your Forces. That you may be as successful as I know you are worthy is my most sincere wish."[2]

Washington was going to need every ounce of wisdom and fortitude to face the coming onslaught, which resumed at Kip's Bay on September 14. Within the next week, New York was in British hands, and a suspicious fire would destroy more than five hundred buildings, mostly on the west side of Broadway, leaving a quarter of the city in ashes. Within three months, the Continental forces were systematically destroyed; Elizabethtown, Perth Amboy, and New Brunswick were occupied by royal troops; and Gen. William Howe could look across the Delaware River from Trenton at the remnants of Washington's army while Congress packed up and fled Philadelphia. Thomas Paine would aptly describe those days as "the times that try men's souls" in *The Crisis*.

Down in Philadelphia on September 11, Nicholas Cresswell was meeting with his Loyalist friends. Arriving the night before, he again noted that the town was full of soldiers and he could not get his former lodgings at The Black Horse on Market Street. "Dined at Mr. Brewer's," he wrote that night. "Spent the afternoon with Mr. Buchhannan. Lodged at Mrs. Stretch's," a boardinghouse on Second Street several doors up from Mrs. Yard's, where John Adams and Ned Rutledge had their quarters. Once more foiled in his attempt to return to England, Nicholas scribbled in despair, "My designs are frustrated. Spend a good deal of money to no sort of purpose. I must return to Virginia and endeavour to get to Canada."[3]

The September 11 edition of *The Pennsylvania Gazette* contained an advertisement from Cresswell's Loyalist friend, the "extravagant fop" to whom he entrusted Mr. Kirk's horse:

PHILIP MARCHINTON HATH removed his stock of GOODS, from his store in Market street, to his store at his Woollen Manufactory, in Front street, between Market and Chestnut streets, which are brown and black broadcloths, English and India black, pink, green, and cloth coloured paduasoys; blue, orange, and cloth coloured, plain and flowered sattin damask; striped and sprigged pink and white, and blue and white tobines; silk lorettas and charlottes; black and cloth coloured silk and hair grograms; cloth coloured silk breeches, black and cloth coloured silk stockings; blue, black and purple, best double top genuine cotton velvets; black and brown best silk and hair plush, &c. He continues taking in Wool; Spinners and Weavers may have full employ.[4]

Marchinton gleefully continued to manufacture and sell wool to uniform his enemies while biding his time, waiting for the revolution to collapse.

Out in Trappe on September 11, Rev. Henry Muhlenberg "received an English letter from Captain Petermann, in Amboy, Jersey, where the camp of the militia is located." The pastor was pleased to learn that "his company expects to return home to Providence next week as they have completed their appointed term of six weeks without suffering injury." Muhlenberg had seen this company off from Augustus Church with blessings in early August, and except for a few deserters, the Providence Company finally made it home intact on September 28.[5]

Adams, Franklin, and Rutledge left New Brunswick under clear skies on September 12 and headed for Philadelphia. How far they traveled that day is unknown, but given the urgency of their mission and their arrival back in town early on the morning of Friday, September 13, they probably pushed to get across the Delaware to get within twenty or so miles of town, perhaps as far as Bristol. The fine, dry weather facilitated their return.

On September 12, "determined to set out to Virginia to-morrow," Nicholas Cresswell made his final farewells to his Loyalist friends. "Dined at Mrs. Stretch's. Supped and spent the evening at *The Golden Fleece*," a tavern on Second Street below Chestnut, only a few yards from the City Tavern, "in company with Marchington, Gresswold, Brewer and Thornbur, all *Sgnik Sdneirf*, very merry." The Loyalists were gloating over the recent turn of events, not yet knowing how the peace conference had turned out. At the tavern, they heard "news that General Prescott and General McDonald were exchanged for G. Sullivan and G. Sterling, *Sleber* took at Long Island."[6] Both American generals were soon back in the field.

The buzz in town grew louder as everyone waited for word from Staten Island. "The people here have been, for several days, fully employed in forming conjectures with respect to the conference between the Commissioners of Congress and Lord Howe," Caesar Rodney of Delaware wrote to George Read on September 13. "They have been various—some [say] Lord Howe has full powers, and if we have not peace it is the fault of Congress—others [say] there is no doubt but they will finally settle matters, and the armies be disbanded—[still] others again are cursed if they believe he has any powers at all." Finally, he was able to state, "However, this business is put an end to by the return of the Committee," who returned to Philadelphia early that morning.[7] The committee delivered an oral report to Congress, which then ordered the facts to be put in writing and presented the following week.

"I returned with Dr. Franklin and Mr. Rutledge from Staten Island, where We met Lord Howe, and had about three hours Conversation with him," John Adams informed Abigail. "It is now plain, that his Lordship has no Power, but what is given him in the Act of Parliament." He went on to describe the essence of the meeting, but that the greatest benefit of it for him was getting out of town. "My ride has been of Service to me," John explained to Abigail. "We were absent but four days. It was an agreable Excursion." As for Admiral Howe, "His Lordship is about fifty Years of Age [and] is a well bred Man but his Address is not so irresistable, as it has been represented," he told his wife. "I could name you many Americans in your own Neighbourhood, whose Art, Address and Abilities are greatly superiour."

To Sam Adams, John wrote a similar description of the meeting, with more political analysis. "I have the pleasure to assure you, that there was no disagreement in Opinion, among the members of the Committee, upon any one point," he said proudly of his colleagues. "They were perfectly united in Sentiment, and in language, as they are in the Result." Looking back on the conference and all of the efforts by Howe to have the conversation, "The whole Affair of the Commission appears to me, as it ever did, to be a bubble, an Ambuscade, a mere insidious Maneuvre, calculated only to decoy and deceive," John acidly commented, "and it is so gross, that they must have a wretched Opinion of our Generalship, to suppose that We can fall into it."[8]

The immediate political benefits in the streets of Philadelphia were only slightly noticeable and of brief duration. "One great point is gained, is to strike the Torys dumb," Congressman William Williams of Connecticut pointed out to Joseph Trumbull that day, "or rather to defeat & kill the impressions they were makeing & wod have made on many Friendly but credulous Minds by their confident & undaunted assertions, that Ld H. was vested with full & ample Powers to Settle the Controversie on the most equitable Terms & Such as would give perfect Satisfaction to all America except the turbulent & haughty, who wishd to continue the War, for their own Honor & Emolument, & was disposed & ardently desirous to do so."[9]

The same day that the committee returned to Philadelphia, Nicholas Cresswell departed the city for good. "Left Philadelphia in company with Messrs. Marchington & Gresswold," two of the Loyalists he had befriended, and headed south. "Crossed Schuylkill at Grey's Ferry. Through Derby, a little place. Dined at Chester, a smart little town on the Delawar River," at that time the seat of Chester County, where Marchinton owned a large farm several miles away. "Here Marchington and Gresswold left me and I joined an Irish Tailor metamorphised into a Captn. and an Irish Blacksmith his

Lieutenant. Both going to Baltimore." Nicholas described his new companions as "rank Paddys," hardly the sort of company he would prefer to be around. "The Captain talks as if he was able to take General Howe in two days with his company," Cresswell snorted. Within the week, the stranded Englishman was once more back in Leesburg, Virginia. "Dined at Mr. Kirk's," he scrawled the following Friday. "Very unhappy."[10]

Out in Trappe on the morning of September 13, "My son Friedrich took me down to Philadelphia with a horse and chaise," Muhlenberg wrote. On their way to the city, a carriage carrying two elderly ladies upset on the road in front of them. Fortunately there were no serious injuries, and after helping the women get back on the road, the Muhlenbergs arrived in Philadelphia "safely in the evening."[11]

Over the next few days, the elder Muhlenberg met with several ministers of other denominations to discuss their growing concerns about the new Pennsylvania constitution. The wording of the constitution did not require officeholders sworn in to be Christians, but only to acknowledge a Supreme Being. "If such an attest were sufficient, then the devil or an ox or an ass could also take part in the government, since devils also believe in a God, and the ox knoweth his owner and the ass his master's crib."[12]

The ministers were alarmed that this might permit non-Christians to hold public office, a situation they found to be inconceivable in a state where the overwhelming majority of citizens were practicing Christians. The state convention was being held in the State House, with Benjamin Franklin as convention president. In an heroic (if futile) attempt to prevent devils, oxen, or asses from being part of the new state government, Muhlenberg and the other ministers requested a meeting with the well-known Deist to lobby for change.

On Tuesday, September 17, "the committee appointed to confer with Lord Howe, agreeable to order, brought in a report in writing, which was read." Franklin, Adams, and Rutledge carefully described the essentials of the conference, and concluded that "Upon the whole, it did not appear to your committee, that his Lordship's commission contained any other authority of importance that what is expressed in the act of parliament, namely, that of granting pardons."[13] The report was entered into the journals of the Continental Congress and ordered to be published in the newspapers. With that, the congressional side of the Staten Island Conference officially concluded.

After presenting the committee's report, Ben Franklin met with Muhlenberg and the other ministers on September 17. "One of us was appointed to speak with the honorable president of the convention, Mr. Fräncklin, and ask him if whether we might not wait on him," Muhlenberg wrote.[14] "The president was condescending enough to come to us, and he took our written draft and promised to lay the matter before the convention." As a result, the state constitution was reworded, but not to the satisfaction of the self-described "old fogey" Muhlenberg; with a righteous fury, he was certain that the wrath of heaven would fall upon Pennsylvania.[15]

One year after the Staten Island Conference, on September 11, 1777, the largest land battle of the War for Independence up to that time raged along Brandywine Creek, thirty miles south of Philadelphia. In a brilliant replay of Long Island, Sir William Howe, knighted for his successful capture of New York, again defeated Washington by outflanking him. The Americans lost more than a thousand men at the Battle of Brandywine, while the British lost half that number, thanks to swift, coordinated bayonet assaults. Once more, as at Long Island, Howe paused after his victory, allowing the bloodied and battered Continental forces to withdraw and regroup.

The British general sent the wounded and prisoners to Wilmington, Delaware, where they established hospitals and awaited the arrival of Admiral Howe's fleet. The fleet was still anchored in the northern Chesapeake below the Elk River on that day, where the army had disembarked three weeks earlier, and Howe and his ships would not arrive in Pennsylvania for another month. Because of the heroic defense of the Delaware by the garrisons at Fort Mifflin and Fort Mercer, Richard Howe and his secretary Ambrose Serle would not set foot in Philadelphia until late November, though his brother's army captured the city in late September.

In Philadelphia on September 11, 1777, John Adams could hear the Battle of Brandywine in the distance, along with everyone else in town. A week later, Congress fled for the second time within the year. Philip Marchinton, the Loyalist cloth merchant, joined Howe's army the day after Brandywine to serve as a guide, along with numerous others, and that army captured Philadelphia on September 26. Loyalism came at a high price, though; after the British evacuation in 1778, Marchinton's property was confiscated by the state of Pennsylvania, and he spent the remainder of his life as a bitter exile in Nova Scotia among tens of thousands of other American Loyalists.

Ben Franklin was in Paris on September 11, 1777, negotiating to secure loans, military necessities, and French recognition of American independence. The American delegation, headed by Silas Deane, encouraged dozens of French and other European officers to offer much-needed professional services to the Continental forces. One eager young man with personal connections at Versailles, the Marquis de la Fayette, had left France in early 1777 after spending several weeks in London and made his way to America to volunteer, ostensibly against the wishes of Louis XVI. Because of his connections at court, Congress commissioned him a major general but initially gave him no troops to command. This nineteen-year-old French aristocrat demonstrated his zeal for the cause of liberty and secured a place in the hearts of Americans in his first battle by being wounded in action at Brandywine on September 11.

Lafayette was shot through the leg while rallying Lord Stirling's division of New Jersey and Pennsylvania troops on the American right wing, commanded by none other than Maj. Gen. John Sullivan. As at Long Island, part of that wing stood firm and momentarily stopped the British light infantry while the other part collapsed under the bayonet assaults of the British Guards and grenadiers. Sullivan was unfairly blamed for this debacle and Congress demanded his recall; Washington deferred the recall and promised a court-martial. This was the second court-martial Sullivan faced in three weeks, the first for a failed attack the hapless general led on, of all places, Staten Island. Sullivan was exonerated in both cases, but bad luck continued to cloud his military career.

Rev. Henry Muhlenberg was also within earshot of the Battle of Brandywine, thirty miles from his home at Trappe. His son, Gen. Peter Muhlenberg, commanded a Virginia brigade that was kept in reserve and saw little (if any) action in the battle. The next day, after hearing of the defeat, the minister wrote with foreboding, "Now prepare thyself, Pennsylvania, to meet the Lord thy God!"[16] In the following weeks, Pastor Muhlenberg would witness his neighborhood in Providence Township picked clean, his homestead invaded, and his beloved Augustus Church trashed and desecrated—by undisciplined Pennsylvania militiamen.

On September 11, 1777, Israel Putnam was commanding the Continental forces stationed in the Hudson Highlands. While this was an important post, Old Put's performance at Long Island relegated him to less active commands for the rest of the war. His former aide, Aaron Burr, was promoted to lieutenant colonel of Malcolm's Additional Continental Regiment in early 1777. Burr was on active duty in the Highlands until late September, when his unit was sent to Pennsylvania.

Margaret Moncrieffe was living with her father on Long Island on September 11, 1777. According to her memoir, she was forced to marry a

British officer, Lt. John Coghlan, in early 1777. Against her wishes, the unhappy marriage was arranged by her father when Margaret was barely fourteen years old. Suffering from an abusive relationship, she was eventually sent by her husband to Britain, where her stormy life continued.

Nicholas Cresswell was in London on September 11, 1777, visiting the British Museum. He had managed to escape from Virginia in early 1777 and made his way by boat to New York. After spending two months in New York waiting for a ship to go home, Nicholas finally set sail for England in July. He wrote at length about what he had seen in America and his impression of the commanders. Of George Washington, "He certainly deserves some merit as a General, that he with his Banditti, can keep General Howe dancing from one town to another for two years together, with such an Army as he has," Cresswell commented. Of William Howe's performance, he fumed, "Confound the great Chucclehead, he will not unmuzzle the mastiffs, or they would eat him [Washington] and his ragged crew in a little time were they properly conducted with a man of resolution and spirit." As he departed, Nicholas commented about the changes the war had wrought on America. "If we have good luck, we shall not be long before we leave sight of this unhappy Country, this Country, turned Topsy Turvy, changed from an earthly paradise to a Hell upon terra firma," he lamented. "I have seen this a happy Country and I have seen it miserable in the short space of three years."[17] His American dream having soured, he returned to Derbyshire and a farmer's life.

John Adams had occasion to remember the Staten Island Conference after he was sent to England in 1785 as the first American ambassador to Great Britain. "When I was afterwards a Minister Plenipotentiary, at the Court of St. James's The King and the Ministry, were often insulted, ridiculed and reproached in the Newspapers, for having conducted with so much folly as to be reduced to the humiliating Necessity of receiving as an Ambassador a Man who stood recorded by the privy Council as a Rebell expressly excepted from Pardon," referring to Lord Howe's "gloomy denunciation of me as 'a decided Character'." This was after John said that the admiral might hold him in any light he wished except that of a British subject. "Some years afterwards, when I resided in England as a public Minister, his Lordship recollected and alluded to this Conversation with great politeness and much good humour." Attending a ball for the queen, "I was at a Loss for the Seats assigned to the foreign Ambassadors and their Ladies," he recalled. Then, John bumped into Lord Howe, and asked him where the ambassadors were supposed to be seated. "His Lordship with his usual politeness, and an unusual Smile of good humour, pointed to the Seats, and manifestly alluding to the Conversation on Staten Island said, 'Aye! Now, We must turn you away among the foreigners!'"

In writing his autobiography, John Adams devoted numerous pages to the Staten Island Conference. "The Conduct of General Sullivan, in consenting to come to Philadelphia, upon so confused an Errand from Lord Howe, though his Situation as a Prisoner was a temptation and may be considered as some Apology for it, appeared to me to betray such Want of Penetration and fortitude, and there was so little precision in the Information he communicated that I felt much resentment and more contempt upon the Occasion than was perhaps just," he admitted, especially after reviewing some of the venomous letters he wrote, describing Sullivan as a "flutterer" and "a decoy duck." He apologized only by saying, "The time was extreamly critical. The Attention of Congress, the Army, the States and the People ought to have been wholly directed to the Defence of the Country. To have it diverted and relaxed by such a poor Artifice and confused tale, appeared very reprehensible." To some of his most confidential friends he expressed how he felt "in a very few Words, which I found time to write," though at the time, John was never short of words. Adams also apologized for the "uncouth freedom" of many of his letters, for he never intended them to be anything but private.[18]

Half a century after the conference, ninety-year-old John Adams died on July 4, 1826—the same day as Thomas Jefferson. Both men had essentially willed themselves to live until that day. A week before his death, Adams was approached by a committee from his hometown to offer a toast for the semicentennial Fourth of July celebration. Physically weak and feeble, but filled with the same fervor he had maintained at the Staten Island Conference, the old patriot acceded to their request:

"I will give you," he said, "Independence forever!"

When asked if he would like to say more, he responded, "Not a word."[19]

EPILOGUE
225 Years Later
❧

I spent much of the summer of 2001 in the Public Record Office (PRO, now the National Archives) in London, researching primary material for my books on the 1777 Philadelphia Campaign. Prior to that, in 1998, my research work for David McCullough's *John Adams* had first taken me to the Conference House on Staten Island, and I was fascinated to see how well it was maintained. The brochure provided at the house briefly described the Staten Island Conference and contained the statement, "It was the last time Britain attempted to speak to America as colonies." That was the first time that the significance of the conference made a lasting impression on me.

Being someone who has had a deep interest in history since early childhood, spawned by family visits to Valley Forge Park, I always try to visit the places where history unfolded and, through primary research, read the documents of those who were there. In 2001, I was able to spend July 4 in the PRO going through the British headquarters papers. Since it was not a national holiday in London for certain historic reasons, the reading rooms were crowded as usual, and my mind wandered as I waited for the documents electronically ordered to arrive by automated conveyor belts. The PRO is a great place for such timeless musings, where huge rolls of medieval parchment are stored together with musty papers from the eighteenth century and carbon-copied dispatches from two more recent world wars.

Realizing that it was the 225th anniversary of American independence, I decided to look through General Howe's letters from July 1776, curious to see just "what they knew and when they knew it" about the Declaration of Independence. It was there that I came across Howe's letter to Lord Germain, written from Staten Island on July 8, with a notation almost as an afterthought that some people had come to Staten Island with a newspaper stating that Congress had declared the colonies free and independent states.

Perusing that original document was an honor and a trust; turning it over, I noticed a small inscription signifying that it had been received in London on August 10. An unexpected realization suddenly dawned on me: I was reading the first notification to the British government that the United States, spawned from the medieval rights contained in some of those very parchment rolls in the PRO, had decided to declare itself a free nation. That realization sent chills up my spine, followed by a downward surge of turning to the page and reading the same copy of the *Pennsylvania Packet* read by General Howe and Lord Germain and heaven knows how many others, containing the text of the Declaration of Independence. My eyes took in the same printed words as their eyes—printed in my hometown, Philadelphia.

A few weeks later, David McCullough contacted me to arrange a meeting with him and another researcher in Washington, DC, to discuss his ideas for a new book, *1776*. I drove down on Sunday morning, September 9, and met David at the Hay-Adams Hotel, across Lafayette Square from the White House. David told us that earlier that morning, when he went out for a walk, he noticed police cars and security activity at St. John's Church across the street from the hotel. Inquiring about what was going on, he was informed that President George W. Bush was going to church that morning. David had met the president earlier that weekend at the Library of Congress, where they chatted about *John Adams* and the irony of fathers and sons serving as president. David and his wife Rosalee decided to attend the service with the president, who was there with only a handful of Secret Service. We chatted about how remarkable it was in America that the head of state could still go out among the people relatively unencumbered. That was on Sunday.

On Tuesday morning, September 11, 2001, I was sitting in the same place where I am writing this epilogue: my desk in Room 104, Carney Hall, at Malvern Preparatory School in Malvern, Pennsylvania. Ten years ago, the juniors who are now taking a U.S. history test as I write were six or seven years old; I was forty-three. That morning, which was sunny, bright, and clear, I had a free first period from 8:25 to 9:10, and it was the first full week of school. I was e-mailing a good friend in London, Col. Graeme Hazelwood of the Royal Logistics Corps, who at that time was assigned to the British Army's GHQ at Horse Guards, a building which would have been well known to General Howe and Lord Cornwallis. I had first met Graeme at Brandywine Battlefield the previous year, when he was on assignment as a liason officer at the Pentagon. Graeme was very interested in the Battle of Brandywine and we were bantering back and forth about British troops being spotted near Brandywine and other such historian nonsense.

Strangely enough, as we were talking Brandywine, I also thought to myself that it was the 225th anniversary of the Staten Island Conference. My imagination wandered to the scene of Adams, Franklin, and Rutledge being rowed across the Arthur Kill around nine o'clock that morning, to be personally greeted by Admiral Howe. I had often wondered what it must have been like to walk between those lines of ferocious-looking Hessian fusiliers, who could have killed the revolutionaries with one command and who would not have hesitated to do so. I also wondered then, as I wondered in the PRO on July 4, about how many people remembered that it was the 225th anniversary of the Staten Island Conference. I figured I was one of very few.

And then, around nine o'clock, the 9/11 attacks began. In the aftermath of that terrible morning, another page in national and world history turned.

Connecting historic events to the present has been one major facet of my life as a teacher and historian. Students often wonder why they need to study history, some complaining that it is "just names and dates," as indeed too many courses in history have been. The connections of the present into the past are vital, and sometimes those connections are not always evident; thus, the challenge of finding the connections. From my own experience, seeing the world as it is now and looking back to as it was reveals some amazing connections. With September 11, 2001, the connections with 1776 are both ironic and remarkable.

In dealing with New York City in 1776, who could have foreseen the fiery destruction of about one-third of the city on September 20? The fire began in the night, probably by American arsonists, after the city fell to the British army. The fire swept up the west side of Broadway and destroyed more than five hundred buildings, including the area where the World Trade Center towers stood. Nicholas Cresswell had entered the city by way of the Paulus Hook ferry, which landed at the foot of Cortlandt Street, on the very site of the Trade Center. That ferry continues operations today. It was in that same general area that David Bushnell's *Turtle* was launched, introducing the submarine into the annals of naval history.

Perhaps the saddest connection of all is that the wreckage of the World Trade Center towers was hauled to Staten Island and deposited at a site only five or so miles from the Conference House.

Remembering these events in history is the challenge for the American people. Those who lived through and witnessed September 11, 2001, will remember it as a major turning point in history and life. Preserving the history and its meaning is an ongoing challenge, as the history of the Conference House, Brandywine Battlefield, and too many other Revolutionary War sites demonstrates when the nation becomes forgetful of its heritage. Let us learn; let us remember.

Notes

PROLOGUE

1. John Adams, *Diary and Autobiography of John Adams*, ed. L. H. Butterfield, et al. (New York: Atheneum, 1961), 3:418. [hereafter Adams]

    Along the same lines, delegate James Smith of York, Pennsylvania, told his wife a few weeks before, "I have prevailed on my Land Lord to rent Littles New House, next Door to the [City] Tavern . . . so that I am quite out of the hurry of the Tavern. I have got a touch of the Rheumatism in my Shoulder by Sleeping with my Windows open. Mr Adams says I very well deserve it, for being so Careless. I told him as Mr Duchee prays for us every Day I thought there was no need to take Care of ourselves. He told me God helps them who help themselves. Mr Hancock is a better Doctor, as he has something of the Gout himself & has promised me some Pine buds to make Tea, however I have shut my Windows these 2 Nights & the Pain is almost gone off, it never hurt my eating & Drinking." James Smith to Elinor Smith, "Philada. Augt. 15, 1776," in *Letters of Delegates to Congress*, ed. Paul H. Smith, et al. (Washington, DC: Library of Congress, 1981), 4:687. [hereafter *LetDel*]

2. Henry Melchior Muhlenberg, *The Journals of Henry Melchior Muhlenberg*, trans. Theodore G. Tappert and John W. Doberstein (Philadelphia: Muhlenberg Press, 1945), 2:731. [hereafter Muhlenberg]

CHAPTER 1

1. Nicholas Cresswell, *The Journal of Nicholas Cresswell, 1774–1777* (London: Jonathan Cape, 1925), 134.

2. Samuel Adams to James Warren, "Philadelphia, April 16, 1776," in Henry Steele Commager and Richard B. Morris, eds. *The Spirit of 'Seventy-Six* (New York, Bonanza Books, 1968), 294. [hereafter Commager]

3. Cresswell, 134.

4. Ibid., 1–2.

5. Ibid., 2, 3, 4, 5.

6. *The Annual Register, or a View of the History, Politics, and Literature, for the Year 1774*, 3rd ed., ed. Edmund Burke (London: Printed for J. Dodsley, 1782.), Chronicle section: 99.

7. "Debate in the Commons, May 2, 1774," Commager, 14.

8. Cresswell, 19.

9. Ibid., 28. Washington wrote in his diary, "July 14: Went up to Alexandria to the Election where I was chosen, together with Majr. [Charles] Broadwater, Burgess. Staid all

Night to a Ball." *Note:* Washington enters up the expense of this election at cakes 13s. 3d. and general expenses £ 3.1/6. George Washington, *The Diaries of George Washington, 1748–1799*, ed. John C. Fitzpatrick (Boston: Houghton Mifflin, 1925), 2:157.

10. Cresswell, 255.

11. Ibid., 251, 257.

12. Ibid., 87.

13. The area is now Big Bone Lick State Park, Kentucky, located a few miles south of Cincinnati. Salt licks abound in the Ohio Valley; they are places where wildlife gathered to lick the salt deposited by natural salt springs. French soldiers noticed the site in 1739 because of the enormous number of mastodon bones strewn there. It was a scientific treasure house noted by Benjamin Franklin and Thomas Jefferson. Unfortunately, nearly all of the fossils were removed in the nineteenth century by naturalists and souvenir collectors.

14. Cresswell, 88, 91–93.

15. Ibid., 136.

16. Ibid., 147–148.

17. Benjamin Rush, *The Autobiography of Benjamin Rush*, ed. George W. Corner (Princeton, NJ: Princeton University Press, 1948), 142.

18. Cresswell, 147–148.

19. Ibid., 149–150.

CHAPTER 2

1. Paul A. W. Wallace, *The Muhlenbergs of Pennsylvania* (Philadelphia: University of Pennsylvania Press, 1950), 120–121.

2. Muhlenberg, 2:717. Among the top national leaders in this category were John Adams and Thomas Jefferson, both of whom were Unitarians, and Thomas Paine, who was at various times a radical Deist, agnostic, or atheist.

3. Muhlenberg, 2:713.

4. Ibid., 2:714.

5. Ibid., 2:720–721.

6. James Read to Edward Shippen, "Reading, May 18, 1776, 8 A.M.," Shippen Papers, vol. 7, 179, Historical Society of Pennsylvania.

7. Muhlenberg, 2:721.

8. Ibid., 2:721–722.

9. Ibid., 2:722.

10. Phineas Pemberton, "Weather Data," "2 Miles Westerly of Philadelphia," at his country house near Gray's Ferry on the Schuylkill River (unpublished manuscript), American Philosophical Society, Philadelphia. Pemberton recorded the temperature and barometric pressure at 7 A.M. and 3 P.M. most days, and sometimes again, along with wind direction and weather conditions. He recorded temperatures inside and outside his house. His thermometer was "a large one made by E. Nairne in Fahrenheit Scale." Pemberton noted on July 11, "A shower about 10 A.M.," which came from the southwest. Muhlenberg was heading northwest to Trappe.

11. Muhlenberg, 2:723.

12. Ibid., 2:722.

CHAPTER 3

1. George Washington to John Hancock, "New York, July 12, 1776," in George Washington, *Papers of George Washington*, Revolutionary War Series, ed. Philander C. Knox, et al. (Charlottesville: University of Virginia, 1995), 5:284. [hereafter Washington, *Papers*]

2. Stephen A. Kemble, "The Kemble Papers," in *Collections of the New York Historical Society* (New York: Printed for the Society, 1883), 1:80. Kemble was the deputy adjutant general of the British Army. [hereafter Kemble]

3. "Diary of the Rev. Mr. Shewkirk of the Moravian Church, entry for July 12, 1776," Commager, 422.

4. *The New-York Gazette*, Monday, July 15, 1776, in *Naval Documents of the American Revolution*, ed. William J. Morgan (Washington DC: Appendices, 1970), 5:1089. [hereafter *Naval Documents*]

5. "Diary of Ensign Caleb Clapp," *Naval Documents*, 5:1042.

6. Ira D. Gruber, *The Howe Brothers and the American Revolution* (Chapel Hill, NC: Institute of Early American History and Culture, 1972), 48.

7. "Admiralty Office 1st June 1776: The present disposition of His Majesty's Ships and vessels in Sea Pay: *Eagle* 64 guns, 520 men, Captain Hon. Henry Duncan, Lieutenants: Samuel Reeves, John Howarth, Harry Harwood, Philip Brown. Commissioned 7th February 1776, cleaned 4th March, Sailed From England May 11 1776." *Naval Documents*, 5:1357.

8. Ambrose Serle, *The American Journal of Ambrose Serle, Secretary to Lord Howe 1776–1778*, ed. Edward H. Tatum Jr. (San Marino, CA: Huntingdon Library, 1940), 14. [hereafter Serle]

9. Serle, 2, 71.

10. Gruber, 48.

11. Serle, 8–9.

12. Ibid. 27.

13. Ibid., 28.

14. William Howe to George Germain, "Head Quarters Staten Island, 7th July 1776," CO 5/93, Box 2, sheets 214–215, National Archives (formerly Public Record Office), London.

15. Serle, 30.

16. Ibid., 31.

17. *Naval Documents*, 6:947.

18. William Howe to George Germain, "Head Quarters Staten Island 8th July 1776," CO 5/93, Box 2, sheet 216, National Archives (formerly Public Record Office), London.

19. Serle, 16.

20. *The Annual Register for 1776* (London: J. Dodson, 1777), 257–258.

21. Richard Howe to George Germain, "Eagle, off Staten Island, 11 August 1776," *Naval Documents*, 6:145–146.

22. Richard Howe to George Washington, "Eagle, off Staten Island, 13 July 1776," Washington, *Papers*, 5:296.

CHAPTER 4

1. Henry Knox to Lucy Knox, "July 15, 1776," Commager, 426–427.
2. Serle, 32.
3. In *Campaign of 1776*, author Henry P. Johnson says, "Another element in the defence was a motley little fleet, made up of schooners, sloops, row-galleys, and whale-boats, and placed under the command of Lieutenant-Colonel Benjamin Tupper, who had distinguished himself by a naval exploit or two in Boston Harbor during the siege. Crews were drafted from the regiments and assigned to the various craft, whose particular mission was to scour the waters along the New Jersey and Long Island coast, to watch for the British fleets, and prevent communication between the Tories and the enemy's ships already lying in the harbor. Tupper, as commodore, appears first in the sloop *Hester* as his flag-ship, and later in the season in the *Lady Washington*, while among his fleet were to be found the *Spitfire*, *General Putnam*, *Shark*, and *Whiting*. The gallant commodore's earliest cruises were made within the Narrows, along the Staten Island shore, and as far down as Sandy Hook, where he attempted the feat of destroying the light-house. But he found this structure, which the enemy had occupied since Major Malcom dismantled it in March, a hard piece of masonry to reduce. He attacked it confidently, June 21st, after demanding its surrender, but retired when he found that an hour's bombardment made no impression upon its walls. He kept a good lookout along these waters, gathered information from deserters, and when reporting on one occasion that the enemy's fleet were short of provisions and the men reduced to half allowance, he added, with unction, 'May God increase their wants!'" Henry P. Johnston, *The Campaign of 1776 around New York and Brooklyn*, (Brooklyn, NY: Long Island Historical Society, 1878), 92. [hereafter Johnston, *Campaign*]
4. "Diary of Ensign Caleb Clapp," *Naval Documents* 5:1073. Clapp was a minuteman at Lexington on April 19, 1775, and served through the entire war, rising to the rank of captain. See F. B. Heitman, *Historical Register of Officers of the Continental Army during the War of the Revolution, April 1775–December 1783* (Washington, DC: W. H. Lowdermilk, 1892).
5. Knox to Knox, Commager, 426–427.
6. George Washington to John Hancock, "New York, July the 14th, 1776," Washington, *Papers*, 5:305–306.
7. Serle, 33.
8. Knox to Knox, Commager, 426–427.
9. George Washington to John Hancock, "New York, July the 14th, 1776," Washington, *Papers*, 5:305–306.
10. George Washington to Adam Stephen, "New York July 20, 1776," Washington, *Papers*, 5:408–409.
11. Serle, 33.
12. Entry for Wednesday, July 17, 1776, *Journals of the Continental Congress, 1774–1789* ed. Worthington C. Ford, et al. (Washington, DC, 1906), 5:567.
13. "Journal of HMS *Eagle*, Captain Henry Duncan," *Naval Documents*, 5:1103.
14. Serle, 35–36.
15. "Webb Journal," *Naval Documents*, 5:401n. Webb was promoted to lieutenant colonel and attached to Washington's staff as an aide-de-camp on June 21, 1776. See General Orders for June 21, 1776 (*Note:* Heitman has the date incorrectly as July 21.). In his

diary, Capt. Archibald Robertson of the British Engineers identified Balfour as the courier: "[July] 19: Captain Balfour went up to Governor's Island with a Flag of truce." Archibald Robertson, *Archibald Robertson, His Diaries and Sketches in America*, ed. Harry Miller Lydenberg (New York: New York Public Library, 1930), 90. [hereafter Robertson]

16. Johnston, *Campaign*, 88.
17. Kemble, 1:82. Capt. Archibald Robertson of the Engineers missed out on the visit, stating, "Colonel Patterson likewise went with a Flag of truce to the Town of new York. I did not get leave to attend him tho' the General at first approv'd it." Robertson, 91.
18. Knox to Knox, "July 22, 1776," Commager, 427.
19. Ibid.
20. Joseph Reed, "Memorandum of an Interview with Lieutenant Colonel James Paterson," *Naval Documents*, 5:398–399.
21. Ibid., 5:402n.
22. Ibid.
23. Ibid., 5:400.
24. Ibid.
25. Cresswell, 139.
26. "A Dialogue between the Ghost of general M and a D, in a wood near Philadelphia," *The Virginia Gazette*, March 8, 1776
27. Knox to Knox, Commager, 427.
28. *Naval Documents*, 5:400–401.
29. Ibid., 5:402n.
30. Knox to Knox, Commager, 427.
31. *Naval Documents*, 5:401n.
32. Knox to Knox, Commager, 428.
33. This reported comment appears in the "Moravian Diary of Reverend Mr. Shewkirk," Johnston, *Campaign*, ii, 112.
34. *Naval Documents*, 5:401n.
35. Ibid., 5:402n.
36. William Howe to George Washington, "Head Quarters Staten Island 1st August 1776," Washington, *Papers*, 5:537–538.
37. George Washington to William Howe, "Head Qrs New York Augt. 17, 1776," Washington, *Papers*, 6:53.

CHAPTER 5

1. Congressional Committee to Committee of Associators meeting at Lancaster, "Philadelphia, July 4, 1776," *LetDel* 4:380–382.
2. Christopher Marshall, "Diary D," entry for July 4, 1776, Historical Society of Pennsylvania.
3. Muhlenberg 2:735–736.
4. Ibid., 2:724–725.
5. Ibid., 2:725.
6. General Orders, "Head Quarters, New York, July 24, 1776," Washington, *Papers*, 5:439.

7. Muhlenberg, 2:725.

8. Ibid., 2:727.

9. Col. Peter Grubb's battalion of six companies totaled 427 men in Philadelphia, August 27, 1776. *Pennsylvania Archives* 2nd series, (Harrisburg, 1876) 2:619. [hereafter *PaArch*]

10. Muhlenberg, 2:729.

11. Ibid.

12. Ibid., 2:731.

CHAPTER 6

1. George Smith, *An Universal Military Dictionary* (London: J. Millan, 1779), 45.

2. The word "kill" here is a Dutch word meaning a large creek or small river. The area of old New Netherland (now New York, New Jersey, Pennsylvania, and Delaware) has many waterways still using "kill," such as Catskill (Kaats kill), Peekskill, Schuylkill, and Broadkill. In some places, the English word "river" has been added (Schuylkill River), although it is technically redundant. Around Staten Island, the Arthur Kill is connected to the Kill van Kull, and freshwater creeks flowing into the Arthur Kill above Billopp's Point are collectively called the Fresh Kills.

3. Hugh Mercer to George Washington, "Eliza. Town, 16 July 1776," Washington, *Papers*, 5:343.

4. George Washington to William Livingston, "Head Quarters New York July 6, 1776, 5 oClock P. M.," in William Livingston, *The Papers of William Livingston*, ed. Carl E. Prince (Trenton: New Jersey Historical Commission, 1979), 1: 75–76. [hereafter Livingston, *Papers*]

5. Hugh Mercer to George Washington, "Perth Amboy, 14 July 1776," Washington, *Papers*, 5:309.

6. George Washington to the Commander of the Pennsylvania Troops at Trenton or elsewhere in New Jersey, "New York Head Quarters, 14 July 1776," Washington, *Papers*, 5:315.

7. Abraham Clark to Elias Dayton, "Elizabeth Town July 14, 1776," *LetDel*, 4:452.

8. Samuel Adams to Richard Henry Lee, "Philada July 15 1777," *LetDel*, 4:459.

9. "Diary of Lieut. James McMichael," entry for July 18, 1776, *PaArch*, 2nd series, 15:196.

10. Josiah Bartlett to John Langdon, "Philadelphia, July 15, 1776," *LetDel*, 4:460.

11. John Adams to Abigail Adams, "Philadelphia, July 15, 1776," *LetDel*, 4:457.

12. Myrmidons were ruthless mercenaries hired by Achilles during the siege of Troy. This word is frequently used by American writers during the Revolution to describe the king's forces.

13. Serle, 36.

14. William Livingston to Samuel Tucker, "Eliz: Town 16th. July 1776," Livingston, *Papers*, 1:100. Livingston also stated in this letter, "No Troops yet from Philadelphia and our People beginning to grow exceeding clamourous about their harvest. If we do not receive succor very speedily it will be of little avail that the Pennsylvanians marched as far as Trenton."

15. Journal entry for Saturday, July 13, 1776. Kemble, 1:81.

16. Serle, 64–65.

17. Nearly a month later, Hessian Quartermaster-General Johann Ludwig von Cochenhausen wrote on August 13, "According to the chart sent over today by General Howe's Quartermaster-General [Lt. Col. William Sheriffe], there is no regular camp to move into." Henry J. Retzer and Donald Londahl-Smidt, "The New York-New Jersey Campaign, 1776–1777: Letters from the von Jungkenn Papers," *Journal of the Johannes Schwalm Historical Association*, 5, no. 4 (1996): 74.

18. Hugh Mercer to George Washington, "Eliza. Town 16 July 1776," Washington, *Papers*, 5:344–346.

19. John Hancock to the New Jersey Convention, "Philada., 22 July 1776," *LetDel*, 4:518.

20. Thomas Jefferson to Fielding Lewis, "Philada., July 16, 1776," in Thomas Jefferson, *The Papers of Thomas Jefferson*, ed. Julian P. Boyd, (Princeton, NJ: Princeton University Press, 1950), 1:467.

21. Mercer to Washington, July 16, 1776, Washington, *Papers*, 5:345.

22. Benjamin Rush to Julia Stockton Rush, "Philada. July 22, 1776," *LetDel*, 4:583. Information about Michael Weaver and his son Henry is found in "Captain Benjamin Loxley's Company-1776, Muster Roll of the First Company of Artillery of Philadelphia, July 24, 1776, Colonel Samuel Mifflin," *PaArch* 6th series, 1:517.

23. Benjamin Rush to Charles Lee, "Philada., July 23, 1776," *LetDel*, 4:528.

24. Thomas Jefferson to Francis Eppes, "Philadelphia, July 23, 1776," *LetDel*, 4:526.

25. Hugh Mercer to George Washington, "Perth Amboy, 24th July 1776," Washington, *Papers*, 5:444.

26. Extract from *The New York Gazette and Weekly Mercury*, July 29, 1776, in *Archives of the State of New Jersey*, 2nd series (Trenton, 1901), 1:154. [hereafter *NJArch*]

27. Hugh Mercer to George Washington, "Perth Amboy 26th July 1776," in George Washington, *George Washington Papers at the Library of Congress*, Series 4: General Correspondence, image 558, www. memory.loc.gov/ammem/gwhtml/gwseries.html.

28. *NJArch*, 1:154.

29. Mercer to Washington, July 26, 1776.

30. *NJArch*. 1:154.

31. Thomas Jefferson to John Page, "Philadelphia, July 30, 1776," *LetDel* Vol. 4, p. 580.

32. William Livingston to Joseph Reed, "New York [Newark] 3 July 1776," Livingston, *Papers*, 1:60.

33. Clark to Dayton, July 14, 1776, *LetDel*, 4:452.

34. Hugh Mercer to George Washington, "Perth Amboy 9th August 1776," Washington, *Papers*, 5:651.

35. John Adams to Daniel Hitchcock, "Philadelphia, August 3, 1776," *LetDel*, 4:615.

36. Report and letter, Report of the Committee of Secret Proceedings/Abraham Clark "To The Honourable Convention of New Jersey at New Brunswick," dated "Phila. Wednesday Evening August 7, 1776," *LetDel* 4:584–585.

37. William Livingston to William Hooper, "Camp at Elizabeth Town point 29 August 1776," Livingston, *Papers*, 1:128–129.

CHAPTER 7

1. Serle, 32.
2. Hugh Mercer to George Washington, "Perth Amboy, 14 July 1776," Washington, *Papers*, 5:309.
3. Serle, 32.
4. Richard Howe to George Germain, *"Eagle,* off Staten Island, 11th August 1776," *Naval Documents*, 6:145.
5. Richard Howe to Benjamin Franklin, "Eagle, off the Coast of the Province of Massachusetts-Bay, June 20th, 1776," (subscripted "Eagle, off Staten Island, 12th July 1776"), in Benjamin Franklin, *The Papers of Benjamin Franklin*, franklinpapers.org, 627095 = 022-483a.html. [hereafter Franklin, *Papers*]
6. Gruber, 54.
7. Howe to Franklin, 12 July 1776.
8. William Ellery to Ezra Stiles?, "[July 20, 1776]," *LetDel* 4:497.
9. Ibid., 4:497–498.
10. Ibid., 4:498.
11. John Adams to Abigail Adams, "Philadelphia 20 July 1776," *LetDel* 4:493.
12. Entry for Saturday, July 20, 1776, *Journals of the Continental Congress*, 5:595.
13. Benjamin Franklin to Richard Howe, "Philadelphia, July 20, 1776," Franklin, *Papers*, franklinpapers.org, 627121 = 022-518a.html.
14. This letter was sent to New York, where it passed through Washington's hands, and probably arrived in Philadelphia on August 20. Franklin wrote a reply on that date that he did not send, later explaining that members of Congress did not like him corresponding with the admiral. Washington's cover letter stated, "New York Augt. 18th. 1776 . . . I also Inclose you a Letter from Lord Howe, sent out (with others) by a Flag in the Afternoon of yesterday." Franklin, *Papers*, franklinpapers.org, 627150 = 022-568b.html.
15. Richard Howe to Benjamin Franklin, "Eagle off Staten Island Augt. the 16: 1776," Franklin, *Papers*, franklinpapers.org, 627146 = 022-565a.html. Franklin wrote a response to this letter from Howe, but evidently did not send it. "Philada Aug 20. 76. My Lord, The Temper (& Disposition) of the Colonies as professed in their several Petitions to the Crown was sincere. The Terms they proposed should then have been closed with, and all might have been Peace. I dare say your L[ordshi]p as well as myself, laments they were not accepted. I remember I told you that better wd never be offered, & I have not forgotten your just Comparison of the Sybyl's Leaves. But the Contempt with which those Petitions were treated, none of them being vouchsaf'd an Answer, and the cruel Measures since taken, have chang'd that Temper. It could not be otherwise. To propose now to the Colonies (a Return to the State of Subjection they were formerly in to the) a Submission to the Crown of Great Britain, would be (useless) fruitless. The Time is past. One might as well propose it to France, on the Footing of a former title." *LetDel*, 5:30.
16. George Washington to Lund Washington, "New York, Augt 19th 1776," Washington *Papers*, 6:83. The question marks were inserted for clarification.

CHAPTER 8

1. Benjamin Rush to Walter Jones, "Philada., July 30, 1776," *LetDel*, 4:583.

2. Margaret Moncrieffe Coughlan, *Memoirs of Mrs. Coughlin, Daughter of the Late Major Moncrieffe, Written by Herself*, (London: Printed for the Author, 1794; reprint, New York: Arno Press, 1971), 22–23. [hereafter Coughlan, *Memoirs*]

 Margaret died in London on June 4, 1787, "in Cavendish Street, Portland-square, Margaret Coughlin, daughter of Col. Moncrieffe." (from *The Gentleman's Magazine*, 1787), and her memoirs were published in 1794 by a friend.

3. "Extracts from the Diary of Dr. James Clitherall, 1776," *Pennsylvania Magazine of History and Biography* 22 (1898): 472.

4. This would have been either on Sunday, July 7, or Sunday, July 14.

5. Coughlin, *Memoirs*, 24. According to a series of letters from Livingston, Pennsylvania troops did not arrive in Elizabethtown until July 18. He wrote to Mathias Ward on July 18 from "HQ. E Town: There being an immediate necessity for the 100 Rifle Men yesterday to the Ferries, they are accordingly ordered down this Morning." Livingston *Papers*, 1:102.

6. Coughlin, *Memoirs*, 25.

7. *Pennsylvania Gazette*, July 24, 1776.

8. Coughlin, *Memoirs*, 25.

9. Mark Mayo Boatner III, *Encyclopedia of the American Revolution* (New York: David McKay, 1966), 902–903.

10. Israel Putnam to Margaret Moncrieffe, "New York, July 26, 1776," in *American Archives*, 5th series, ed. Peter Force (Washington, DC: M. St. Clair and Peter Force, 1848), 471. Given Putnam's abysmal level of literacy, the grammar of this letter was no doubt extensively 'cleaned up' by Peter Force's editorial staff.

11. It is unlikely that Margaret was introduced to Martha Washington, for General Washington wrote to his brother John Augustine on July 22, "Mrs. Washington is now at Philadelphia & has thoughts of returning to Virginia as there is little or no prospect of her being with me any part of this Summer." Martha wrote to her sister Anna Maria Dandridge Bassett from Philadelphia on August 28, "I am still in this town and Noe prospects at present of my leveing it." George Washington to John Augustine Washington, "New York July 22d 1776," Washington, *Papers* 5: 429–30, n. 3.

12. Coughlin, *Memoirs*, 27–28. This narrative was written years after the war; General Howe did not receive his title "Sir" until after the New York Campaign, when he was made a "Knight of the Bath" by the king for his military successes. Margaret also refers to numerous officers by ranks as she remembered them, not necessarily the ranks they held in 1776.

13. Ibid., 28. This outrageous claim by Margaret has not been substantiated from any other sources. "The commander in chief, whose influence governed the congress, soon prevailed on them to consider me as a person whose situation required their strict attention* [footnote: "My father's knowledge of the country induced General Washington to use every expedient in order to seduce him from the Royal cause, and he knew there was none more likely to succeed than that of attacking his parental

feelings."]; and, that I might not escape, they ordered me to King's-Bridge, where, in justice, I must say, that I was treated with the utmost tenderness: General Mifflin there commanded; his lady was a most accomplished, beautiful woman, a quaker." Nowhere in the writings of Congress does her name come up.

14. Ibid., 29.

15. "General Orders, June 22: Aaron Burr Esqr: is appointed Aide du Camp to Genl. Putnam in the room of Major Webb promoted." Washington, *Papers*, 5:75.

16. Boatner, 145.

17. Coughlin, *Memoirs*, 31.

18. Ibid., 29. Of Aaron Burr and his personal morals, author Lewis Burd Walker wrote in 1901, "A greater scamp does not walk the history of America. . . . When aide-decamp to General Putnam, in 1776, his position brought him into contact with Margaret Moncrieffe, who had by the fortunes of war become separated from her father, Major Moncrieffe, an officer of the British Army. While she, a girl of less than fourteen years of age, was under the care of General Putnam, Burr seduced her." Historian Matthew Livingston Davis wrote, "Miss Moncrieffe before she had reached her fourteenth year, was probably the victim of seduction." Aaron Burr, *Memoirs of Aaron Burr* ed. Matthew Livingston Davis (1840), 1:90. For further comments, see Lewis Burd Walker, "Life of Margaret Shippen, Wife of Benedict Arnold," *Pennsylvania Magazine of History and Biography* 25 (1901): 154.

19. Coughlin, *Memoirs*, 31–32.

20. Ibid., 32.

21. Kemble, 1:83.

22. Coughlin, *Memoirs*, 33.

23. Ibid., 33–34. "On 23 October 1768 Captain William Sherriffe had been appointed Deputy Quartermaster General to the Forces serving in North America with the rank of Major effective 25 July 1768 . . . On 17 May 1776 Major Sherriffe was promoted to the rank of lieutenant colonel because of his services in America. A Quartermaster General to the forces in North America was not appointed until 7 October 1776, when Brigadier General Sir William Erskine assumed that office." *Journal of the Johannes Schwalm Historical Association* 5, no. 4 (1996): 79, note 6.

24. Coughlin, *Memoirs*, 34–35.

25. Entry for August 18, 1776, in Serle, 69.

26. Adams wrote, "I have written with great Freedom, in Confidence that no ill use will be made of it. I wish your Sentiments upon these subjects with the Same Candor." In the same letter, Adams wrote, "But in the other Cases it was not Wrong. Mercer, Lewis, More, and How were not only Men of Fortune, and Figure, in their Countries and in civil Imployments, but they were all veteran Soldiers, and had been Collonells in a former War. It is true, their Provincial Legislatures had made them only Collonells last year, and the Reason was because they only raised Regiments, not Brigades. But as soon as those Colonies came to raise Brigades, it was but reasonable these officers should be appointed Brigadiers. These officers stood in the Light of Thomas, Fry, Whitcomb, Putnam, &c &c with this difference, that the Gentlemen themselves were Superiour in Point of Property and Education. Besides, it has been our constant Endeavour, that each State should have a reasonable Number of Gen-

eral officers in Proportion to the Number of Troops they raise. It should be considered that We have constituents to satisfy as well as the Army, and Colonies to rank as well as Collonells and Generals. Massachusetts has most Cause of Complaint upon this Head. That there have not been many Promotions of Collonells to the Northward, is true. But how can it be avoided. If I were left to myself, to my Judgment and Inclination, I should not hesitate a Moment. But We must not deviate from the Line of Succession. If We do, We are threatened with Disgust and Resignations. And how can We follow the Lined Wooster, Heath and Spencer ought to be made Major Generals, But is this the opinion of the Army?" John Adams to Daniel Hitchcock, August 3, 1776, *LetDel* 4:614–615.

27. Coughlin, *Memoirs*, 35–36.

CHAPTER 9

1. Serle, 52.
2. Ibid., 54.
3. George Washington to Charles Lee, "New York Augt 12th1776," Washington, *Papers*, 5:681–682.
4. Serle, 62.
5. Nathanael Greene to George Washington, "Camp at Brookland [Brooklyn] Augt 12—1776," Washington, *Papers*, 5:676.
6. Serle, 62.
7. William Livingston to George Washington, "Eliz. Town 12 Augt 1776," Washington, *Papers*, 5:684.
8. Hugh Mercer to George Washington, "Woodbridge, 12 Augt 1776," Washington, *Papers*, 5:685.
9. Livingston to Washington, August 12, 1776, Washington, *Papers*, 684.
10. The first transport ship with Hessians aboard arrived off Staten Island on July 29 was the *Speedwell*, carrying Lt. Col. Justus Heinrich Block with part of a composite grenadier battalion. This ship was part of a small squadron escorted by the HMS *Niger*. The *Malaga*, *Polly*, and *Surprise* arrived on August 4 with more Hessian troops. See Donald Londahl-Smidt, et al., "On Board the *Speedwell*: The First Hessians Arrive at New York," *Journal of the Johannes Schwalm Historical Association* 5, no. 2 (1994): 9–12.
11. Henry J. Retzer and Donald M. Londahl-Smidt, "The Journal of Ensign/Lt. Wilhelm Johann Ernst Freyenhagen, 1776–1778," *Journal of the Johannes Schwalm Historical Association* 13 (2010): 15.
12. This regiment was regarded as one of the most elite of the Hessians units sent to America. The German name literally means "Life Regiment" and the literal French translation is "Regiment of the Body," implying bodyguards. The correct translation is rendered idiomatically into English as the Household Regiment. This unit was detached from the household guards of Prince Friedrich, the Landgraf of Hesse-Cassel. To avoid confusion with the British Brigade of Guards, which was also with the flotilla arriving August 12, the unit will be called the Leib Regiment.

From Paris to Berlin to St. Petersburg, French was the language of many continental European courts in the eighteenth century and was also the international language of diplomacy and the military. Frederick the Great of Prussia used it extensively, as he

considered German to be the language of peasants. Hessian and other German officers who did not speak English often used French when communicating with British
officers who did not speak German. Many British officers had some basic knowledge
of French, if not a working fluency. In writings from the period, French terms are frequently used with reference to Hessian forces, such as General de Heister instead of
von Heister; Regiment de Knyphausen instead of von Knyphausen; and the British
use of the word *"chasseur"* for German *"jäger"* (both words mean "hunter"). Even in
the American forces, two former Prussian officers, Baron d'Arendt and Baron de Kalb
use "de" instead of "von," and drillmaster "Baron" von Steuben is sometimes called
de Steuben.

13. Lotheisen, "Journal of the Remarkable Events which occurred to the Hon. Leib
    Infantry Regiment entitled Crown Prince, Commenced in February 1776, when it
    marched out to America. Completed end of May 1784, when on its return from
    America, it marched to its appointed Garrison at Marburg in Ober-Hesse. Written
    by Staff Secretary and Regimental Quarter-Master Lotheisen," V. 2, *Hessian Documents
    of the American Revolution*, Letter V: Journal of the Leib Infantry Regiment, Morristown
    National Historical Park, microfiche.
14. Lotheisen, V7.
15. Lotheisen, V7–V8.
16. Lotheisen, V8.
17. Lotheisen, V8–V9.
18. Benjamin Franklin to Thomas McKean, "Philadelphia, August 24, 1776," *LetDel*,
    5:56.
19. Deserter advertisement from *Pennsylvania Packet*, September 10, 1776. "Extracts from
    American Newspapers," *NJArch*, 2nd series, 1:184. The boldface section was added by
    the author for emphasis.
20. Muhlenberg, 2:729.

CHAPTER 10

1. Thomas Sullivan, *From Redcoat to Rebel: The Thomas Sullivan Journal*, ed. Joseph Lee Boyle
   (Bowie, MD: Heritage Books, 1997), 48–49. [hereafter Sullivan, *Journal*]
2. Thomas Jefferson to Edmund Pendleton, "Philadelphia, August 26, 1776," *LetDel*
   5:68.
3. "Journal of Colonel Samuel Miles Concerning the Battle of Long Island," *PaArch*,
   2nd series, 1:520.
4. William Dansey to Catherine Malit, "Bedford on Long Island near New York, 30th
   Augt. 1776"; also a fragment of another letter, undated, probably to his mother,
   widow of a career army officer, Dansey Letters, Delaware Historical Society. Punctu-
   ation added in places for clarity.
5. *PaArch*, 1:521–522.
6. Coughlin, *Memoirs*, 37–38.
7. Joseph Plumb Martin and George F. Scheer, *Private Yankee Doodle* (Boston: Little,
   Brown, 1962), 25.
8. *PaArch*, 1:521–522.

9. Coughlin, *Memoirs*, 38.

10. *PaArch*, 1:521–522.

11. *Journal of the Johannes Schwalm Historical Association* 13 (2010): 5.

12. Hugh Percy, *Letters of Hugh, Earl Percy, from Boston and New York, 1774–1776*, ed. Charles Knowles Bolton (Boston: Gregg Press, 1972), 68–69. [hereafter Percy, *Letters*]

In another letter "to a Gentleman in London," Percy wrote, "It was the General's orders that the troops should receive the Rebels' first fire, and then rush on them before they had recovered their arms, with their bayonets, which threw them into the utmost disorder and confusion, they being unacquainted with such a manoeuvre," 71.

13. William Howe to George Germain, "New York 3 September 1776," CO 5/93, Box 2, sheet 258, National Archives (formerly Public Record Office), London.

14. Percy, *Letters*, 69.

15. James Murray to Bessie Murray Smythe, "Newton [Newtown] Kilns, Long Island. August 31st, 1776," in James Murray, *Letters from America 1773 to 1780*, ed. Eric Robson (Manchester: Manchester University Press, 1951), 33.

16. John Haslet to Caesar Rodney, "Camp at New York, August 31, 1776," in Caesar Rodney, *Letters to and from Caesar Rodney, 1756–1784*, ed. George Herbert Ryden (Philadelphia: University of Pennsylvania Press, 1933), 108–109.

17. Caesar Rodney to George Read, "Philadelphia, September 4, 1776," *LetDel* 5:106.

18. Loftus Cliffe to Bartholomew Cliffe, "Camp York Island [Manhattan] September 21, 1776," Loftus Cliffe Letters, Clements Library.

19. See Boatner, 647–656.

20. Cliffe to Cliffe, September 21, 1776.

21. James Wilson to Jasper Yeates, "Woodstock 14th September 1776," *LetDel* 5:171.

22. Muhlenberg, 2:757.

23. Jasper Ewing to Judge Yeates, "New York, August 30, 1776," Johnston, *Campaign*, p. ii 50.

24. Commager, 443.

25. *Journal of the Johannes Schwalm Historical Association* 5, no. 4 (1996): 75.

26. Daniel Brodhead to unknown member of the Pennsylvania Convention, "Camp near Kingsbridge, 5th Sep'r 1776," *PaArch* 1st series, 5:22–23.

27. Charles Stuart to Lord Bute, "Newtown Camp, Sept. 3, 1776," in Mrs. E. Stuart Wortley, *A Prime Minister and His Son* (London: John Murray, 1925), 84.

28. James Grant to Edward Harvey, "Long Island 2nd Septemr 1776," Grant Papers.

29. Cliffe to Cliffe, September 21, 1776.

30. Orderly Book of Ensign Thomas Glyn, 10a, Princeton University Library.

31. Loftus Cliffe to Jack Cliffe, "Camp York Island [Manhattan] September 21, 1776," Cliffe Letters, Clements Library.

32. Rev. Mr./Brother Shewkirk, "Occupation of New York City By the British, 1776: Extracts from the Diary of the Moravian Congregation," *Pennsylvania Magazine of History and Biography*, 1 (1877): 148.

33. George Washington to John Hancock, "New York Headqrs Septr 8th 1776," Washington, *Papers*, 6:251–252.

CHAPTER 11

1. Cresswell, 151.
2. Research in county and town histories thus far has not uncovered any record of a tavern by this name in York. The Court of Quarter Sessions records in the York County Archives list only the names of tavern keepers, not the tavern names. In York Town, about a dozen names were listed in 1773, 1774, and 1775, many of which are German or Anglicized German. The records for 1776 and 1777 are not available, probably because of the disruption of government. The oldest tavern in town was kept by Baltzer Spangler, a prominent community leader; another "Dutchman with a confounded hard name" was Gottlieb Ziegle. Yet another tavern was kept by one Henry Boozer.

    Lewis Miller, a York carpenter, made a series of hundreds of drawings of York in the early nineteenth century. One is labeled "The Old Brewhouse in the year 1801, The[y] made Good Beer." This may have been the establishment where Cresswell stayed. See Cleveland Amory, et al., *The American Heritage Cookbook* (New York: American Heritage Publishing, 1964), 181.
3. Cresswell, 152. This tavern stood at the southeast corner of East King Street and Center Square. No trace of it remains. See H. Ray Woerner, "The Taverns of Early Lancaster and the Later-Day Hotels," *Journal of the Lancaster County Historical Society* 73 (1969): 45.
4. Extract of a letter from Andre to his mother, quoted in James Thomas Flexner, *The Traitor and the Spy* (Boston: Little, Brown, 1953), 146. Ironically, the 26th Old Cameronians, one of the oldest Scottish regiments in the British army, descended directly from a regiment made up of lowland Scottish Presbyterian Covenanters.
5. The Sign of the Duke of Cumberland Tavern was in Leacock Township, "about 10 miles from Lancaster" (*Pennsylvania Gazette*, September 29, 1773) and kept by James Mercer. If the tavern building survives, it has been greatly altered and may be a nearby farmhouse. The Old Leacock Presbyterian Church is still in use and is well preserved, standing on Route 340 about two miles west of Intercourse, Pennsylvania.
6. *Pennsylvania Gazette*, December 12, 1778: "bounded on the south by the Conestogo great road, and on the east by the road leading from the sign of the White Horse to the Yellow Springs, and adjoining the White Horse tract, as also the land in tenure of Mr. Jacobs at the sign of the Cross Keys." This tavern stood somewhere on the north side of Swedesford Road near Bacton Hill Road. If the building survives, it has been greatly altered and is unidentified. It was somewhere across the road from the White Horse Tavern, one of the earliest and most famous taverns in Chester County. The White Horse still stands with some alterations on the south side of Swedesford Road, west of Planebrook Road.
7. "North side between 4th and 5th street . . . William Graham keeper, 1776." *Pennsylvania Gazette*, June 26, 1776.
8. Cresswell, 155.
9. Ibid., 156. In colonial days, New Jersey was divided into East and West Jersey, with its seats of government alternating respectively between Perth Amboy and Burlington. The province was commonly called "The Jerseys" or "The Jersies."
10. Christopher Marshall, "Diary D," entry for August 27, 1776, Historical Society of Pennsylvania.

11. "Return of Troops Quartered In and Near the City, Phila'a, August 27th, 1776," *PaArch*, 2nd series, 1:619–620.

12. Cresswell, 155.

13. Ibid., 156.

14. Marshall, "Diary D," entry for August 28, 1776, HSP. Jeremiah Warder advertisements are found throughout the *Pennsylvania Gazette*, 1776.

15. Cresswell, 155.

16. *Dictionary of Canadian Biography Online, Vol. 5, 1801–1820.* University of Toronto, 2000. www.biographi.ca/009004

17. *Pennsylvania Gazette*, November 10, 1773.

18. *Pennsylvania Gazette*, May 11, 1774.

19. His December ad included "woollen and linen drapery, silk mercery, hoisery, and haberdashery," and "a large quantity of Boston shoes and Barcelona handkerchiefs." *Pennsylvania Gazette*, December 11, 1774.

20. *Pennsylvania Gazette*, June 14, 1776. Emphasis added.

21. *Pennsylvania Gazette*, August 14, 1776. Marchinton's activities continued well into the next year. In February 1777, Col. Thomas Hartley, who was raising an elite "additional" Continental regiment, wrote to Washington from York County, Pennsylvania, "in many Parts of this Province (this County in particular)—there are several Discouraging Circumstances against the Recruiting Service . . . In Maryland I have three Companies . . . In Virginia I have one . . . The Uniform Blue faced with white after the cut of your Excellency's Uniform . . . In my Attestations I call my Regement Guards but have left blank for any other Distinction." Thomas Hartley to George Washington, "York Town Pennsylvania February the 12th 1777," Washington, *Papers*, 8:317–318. Ten days later, Hartley wrote to Washington from Lancaster, "Cloathing I hope Mr. Mease will have ready—**one Mr Merchanton of Philada offered to furnish me with blue and White Cloth for a Regiment** . . . Several Matters such as Marking Buttons Caps &c. render it necessary if it is agreeable to you, to have my Regiment, distinguished by some Number in the Guards." Ibid., 411.

22. "Philadelphia, July 11, 1776, The Examination of Isaac Atwood, Comb maker, who has resided in this city since 1773. He is an Englishman." "They sometimes meet now at Hale's and at the House of Johnson, the Coach Maker [John Johnson, Coachmaker, Market Street between 5th and 6th, *Pennsylvania Gazette*, May 15, 1776], and sometimes at Griegson's" *PaArch*, 2nd series, 1:611–613.

23. Cresswell, 155.

24. John Adams to Benjamin Rush, quoted in Page Smith, *John Adams*, (New York: Doubleday, 1962), 2:802.

25. This was the 3rd Pennsylvania Battalion in the Continental Army, not the 3rd Battalion of Philadelphia Associators, who at that time were under their own jurisdiction. Graydon's unit later became the 4th Pennsylvania Regiment of the Continental Line.

26. Alexander Graydon, *Memoirs of a Life Chiefly Passed in Pennsylvania within the Last Sixty Years* (Edinburgh: William Blackwood and T. Caldell, 1822), 156–157.

27. Cresswell, 154.

CHAPTER 12

1. John Sullivan, *Letters and Papers of Major-General John Sullivan*, ed. Otis G. Hammond, (Concord, NH: New Hampshire Historical Society, 1930), 1:4–5. Many sources incorrectly state that Sullivan was born in Maine. [hereafter Sullivan, *Papers*]
2. George Washington to John Hancock, "New York June 17, 1776," Washington, *Papers*, 5:21.
3. John Sullivan to Philip Schuyler, "Crown Point July 6, 1776," Sullivan, *Papers*, 1:280–281.
4. John Adams to Abigail Adams, "Philadelphia July 27, 1776," *LetDel*, 4:551.
5. Charles Thomson to John Dickinson, "Summerville July 29, 1776," *LetDel*, 4:563.
6. Thomas Jefferson to Richard Henry Lee, "Philadelphia July 29, 1776," *LetDel*, 4:562.
7. John Hancock to George Washington, "Philadelphia, July 31, 1776," *LetDel*, 4:590.
8. Serle, 81–82.
9. John Sullivan to Richard Howe, "New York, 30 August 1776," in *Journals of the Continental Congress*, 5:731–732.
10. Serle, 83.
11. Entry for Tuesday, September 3, 1776, *Journals of the Continental Congress*, 5:731.
12. Serle, 83.
13. Will Hooper to William Livingston, "September 2, 1776 Philadelphia," *LetDel* 5:94.
14. The reasons had nothing to do with fear of the British army or of imminent defeat; they had to do mostly with personal business and fatigue. For example, John Adams was waiting for a replacement, because of exhaustion and his large family of small children being inoculated with smallpox. Not surprisingly, the work of Congress had to be taken up by fewer and newer members, which added to the burdens and fatigue of the more experienced members.
15. Josiah Bartlett to William Whipple, "Philadelphia, September 3, 1776," *LetDel* 5:94.
16. Ibid.
17. Adams, 3:415.
18. Rush, *Autobiography*, 140.
19. Extract of a letter from John Adams to William Tudor, dated Philadelphia August 29 and continued to September 2, 1776. *Adams Family Papers: An Electronic Archive.* Massachusetts Historical Society. http://www.masshist.org/digitaladams.

CHAPTER 13

1. Josiah Bartlett to William Whipple, "Philadelphia, September 3, 1776," *LetDel* 5:94–95.
2. Will Hooper to William Livingston, "September 2nd 1776 Philadelphia," *LetDel* 5:93–94.
3. John Adams to James Warren, "Philadelphia, September 4, 1776," *LetDel* 5: 103.
4. Adams, 3:416.
5. Rush, *Autobiography*, 120.
6. Boatner, 1214–1215.
7. John Witherspoon's Speech in Congress, [September 5? 1776], *LetDel*, 5: 109–110.
8. Ibid., 5:110.

9. Ibid., 5:110–111.
10. Ibid., 5:111.
11. Ibid., 5:111–112.
12. Ibid., 5:112.
13. Ibid., 5:112–113.
14. Entry for September 9, in Serle, 96.
15. John Adams to Abigail Adams, "Fryday, September 6," *LetDel*, 5:114–115.
16. Adams, 3:425–426.
17. Benjamin Franklin to Richard Howe, "Philada. Sept. 8, 1776," Franklin, *Papers*. franklinpapers.org, 627167 = 022-591a.html.
18. Benjamin Franklin to George Washington, "Philada. Sept 8, 1776," Franklin, *Papers*, franklinpapers.org, 627168 = 022-593a.html.
19. Richard Howe to George Germain, "Eagle, off Bedloe's Island, September 20, 1776," C.O. 5, 177:38 40, National Archives (formerly Public Record Office), London.
20. Richard Howe to Benjamin Franklin, "Eagle off Bedlows Island Sepr. 10: 1776." Franklin, *Papers*, franklinpapers.org, 627171 = 022-597a.html.

CHAPTER 14

1. Cresswell, 154.
2. This price was given in Pennsylvania shillings, twenty of which equaled one pound. The price was also advertised at $4, meaning four Spanish silver dollars. The Pennsylvania pound was officially valued at seven-tenths the value of a pound Sterling. Translating the values into modern money is nearly impossible, but at a reckoning of £1 sterling = $200, the cost of Cresswell's trip would be about $150. This would have been beyond the means of most average people in America at the time.

   Cresswell states that he paid twenty-one shillings for the trip—a price increase due, no doubt, to wartime inflation.
3. *Pennsylvania Gazette*, November 14, 1771. There were other "stage lines" between Philadelphia and New York before this, but they involved "stage boats" up the Delaware from Philadelphia to Burlington and again from Staten Island to New York. They also took three or more days to complete. Apparently this was the first "direct" and speedy land service.
4. Kenneth Roberts and Anna M. Roberts, *Moreau de St. Mery's American Journey* (Garden City, NY: Doubleday, 1947), 96–97.
5. Ibid., 96. Travel discomforts being relative to time and place, the closest modern equivalent of this mode of transportation would probably be common airport limousine service between Philadelphia and Newark or JFK airports. Tight sitting, multiple stops, baggage crammed in, and even luggage sitting on laps are notable features. Fortunately, the time of such a trip is limited to a few hours, unless traffic is backed up, which can make it seem like days.
6. Pemberton, "Weather Observations for 1776," made from a house two miles west of Philadelphia near the Schuylkill, American Philosophical Society, Philadelphia.
7. Cresswell, 154.
8. Charles S. Boyer, *Old Inns and Taverns in West Jersey* (Camden: Camden County Historical Society, 1962), 200. From *Pennsylvania Gazette*, February 3, 1773: "Extract of a Letter

from Princeton, New Jersey, January 23. Yesterday Morning, between Three and Four o'Clock, I was awaked by the Cry of Fire: I immediately arose, and having dressed myself, hastened out, and enquired where the Fire was; I was informed it was at the House of Mr. Jacob Hyer, at the *Sign of Hudibras*. I ran immediately to the Place, and found the Northeast Corner in Flames without, also the Garret within. The College Fire Engine and Buckets being brought, all possible Means were used to extinguish the Flames, but to no Purpose; the Fire burnt till Seven o'Clock, when the whole House was laid in Ashes. Mr. Hyer lost all his Winter Provision, Beds, and other Furniture. By the Carefulness of the Students, Mr. Patterson's House was saved, although adjoining; the Roof catched several Times, and was put out as often by the Help of the Fire Engines: The Students on this Occasion behaved with a becoming Boldness, which does them Honour. Mr. Hyer's Kitchen, Shop, &c. were also saved, by pulling down the Entry that leads from the Kitchen to the House. The Fire is supposed to have been occasioned by the Carelessness of a Negroe Wench, who left a Candle burning when she went to Bed, which fell down and catched the Floor, and having burnt a Hole through, communicated it to the Laths between the Ceiling and the Floor. 'Tis to be hoped this Accident will cause People to be careful in putting out their Candles before they go to sleep." See also William H. Benedict, *New Brunswick in History* (New Brunswick, NJ: Published by the Author, 1925), 80–81.

9. Adams, 2:112.

10. Ibid., 2:111.

11. "Journal of H. M. S. Eagle," in *Naval Documents*, 6:737.

12. Cresswell, 157.

13. Joseph Reed to his wife, "New York, September 6th, 1776," in Commager, 458.

14. Samuel Blachley Webb, *Correspondence and Journals of Samuel Blachley Webb*, ed. Worthington Chauncey Ford (New York, 1893; reprint, New York: Arno Press, 1969), 148–149, 150n.

15. Cresswell, 157–158.

16. Loammi Baldwin to Mary Baldwin, "North River, New York, June 12, 1776," in Commager, 420–421.

17. Cresswell, 158. John Austin Stevens, *Progress of New York in a Century, 1776–1876* (New York: New York Historical Society, 1876), 21–22. "Also Hull, Robert. Of New York. 'At Hull's Tavern, No. 18 Broadway.' In 1776 an Addresser of Lord and Sir William Howe." Lorenzo Sabine, *Biographical Sketches of Loyalists of the American Revolution* (Boston: Little, Brown, 1864), 2:533. This tavern stood two blocks above Wall Street. The modern site is one block east and south of the World Trade Center site.

18. Cresswell, 158–159.

19. *Naval Documents*, 6:737.

20. Ibid., 6:1509. According to historical meteorological data, the moonrise was at 12:25 A.M. on September 8, 1776, moon waning 23 percent visible. Lee wrote that the moon was "about 2 hours high and the daylight about one."

21. Ibid., 6:1510.

22. Cresswell, 159. The word *supposed* is italicized for emphasis. While the cannonade at Hell Gate is documented by Kemble and also by Capt. Archibald Robertson, who built the batteries, witnessed the cannonade, and made a wash drawing of the event, it seems

odd that the explosion of the *Turtle's* torpedo around the same time would not have been noted by anyone. On the other hand, with the operation so secret and without any other known plausible explanation, an explosion of 150 pounds of powder in water early on a Sunday morning might have seemed like a cannonade at a distance, if it happened while Cresswell was on the ferry. British accounts say nothing further about the episode other than the guard boats firing at American rowboats the night before.

The torpedo explosion would have occurred in the East River somewhere between Brooklyn, Governor's Island, and the lower tip of Manhattan, southeast of the Paulus Hook ferry, while the cannonade was several miles northeast of the ferry. The city buildings would have been between the explosion and the ferry, and given the numerous hills and woods of most of Manhattan at that time, the sound would have deflected up and down the East River.

23. Kemble, 1:87.
24. Cresswell, 159, 224. Cresswell returned to New York the following June after escaping from Virginia for good.
25. Ibid., 159.
26. Ibid., 227–228.
27. Ibid., 159.

CHAPTER 15

1. In addition to the political and military situation, John worried endlessly about his family, especially as Abigail and the children underwent smallpox inoculation. A hot and humid summer in Philadelphia, with thousands of soldiers continuously passing through, left residents prone to outbreaks of all sorts of fevers and "agues" brought into town from the army camps and from worsening unsanitary conditions in town itself. Additionally, John suffered from a chronic fear of "night air" as an agent of illness and slept with the windows shut tight, even on thick, warm nights. The strain of it all was wearing him out; at one point on this road trip, John described himself as "an invalid."

His remembered mode of transportation is questionable, for although he had written repeatedly to Abigail to send a good horse to him (and the horse arrived on September 6), the diary he kept at the time, spotty as it is, suggests a different tale. In October, a month after the conference, he set out for home, writing, "Oated at the Red Lyon, dined at Bristol, crossed Trenton ferry, long before Sun set, drank Coffee at the Ferry House on the east Side of Delaware, where I putt up—partly to avoid riding in the Evening Air, and partly because 30 miles is enough for the first day, as my Tendons are delicate, not having been once on Horse back since the Eighth day of last February." See Adams, 2:251, 3:417–418.

2. Ibid., 3:417–418.
3. Benjamin Franklin to William Temple Franklin, "Brunswick, Sept. 10, 1776," *LetDel* 5:138.
4. *Naval Documents*, 6:782.
5. Lotheisen, V9.
6. Adams, 3:419.
7. Ibid., 3:419.

8. Henry Strachey, "Notes," in *LetDel*, 5:138.

9. Adams, 3:419.

10. Lotheisen, V9–V10.

11. Strachey, *LetDel*, 5:138.

12. Adams, 3:419–420.

13. Serle, 77, 86-87.

14. Strachey, *LetDel*, 138.

15. Adams, 3:422–423.

16. Strachey, *LetDel*, 139.

17. Ibid.

18. Adams, 3:422–423. Of this remark, John wrote, "I now believe it meant more, than either of my Colleagues or myself understood at the time. In our report to Congress We supposed that the Commissioners, Lord and General Howe, had by their Commission Power to [except] from Pardon all that they should think proper. But I was informed in England, afterwards, that a Number were expressly excepted by Name from Pardon, by the privy Council, and that John Adams was one of them, and that this List of Exceptions was given as an Instruction to the two Howes, with their Commission. When I was afterwards a Minister Plenipotentiary, at the Court of St. James's The King and the Ministry, were often insulted, ridiculed and reproached in the Newspapers, for having conducted with so much folly as to be reduced to the humiliating Necessity of receiving as an Ambassador a Man who stood recorded by the privy Council as a Rebell expressly excepted from Pardon. If this is true it will account for his Lordships gloomy denunciation of me, as 'a decided Character.' Some years afterwards, when I resided in England as a public Minister, his Lordship recollected and alluded to this Conversation with great politeness and much good humour. Att the Ball, on the Queens Birthnight, I was at a Loss for the Seats assigned to the foreign Ambassadors and their Ladies. Fortunately meeting Lord How at the Door I asked his Lordship, where were the Ambassadors Seats. His Lordship with his usual politeness, and an unusual Smile of good humour, pointed to the Seats, and manifestly alluding to the Conversation on Staten Island said, 'Aye! Now, We must turn you away among the foreigners.'" No corroborating evidence of or reference to this list has been found in contemporary sources.

19. Strachey, *LetDel*, 139.

20. Ibid., 139–140.

21. Ibid., 140.

22. Boatner, 953. On first meeting Edward Rutledge in September, 1774, John Adams wrote in his diary: "Young Rutledge told me, he studied 3 Years at the Temple. He thinks this a great Distinction. Says he took a Volume of Notes, which J. Quincy transcribed. Says that young Gentlemen ought to travel early, because that freedom and Ease of Behaviour, which is so necessary, cannot be acquired but in early Life. This Rutledge is young—sprightly but not deep. He has the most indistinct, inarticulate Way of Speaking. Speaks through his nose—a wretched Speaker in Conversation. How he will shine in public I dont yet know. He seems good natured tho conceited." Adams, 2:121.

23. Strachey, *LetDel*, 140–141.

24. Adams, 3:422–423.
25. Strachey, 141.
26. Strachey, 141–142.
27. Richard Howe to George Germain, September 20, 1776, C.O. 5, 177:38 40. National Archives (formerly Public Record Office), London.

CHAPTER 16

1. Entry for Friday, September 13, in Serle, 106.
2. Edward Rutledge to George Washington, "Brunswick Wednesday Evening 10 o'Clock [September 11, 1776]," *LetDel*, 5:138.
3. Cresswell, 160.
4. *Pennsylvania Gazette*, September 11, 1776.
5. Muhlenberg 2:739, 2:744.
6. Cresswell, 160.
7. Caesar Rodney to George Read, "Philadelphia, September 13, 1776," *LetDel* 5:117.
8. Adams, 3:429–430.
9. William Williams to Joseph Trumbull, "Sepr 13 PM," *LetDel* 5:159.
10. Cresswell, 160–162.
11. Muhlenberg, 2:739–740.
12. Ibid., 2:742.
13. Journals of the Continental Congress, entry for Tuesday, September 17, 1776, 5:765.
14. Muhlenberg, 2:742.
15. As a final wrap-up to the controversy, Muhlenberg writes on Sunday October 6, in a letter from his fellow pastor Rev. Kuntze: "Inclosed was the new printed plan of government of the provincial convention in which our desired paragraph is incorporated in Section 45 . . . In Section 10 the pledge of loyalty which the members of the new government are to make is altered to read as follows: "I believe in one God, the Creator and Ruler of the whole world, the Rewarder of the good and Punisher of the wicked. And I acknowledge the Scriptures of the Old and New Testaments given through divine inspiration. And nothing further, nor any other religious testimony, shall henceforth be required of civil servants of the government in this republic." Muhlenberg accepted the rewording as the best that could be done, but was not at all satisfied with it: "Very well, you smart chief-fabricators with your refined taste, you have acted very cleverly in allowing nothing concerning a Saviour of the world and His religion to slip in. For that is too old fashioned and countrified. You could not get along without the Old and new Testaments because otherwise you would have nothing on which to swear in Jews and Christians. Your ingenious edifice is founded on quicksand and will not survive many stormy winds and rains. Your heathen morality has putrid sources and your wild and tainted flesh abhors the salt of Christian morality. You will satisfy your refined taste with grapes from thorns and figs from thistles." Muhlenberg, 2:747–748.
16. Ibid., 3:74.
17. Cresswell, 257, 259.
18. Adams, 3:430–431.
19. Quoted in David McCullough, *John Adams* (New York: Simon and Schuster, 2001), 645.

INDEX

Adams, Abigail, 15, 60, 74, 124–125, 139, 171
Adams, John, 1, 5, 11, 13, 41, 60, 68, 72, 87, 120, 121, 124–125, 137, 148, 173
  as ambassador to Great Britain, 175–176
  autobiography of, 130, 157–158, 176
  Billopp House described by, 161
  death of, 176
  First Continental Congress and, 146–147
  Hessians described by, 160
  Howe meeting, aftermath of, 168, 170–172, 175–176
  Howe meeting, details of, 159–167
  independence debate and, 14, 15, 24
  peace mission and, 2–3, 74, 130, 134, 135, 139–142, 156–168, 170–172, 175–176
Adams, Samuel, 11, 59, 72, 140, 141, 171
Alexander, William. See Stirling, Lord
Amherst, Jeffrey Lord, 79
André, John, 113–114
Anglicans, 18–19, 114
Army of Observation. See Flying Camp
Arnold, Benedict, 124
Arnold, James, 102
Articles of Association, 9
Asia, HMS, 151
Associators, 9, 119
  Maryland, 117

Pennsylvania, 14, 24, 49–50, 53, 58, 59, 64, 69, 80–81, 90, 94, 113–117
Atlee, William, 90
Atwood, Isaac, 119–120
Augustus Lutheran Church (Trappe, Pennsylvania), 20, 53–54, 95, 170
  building of, 17–18
  trashing and desecration of, 174

Baldwin, Loammi, 150
Baldwin, Mrs. Loammi, 150
Balfour, Nisbet, 43, 81
Bartlett, Josiah, 59–60, 129, 133–134
Bathurst, John, 94
Bell, Andrew, 94
Berks Committee of Safety, 22
Bessonett, Charles, 144, 145
Bessonett's Flying Machines (stage wagons), Cresswell's journey via, 143–148, 156
Billopp, Christopher, 65–66
Billopp family, 65–66, 162
Billopp House, 3, 65–66, 141
  described by Adams, 161
  described by Serle, 162
  Howe meeting with Adams, Franklin, and Rutledge, details of, 159–167
Blennerhasset, Lieutenant, 60–61
Board of War, 125
Bossiers, Joseph, 12
Boston, American blockade/siege and British evacuation of, 9, 10, 15, 56, 123, 124

Boston Tea Party (1773), 8–9, 118
Braddock, Edward, 6, 41, 96–97, 101
Brandywine, Battle of, 173, 174
Breed's Hill, Battle of, 45, 97, 98, 110
Brewer, Joseph, 118, 120, 169, 170
Brodhead, Daniel (Lieutenant Colonel),
    108–109
Brodhead, Ensign, 102
Brown, Philip, 28, 35–39, 41, 85–86
Bryan, John, 94
Buchhannan, Mr., 118, 120, 169
Bull, John, 53, 94
Burr, Aaron, 67, 84–85, 174
Bushnell, David, 152, 154
Bute, Lord, 109

Cadwallader, Colonel, 59
Calvinists, 55, 150
Campbell, Archibald, 108
Carleton, Sir Guy, 124
Centurion, HMS, 97
Charles II, king of England, 65
Christ Church (Philadelphia), 24, 116
Clapp, Caleb, 38
Clark, Abraham, 59, 67, 68
Cliffe, Loftus, 106–107, 109–111
Clift, Captain van, 107
Clinton, Henry, 89, 99–100, 106–107,
    109
Clitherall, James, 80
Coercive Acts (Intolerable Acts) (1774),
    9, 10
Coghlan, John, 175
College of New Jersey (now Princeton
    University), 84, 135
    described, 146
Collins, Mr., 148, 151
Committees of Safety, 49–50, 117
    Berks Committee, 22
    Philadelphia, 63
Committee of Secret Correspondence, 68
Common Sense (Paine), 13
Concord, Battle of (1775), 11, 96
Congress of the United States, 1
    Committee of Secret Correspondence,
    68
    Continental Army and, 46, 56, 62,
    105–106, 111, 119

Declaration of Independence and,
    14, 23–24, 33–34, 49, 60, 74,
    135, 138, 165–166
First Continental Congress (1774),
    9, 10, 64, 80, 123, 146–147
Flying Camp and, 58–59, 62, 68, 69
France, diplomatic mission to,
    173–174
military appointments, controversy
    over, 124–125
Olive Branch Petition and, 163
paper money issued by, 21
peace mission and, 72–77, 127–143,
    146, 156–172, 175–176
Philadelphia, flight from, 169
Plan of Union and, 64
prisoners of war and, 82, 127–132
Second Continental Congress
    (1775–1781), 3, 13–15, 21–24,
    27, 33–34, 38, 42, 46, 49–50,
    58–60, 62, 63, 65, 67–69, 72,
    80, 94, 98, 105–107, 112, 117,
    120–125, 127–143, 146, 156–176
Washington and, 10, 27, 38, 42, 46,
    58, 71, 98, 111, 128, 134–135,
    141, 168–169, 174
Connecticut military forces, 82
Constitutional Gazette, 33
Continental Army, 36, 54, 59, 64, 67,
    113, 123, 149, 151, 169, 174
    Battle of Brandywine and, 173
    Battle of Long Island and, 3, 96–100,
    105–106, 109–110, 173
    Congress and, 46, 56, 62, 105–106,
    119
    uniforms for, 81, 119
Cooper, Alexander, 112–115
Cornwallis, Charles, 89
Cotton, Lieutenant, 100
Cresswell, Nicholas, 3, 9, 11–16, 18,
    46, 112–118, 121–122, 129,
    143–144, 157, 158, 171–172
    background of, 5–8
    Bessonett's Flying Machines (stage
    wagons) journey, 143–148
    Howe (General) described by, 175
    Loyalists, meetings with, 118–120,
    169–171

map of his travels in American, 115
New York City described by,
    148–152, 154–155
Thomson, trouble with the
    Presbyterian Rev. Mr., 114,
    155–156
Washington described by, 10–11, 175
Crisis, The (Paine), 169

Dansey, William, 100–101
Dayton, Elias, 59, 67
Deane, Silas, 173–174
Declaration of Independence, 39, 40,
    50, 56, 64, 74, 121, 122, 138,
    163–166
    British government receives, 33–34
    debate over, 14, 24, 49, 60, 74, 135
    first public reading of, 23–24, 49,
        150
    printing of, 33, 49
De Hart, John, 80
De Hart, Sarah Dagworthy, 80
Deists, 13, 20, 172
Delaware (Lenni Lenape) Indians, 12–13
Delaware military forces, 60, 105–106
Dickinson, John, 50, 59, 90, 125
    independence debate and, 14, 15, 24
    Letters from a Farmer in Pennsylvania, 72
    peace mission and, 34, 72, 74
Dinwiddie, Robert, 40, 41
Donop, Karl Emil von, 99, 103, 104
Draper, Richard, 15
Drummond, Lord, 134–136
Duncan, Henry, 28, 42, 152, 159
Dunlap, Mr., 64
Dunlap, Mrs., 64
Dunlap, Sally, 64
Dunmore, John Murray Lord, 14, 16,
    33, 161–162
Dunmore's War, 11–12

Eagle, HMS, 35, 36, 38, 41, 42, 48, 70,
    71, 85–86, 97, 123, 128, 141,
    142, 148, 151, 159
    arrival in America, 26–31, 90
    described, 28
    Turtle (submarine) mission to destroy,
        152–154

Edwards, John, 94
Edwards, Jonathan, 84
Ellery, William, 72–74
Eppes, Francis, 65
Ewing, Jasper, 108

Flying Camp (Army of Observation),
    54, 60, 70, 74, 79, 81, 92–93,
    100, 125
    Congress and, 58–59, 62, 68, 69
    creation of, 56–57, 71
    problems in, 62–63, 65–69, 94
    Washington and, 56–59, 61–63,
        65–67, 70, 90
Fort Duquesne, 40–41
Fort Mercer, 173
Fort Mifflin, 173
Fort Necessity, 6, 41
Fort Pitt, 6, 11
Fort St. Johns, 113
Fort Ticonderoga, 113, 125, 162
Fort Washington, 121
Fox, Charles James, 9, 75
France, Franklin's diplomatic mssion to,
    173–174
Franklin, Benjamin, 1, 33, 50, 64, 69,
    70, 94, 117, 121
    as Deist, 20, 172
    France, diplomatic mssion to,
        173–174
    Howe meeting, aftermath of, 168,
        170–172
    Howe meeting, details of, 159–167
    Muhlenberg, meeting with,
        172–173
    peace mission and, 2–3, 34, 71–78,
        140–142, 156–168, 170–172
    Pennsylvania Convention and, 117,
        172–173
Franklin, Elizabeth (wife of William),
    56, 158
Franklin, William (son of Benjamin), 33,
    56, 57, 69, 70, 135
Franklin, William Temple (grandson of
    Benjamin), 56, 141, 158–159
French and Indian War, 6, 82, 96–97,
    146, 162
Freyenhagen, Wilhelm, 91, 103

Gage, Thomas, 9, 79, 97
Galloway, Joseph, 64
Gates, Horatio, 124–125
George III, king of England, 6, 32, 40,
    62, 110, 150, 175
    Boston Tea Party and, 8, 9
    Declaration of Independence and, 33
    Olive Branch Petition and, 163
    peace mission and, 34, 35, 46, 47, 72,
        75, 77, 135, 136, 164–167
Germain, George Sackville Lord, 23
    Howe (Admiral), report from 71
    Howe (General), reports from,
        32–34, 48, 104
Gerry, Elbridge, 141
Gist, Mordecai, 105
Glyn, Thomas, 110
Godard, Postmaster, 151
Goercke, Artillery-Lieutenant, 93
Graham, William, 116
Grant, James, 99, 106, 109
Graydon, Alexander, 121
Great War for Empire, 6
Greene, Nathanael, 90, 98, 125–126
Griswold, Joseph, 120, 170, 171
Groves, William, 94
Grub, Colonel, 52

Hancock, John, 62, 73, 74, 141, 143
    Washington and, 27, 38, 39, 111,
        124, 125, 134–135
Hand, Edward, 97–98
Hart, John, 80
Harvey, Edward, 109
Harwood, Harry, 28
Haslet, John, 105–106
Haywood, Mr., 129
Heister, Philip von, 99, 103, 106
Henry, Patrick, 15–16, 63
Hessians, 1, 14, 89, 91–94, 159, 161
    Battle of Long Island and, 96, 98, 99,
        102–104, 106–108
    described by Adams, 160
    described by Serle, 161–162
    reputation as savage fighters, 107–108
Hickey, Thomas, 149
High, George, 94
Hinkle, Jacob, 115

Hooper, Will, 69, 129, 134
Hopkinson, Francis, 50
Hotham, Commodore, 90, 92
House of Commons, 8, 9, 30, 31
House of Lords, 9, 40
Howarth, John, 28
Howe, Caroline, 28, 71, 76
Howe, George Augustus, 96–97, 162
Howe, Richard Earl (4th Viscount
    Howe, Admiral Howe), 15, 44,
    47–48, 64, 87, 173
    background of, 2, 28, 30
    Battle of Long Island and, 97, 123,
        126
    Declaration of Independence and,
        163–165
    flagship (HMS *Eagle*), 26–31, 35,
        36, 38, 41, 42, 48, 70, 71, 85–86,
        90, 97, 123, 128, 141, 151–154,
        159
    Franklin letters, 71–78
    Germain, report to, 71
    meeting with Adams, Franklin, and
        Rutledge, aftermath of, 168–172,
        175–176
    meeting with Adams, Franklin, and
        Rutledge, details of, 159–167
    peace mission and, 2–3, 31–43,
        46–47, 70–78, 85–86, 126–143,
        146, 151, 156–172, 175–176
    Staten Island, capture of, 23, 27–28,
        66, 90
    Turtle (submarine) mission to destroy
        flagship of, 152–154
    Washington letters, 35–42, 46–47,
        70–71, 75, 78, 85–86, 136
Howe, William (5th Viscount Howe,
    General Howe), 27, 28, 30, 38,
    41, 83, 86, 87, 151, 169, 172
    background of, 96–97
    Battle of Brandywine and, 173
    Battle of Breed's Hill and, 97, 110
    Battle of Long Island and, 96–100,
        103–106, 110, 126, 173
    Battle of the Monongahela and,
        96–97
    described by Creswell, 175
    Germain, reports to, 32–34, 48, 104

peace mission and, 2–3, 31, 32, 34,
46–48, 74, 81, 141–142, 163
Philadelphia, capture of, 173
Staten Island, capture of, 23, 33, 56,
60, 65, 67, 89, 91, 92
Washington letters, 42–48, 81
Hull, Robert, 151
Hutchinson, Thomas, 76, 140
Hyer, Jacob, 147

Intolerable Acts (Coercive Acts) (1774),
9, 10

Jacobs, Richard, 115
Jay, Frederick, 80
Jay, John, 80
Jefferson, Thomas, 98, 112, 121, 125,
129, 143
death of, 176
Declaration of Independence and,
40, 122
Flying Camp and, 63–66
Jones, Cadwalader, 94
Jungkenn, Karl von, 108

Kemble, Stephen, 43, 60–61, 85, 154
Kennedy, Captain, 43
King's College (now Columbia University), 79
Kirk, Mr., 112, 143, 169, 172
Knox, Henry, 38–39, 43–44, 47,
85, 86
Knox, Lucy, 38, 44

Lafayette, Marquis de, 174
Leacock Presbyterian Church (Leacock
Township, Pennsylvania), 114
Lee, Charles, 64, 89–90
Lee, Ezra, 153–154
Lee, Francis Lightfoot, 112, 121
Lee, Richard Henry, 14, 59, 125, 129
peace mission and, 140
Lenni Lenape (Delaware) Indians, 12–13
Letters from a Farmer in Pennsylvania
(Dickinson), 72
Lexington, Battle of (1775), 11, 96
Liberty Bell, 49, 121
Liverpool, HMS, 21–22

Livingston, Robert R., 50
Livingston, William
as general, 57–58, 60, 67, 69, 80, 81,
90–91
as governor of New Jersey, 69, 80, 81,
129, 134
Livingston, William Smith (Major, New
York), 82–83
Long Island, Battle of, 3, 120, 123,
125–128, 133, 134, 137, 173, 174
details of, 96–111
map of, 99
Loos, Johann von, 108
Lord Howe, HMS, 92
Lossberg, Colonel von, 92
Lotheisen, Regimental Quartermaster /
Staff Secretary, 91–93, 159–161
Louis XVI, king of France, 174
Lowell, Mr. (prisoner of war), 82
Loxley, Captain, 64
Loyalists (American Tories), 14, 18, 32,
64, 68, 74, 81, 133, 138
Billopp family, 65–66, 162
Cresswell's meetings with, 118–120,
169–171
Franklin, William, 33, 56, 57, 69,
70, 135
Marchinton, Philip, 118–120, 143,
169–171, 173
Washington, plot to assassinate, 58,
149
Witherspoon's description of,
138–139
Ludwick, Christopher, 94
Luther, Martin, 52
Lutherans, 22
See also Muhlenberg, Henry Melchior
doctrine, 18, 51

MacDonald, Donald, 129, 170
Marchinton, Philip, 118–120, 143,
169–171, 173
Marshall, Christopher, 50, 116, 118
Martin, Joseph Plumb, 102
Maryland military forces, 59–60, 105,
106
Associators, 117
Mason, George, 15

Mason, Thomson, 15–16, 112, 121, 152, 155
Massachusetts Gazette, 15
Mathew, Edward, 104–105
Matthews, David, 149
McDonough, Thomas, 105
McKean, Thomas, 59, 94
McMichael, James, 59
Menzies, Robert, 108
Mercer, Hugh, 35, 58, 61–63, 65–67, 90
   appointed commander of Flying Camp, 56–57, 71
   background of, 70–71
Mercer, James, 114
Mersereau, John, 62
Mifflin, Thomas, 84, 120
Miles, Samuel, 59, 60, 90, 98, 100–103
Moncrieffe, Edward Cornwallis, 79
Moncrieffe, Margaret, 3, 79–88, 102–103, 174–175
Moncrieffe, Thomas, 79–88, 102–103, 174
Monongahela, Battle of the, 6, 41, 96–97
Montgomery, Richard, 46–47, 84, 124
Montrésor, Frances Tucker, 86
Montrésor, John, 86
Moore's Creek Bridge, Battle of, 129
Moravians, 28, 111
Motz, Captain von, 92
Muhlenberg, Frederick, 18, 23, 172
Muhlenberg, Henry Melchior, 3, 20–25, 50–54, 67, 107, 172, 174
   Augustus Lutheran Church (Trappe, Pennsylvania), 17–18, 20, 53–54, 95, 170
   background of, 17–18
   Franklin, meeting with, 172–173
Muhlenberg, Mrs. Henry, 24
Muhlenberg, Peter, 18, 20, 174
Murray, Bessie, 105
Murray, Sir James, 105

Nalen, Jacob, 12
New Hanover Church (Pennsylvania), 51
New Jersey Convention, 62, 68, 69, 80
New Jersey military forces, 50, 57–60, 66–69, 80, 81, 147, 174

New York Convention, 60
New York Harbor
   British reinforcements in, 89–90
   map of, 37
New-York Gazette, 28
New York Gazette and Weekly Mercury, 66
New York military forces, 82–83
Noland, Lieutenant, 156
North, Frederick Lord, 31
Northumberland, Duke of (father of Lord Percy), 104, 105

O'Brien, Tom, 12
Olive Branch Petition, 163
Osborn, Sir George, 104

Pain, Captain, 106
Paine, Thomas, 149
   Common Sense, 13
   Crisis, The, 169
Parliament, British, 14, 32, 39–40, 82
   Coercive Acts (Intolerable Acts) (1774), 9, 10
   House of Commons, 8, 9, 30, 31
   House of Lords, 9, 40
   Olive Branch Petition and, 163
   peace mission and, 31, 32, 74, 78, 129, 130, 136, 164–166, 171, 172
Parker, Sir Peter, 89
Paterson, James, 43–47, 75, 81, 82, 87, 136
Patton, Major, 60
Penn, John, 33, 64
Penn, William, 33
Pennsylvania Assembly, 64
Pennsylvania Board of War, 50, 116, 146
Pennsylvania Constitution, 172, 173
Pennsylvania Convention, 53, 117, 172–173
Pennsylvania Gazette, 42, 81, 118, 144, 169
Pennsylvania military forces, 52–54, 60, 62–69, 84, 90–91, 114, 121
   Associators, 14, 24, 49–50, 53, 58, 59, 64, 69, 80–81, 90, 94, 100, 113–117
   Battle of Brandywine and, 174
   Battle of Long Island and, 97–98, 100–103, 107–109

Navy, 22
Pennsylvania Packet, 94
Percy, Hugh Lord, 87–88, 102, 104–105
Peterman, Jacob, 53–54, 170
Philadelphia, British capture of, 173
  Congress flees, 169
Philadelphia Committee of Safety, 63
Philadelphia Council of Safety, 146
Phoenix, HMS, 27–28
Pitt, Sir William (Earl of Chatham), 150–151
Plan of Union, 64
Porter, Phineas, 102
Presbyterians, 13, 114, 135, 146, 155–156
Prescott, Richard, 45, 129, 170
Privy Council, 76, 164, 175
Puritans, 55
Putnam, Israel, 43, 67, 82–87, 120
  background of, 82
  Battle of Long Island and, 98, 109, 126, 174
Putnam, Mrs. Israel, 83

Quakers, 22, 118
  pacifism, 52–53, 55

Read, George, 170
Read, James, 22–23
Reed, Joseph, 36–39, 43, 44, 47, 67, 149
Reed, Mrs. Joseph, 149
Reeve, Samuel, 28, 35, 70
Reknown, HMS, 89
Reynolds, Sir Joshua, 28
Rittenhouse, David, 146
Roberdeau, Daniel, 59
Rodney, Caesar, 105–106, 170
Roebuck, HMS, 21–22, 151
Rogers, John, 112
Rose, HMS, 27–28
Ross, George, 135
Ross, William, 113
Rush, Benjamin, 14, 63–64, 79, 121
  peace mission and, 130, 135
Rush, Julia, 63–64
Rutledge, Edward "Ned," 80

Howe meeting, aftermath of, 168–172
Howe meeting, details of, 159–167
peace mission and, 2–3, 140–142, 156–172

Sandwich, John Montagu Lord, 31
Schrack, Henrich, 54
Schrack, Jacob, 54
Schrack, Magdelena, 54
Schuyler, Philip, 124
Scottish Highlanders, 14, 66
  Battle of Long Island and, 97, 106, 108
  reputation as savage fighters, 108
Serle, Ambrose, 29–34, 38, 41–43, 60, 61, 70, 87, 89, 90, 123, 126, 128, 139, 152
  Billopp House described by, 162
  Hessians described by, 161–162
  Howe brothers described by, 30
  Howe meeting with Adams, Franklin, and Rutledge described by, 168
Seven Years' War, 6
Shambough, Joseph, 94
Shawnee Indians, 12
Sheriff, William, 86
Shewkirk, Rev. Mr., 28, 111
Shrack, John, 94
Shuldham, Molyneux, 31, 32
Skeen, Abram, 94
Skene, Governor (prisoner of war), 82
Small, John, 87–88
Sons of Liberty, 8, 149
Staten Island, British capture of, 23, 24, 26–31, 50, 56, 60–62, 65–67, 80
  map of, 61
  reinforcements arrive, 89–93
St. Clair, Daniel, 113
Stephen, Adam, 41
St. George's Chapel (New York City), 150
Stiles, Ezra, 72, 74
Stirling, Lord (William Alexander), 98, 99, 105
  Battle of Brandywine and, 174
  released as part of prisoner exchange, 170

taken prisoner of war, 106, 123,
126–128
Stirn, Major General, 91
Stockton, Richard, 63, 72, 135
Stone, Thomas, 112
St. Paul's Church (New York City), 150
Strachey, Henry, 160–162, 165
Stretch, Mrs., 169, 170
Stuart, Charles (Colonel), 109
Stuart, Charles Edward (Bonnie Prince
Charlie), 70–71, 137
Sullivan, John, 98
Sullivan, Thomas, 97–100, 103, 109,
124–125
background of, 123–124, 131–132
Battle of Brandywine and, 174
peace mission and, 126–134, 136,
139, 141, 143, 166, 176
released as part of prisoner exchange,
170
taken prisoner of war, 104, 123,
126–128

Taney, Daniel, 94
Taney, Jacob, 94
Thomson, Charles, 125
Thomson, Rev. Mr., 114, 155–156
Thornbur, Thomas, 120, 170
Tories, American. *See* Loyalists
Tories, British, 31, 75
peace mission and, 32, 46, 127,
133–134, 171
Trinity Church (New York City), 28,
150
Trumbull, Joseph, 171
Tryon, William, 33
Tupper, Benjamin, 38
Turtle (submarine), 152–154

Vanderslice, Thomas, 94
Virginia Gazette, 46
Virginia House of Burgesses, 10, 18, 40
Virginia military forces, 18–19, 65, 155,
174
Voltaire, 6

Warder, Jeremiah, 118–120
Warren, James, 15, 134, 140–141

Washington, George, 32, 82–84, 86, 87,
89–91, 102, 118, 120, 121, 124,
130, 149, 151
Battle of Brandywine and, 173,
174
Battle of Long Island and, 96, 98,
100, 106, 110, 111, 125–126,
128
Congress and, 10, 27, 38, 42, 46, 58,
71, 98, 111, 128, 134–135, 141,
168–169, 174
described, 10–11, 43–44, 175
Flying Camp and, 56–59, 61–63,
65–67, 70, 90
Fort Duquesne and, 40–41
Fort Necessity and, 6, 41
Howe (Admiral) letters, 35–42,
46–47, 70–71, 75, 78, 85–86,
136, 141
Howe (General) letters, 42–48, 81
Loyalist plot to assassinate, 58, 149
New York City evacuation ordered
by, 150
orders regarding dress for troops,
51–52
Virginia House of Burgesses
and, 18
Washington, Martha, 10, 83
Way, Caleb, Jr., 114
Weaver, Henry, 64
Weaver, Michael, 64
Webb, Samuel, 43, 47, 83, 84, 149
Wedderburn, Lord, 76
Whigs
American, 14, 18, 39–40, 75, 127,
138, 139, 151
British, 9, 31, 32, 134
Whipple, William, 129
Williams, William, 171
Wilson, James, 107
Witherspoon, John, 135–139, 146
Wolfe, James, 82
Wurmb, Colonel Friedrich von, 92, 93,
160–162
Wurmb, Major von, 92, 93

Yard, Mrs., 120
Yeates, Jasper, 107, 113